READERS' GUIDES TO ESSENTIAL CRITICISM

CONSULTANT EDITOR: NICOLAS TREDELL

Nick Selby	T. S. Eliot: *The Waste Land*
Nick Selby	Herman Melville: *Moby Dick*
Nick Selby	The Poetry of Walt Whitman
David Smale	Salman Rushdie: *Midnight's Children – The Satanic Verses*
Patsy Stoneman	Emily Brontë: *Wuthering Heights*
Susie Thomas	Hanif Kureishi
Nicolas Tredell	F. Scott Fitzgerald: *The Great Gatsby*
Nicolas Tredell	Joseph Conrad: *Heart of Darkness*
Nicolas Tredell	Charles Dickens: *Great Expectations*
Nicolas Tredell	William Faulkner: *The Sound and the Fury – As I Lay Dying*
Nicolas Tredell	Shakespeare: *Macbeth*
Nicolas Tredell	The Fiction of Martin Amis
Angela Wright	Gothic Fiction

Forthcoming

Pascale Aebischer	Jacobean Drama
Simon Avery	Thomas Hardy: *The Mayor of Casterbridge – Jude the Obscure*
Annika Bautz	Jane Austen: *Sense and Sensibility – Pride and Prejudice – Emma*
Matthew Beedham	The Novels of Kazuo Ishiguro
Justin Edwards	Postcolonial Literature
Jodi-Anne George	*Beowulf*
William Hughes	Bram Stoker: *Dracula*
Matthew Jordan	Milton: *Paradise Lost*
Sara Lodge	Charlotte Brontë: *Jane Eyre*
Matthew McGuire	Contemporary Scottish Literature
Timothy Milnes	Wordsworth: *The Prelude*
Steven Price	The Plays, Screenplays and Films of David Mamet
Stephen Regan	The Poetry of Philip Larkin
Michael Whitworth	Virginia Woolf: *Mrs Dalloway*
Gina Wisker	The Fiction of Margaret Atwood
Matthew Woodcock	Shakespeare: *Henry V*

Readers' Guides to Essential Criticism
Series Standing Order
ISBN 1–4039–0108–2
(*outside North America only*)

You can receive future titles in this series as they are published by placing a standing order. Please contact your bookseller or, in the case of difficulty, write to us at the address below with your name and address, the title of the series and the ISBN quoted above.

Customer Services Department, Macmillan Distribution Ltd
Houndmills, Basingstoke, Hampshire RG21 6XS, England

Twentieth-Century Irish Literature

AARON KELLY

Consultant editor: Nicolas Tredell

First published 2008 by
PALGRAVE MACMILLAN
Houndmills, Basingstoke, Hampshire RG21 6XS and
175 Fifth Avenue, New York, N.Y. 10010
Companies and representatives throughout the world

PALGRAVE MACMILLAN is the global academic imprint of the Palgrave Macmillan division of St. Martin's Press, LLC and of Palgrave Macmillan Ltd. Macmillan® is a registered trademark in the United States, United Kingdom and other countries. Palgrave is a registered trademark in the European Union and other countries.

ISBN-13: 978-0230-51718-9   hardback
ISBN-10: 0230-51718-8   hardback
ISBN-13: 978-0230-51719-6   paperback
ISBN-10: 0230-51719-6   paperback

This book is printed on paper suitable for recycling and made from fully managed and sustained forest sources. Logging, pulping and manufacturing processes are expected to conform to the environmental regulations of the country of origin.

A catalogue record for this book is available from the British Library.

A catalog record for this book is available from the Library of Congress.

10   9   8   7   6   5   4   3   2   1
17   16   15   14   13   12   11   10   09   08

Printed and bound in China

In Memory of
James and Sarah Kelly
William and Ellen Childs

And dedicated to
Jim, Greta, Phil, Sarah and Erin Kelly
With love

CONTENTS

Hanna Bell, MacNeice in relation to Northern Ireland. Concludes with an account of the increasing interest of international critics in Irish writing in the second half of the twentieth century up to the more institutional development of Irish Studies. Explains the impact of New Criticism in this movement and analyses the work of scholars such as Denis Donoghue, Donald Davie, Vivian Mercier, Richard Ellmann and Hugh Kenner. Observes that Irish Studies was slowly being brought into being as an academic discipline.

CHAPTER THREE   59

The Development of Irish Studies: Contesting the Revival

Traces the institutional development of Irish Studies in the academy and outlines the key debates and competing interpretative schools of Revisionism and Postcolonialism, together with an account of the Field Day project. Addresses the differing interpretative lenses used to interpret the literature of the Revival, especially in relation to Modernism and to the contested legacies of the Revival with Ireland's relation to empire. Uses the differing accounts of the Revival in Irish Studies to tease out the motivations behind current critical approaches. Relates debates within current literary studies to social change and upheaval in both the Republic and the North of Ireland. Critics discussed include Declan Kiberd, Seamus Deane, David Lloyd, Edna Longley, Roy Foster, Fredric Jameson and Edward Said.

CHAPTER FOUR   82

Irish Studies Paradigms and Literature after Partition

Continues the assessment of contemporary Irish Studies paradigms and examines specifically their attitudes to the Northern Irish and Irish Republic States. Focusing on the critiques offered to the direction of each state with reference to the writing of O'Casey, Kavanagh, Beckett, Flann O'Brien, Hewitt, W. R. Rodgers and others. Critics assessed include Kiberd, Deane, Lloyd, Longley and Nicholas Grene. In particular, discusses Lloyd's theories of a 'republic of difference' in opposition to state nationalism with regard to Beckett, and Deane's account of Flann O'Brien in similar terms. Also evaluates Revisionist accounts of the poetry of MacNeice, Hewitt and Northern writing by Longley, John Wilson Foster and Peter McDonald.

Discusses the new global dispensation and debates about pluralism and multiculturalism in companion pieces by Longley and Kiberd, both of whom also point out a rise in racism in Ireland, a troubling dimension taken up by Suzanna Chan's work. Both Francis Mulhern and Terry Eagleton challenge the postmodern condition and its cultural relativism which they believe disables judgement and critique. Finally, David Lloyd and Colin Graham address the impact of a globalized world on Irish culture.

ACKNOWLEDGEMENTS

I am deeply grateful to the series editor, Nicolas Tredell, Sonya Barker and all the team at Palgrave Macmillan for their invaluable help, advice, encouragement and patience during the writing of this book. All their efforts are very much appreciated. I would like to thank David Salter and Alan Gillis for their assistance and friendship. I am also beholden to the following friends, colleagues, peers or teachers for their support over the years: Michael Allen, Nicholas Allen, Steffi Bachorz, Eleanor Bell, Ester Carrillo, Cairns Craig, Noreen Doody, Sarah Dunnigan, Lynne Ellis, Alice Ferrebe, Sarah Gamble, Peter Garratt, Luke Gibbons, Colin Graham, Stipe Grgas, Patsy Horton, Eamonn Hughes, Keith Hughes, Bob Irvine, Mark Jamieson, Jim Kelly, Declan Kiberd, Thomas Legendre, Steffi Lehner, Edna Longley, P. J. Matthews, Michael McAteer, Matt McGuire, Julie Marney, Kate Nicol, Allyson Stack, Julie Anne Stevens, Randall Stevenson and Wendy Townsend.

Finally, this book is for my family and it is dedicated with love to Jim, Greta, Phil, Sarah and Erin Kelly.

Introduction

This Guide to Essential Criticism of twentieth-century Irish literature written in English necessarily addresses issues pertaining to a nationally specific culture. However, while Irish literary criticism permits us to think deeply about Ireland and nationality, it is, equally, not bound by the nation as an already agreed concept or a homogeneous entity. In fact, Irish literature continually rethinks the parameters of its own national context in terms of ideas of identity, culture, gender, social class and so forth. The global scope of Irish writing makes plain that it harbours an international range of important themes that cannot be simply reduced to a hermetically sealed nation. This guide seeks to deal with Irish literary criticism in its specificity without peculiarizing it or cordoning it off from the rest of the world. The wilful internationalism of writers such as James Joyce (1882–1941) or Samuel Beckett (1906–89), the internationally informed debates within Irish Studies itself, together with the engagement with Irish writing by a host of internationally renowned scholars such as Edward W. Said (1935–2003) and Fredric Jameson (born 1934), all affirm that Irish literature is able to think about its borders, boundaries and divisions and simultaneously to think beyond them. In tracing the paths of Irish literature and literary criticism in the twentieth-century, the highly charged contexts and debates which emerge are given specific forms by Irish society but they are also shaped by, and indeed help to shape, international dialogues concerning tradition and modernity; war and social conflict; profound economic change; nationalism, colonialism and postcolonialism; emancipation projects of class and gender; and the onset of a global age.

The aesthetic shapes and formal modes of Irish writing negotiate with the historical pressures of the twentieth century as part of the particular constellations which they assume in Irish society. At the beginning of the twentieth century Irish literature and criticism were in the midst of a whole array of re-imaginings and negotiations with the world that were conducted in varying degrees of optimism, idealism, pessimism and scorn. Most particularly, the Irish Literary Revival crystallizes many of these energies and currents without fully exhausting or encompassing all of them. The Revival constituted an ongoing and concerted effort through the second half of the nineteenth century into the twentieth that was wedded to broader social, cultural and political projects, the main aim of which was to redefine or revive Irishness. The fact that a revivification was necessary obviously implies that there was a prevailing

1

sense that Irishness was lost or moribund, that it had been overcome to an almost fatal degree by British culture and society. So the very designation of the Irish Literary Revival contains a sense of revivification, of bringing something back to life. Yet even the Revival's most celebrated proponents such as William Butler Yeats (1865–1939) often harboured a pessimism as to how far the past could be brought back to life and revived successfully (as in 'September 1913'). And from a differing viewpoint, our reading of Joyce's indictment of his contemporary Irish Society, *Dubliners* (1914), is literally and retroactively haunted by its final story 'The Dead'. Nevertheless, the coalescence of cultural and political nationalism in the period produces a sustained effort of renewed national self-definition and re-articulation. Yet these imaginatively recovered and divergent nations in turn bring forth – whether knowingly or disquietedly – issues such as the position of women in society, sexuality, social class, religion and region.

Indeed, the literary Revival was interwoven with convulsive political upheavals, most notably the Irish Republican Easter Rising in 1916 which sought to take advantage of the British involvement in the First World War (1914–18). The execution of the leaders of the Easter Rising, including Pádraic Pearse (1879–1916), the socialist James Connolly (1868–1916) and the poet and critic Thomas MacDonagh (1878–1916), backfired badly on the British authorities and gave renewed resonance to the proclamation of the Republic voiced by the Rising. Sinn Féin, whose constitution had changed to advocate an independent republic, swept to a landslide victory in the 1918 election. The Republican establishment of the *Dáil*, or independent Irish Parliament, by the majority of Irish MPs was followed in January 1919 by the beginning of the Anglo-Irish War or War of Independence. Even after the signing of the Anglo-Irish Treaty in 1921 the uneasy truce could not prevent further killings on sectarian lines in the North, and within Nationalism a fractious Civil War ensued between those supporting and opposed to the signing of the Treaty and it continued until 1923.

Following the Government of Ireland Act in 1920, which instantiated partition and the establishment of the six-county Northern Irish State, both the dominant ideologies in Ireland – Irish Nationalism and Unionism – had control over their own state and political institutions. Literature and literary criticism has often taken both prevailing ideologies to task, especially in relation to the profound discrepancy between their more idealized rhetoric or formative self-imagining and the reality of life in their respective states. Literature and literary criticism here speak directly not only to nationhood or national collective belonging but also to the live issues of gender, sexuality, class inequality, state power and repression. Terence Brown (born 1944) posits that the overwhelming Catholic, Nationalist majority in the Irish Free State resulted in 'a small country made drastically smaller by a border that had set six of its counties adrift'.[1] However, as countered by Thomas Kinsella (born 1928), it should also be acknowledged that partition created an insular, repressive state in the North. Kinsella rebukes Brown thus: 'There is no comment on the transformation of the Unionist minority in the North, by the same act, into a supremacist permanent majority which proceeded, in the name of democracy, to discriminate methodically against the newly created Catholic Nationalist minority'.[2]

Kinsella also presciently reminds us that Irish culture has a troubled, dual inheritance: 'Irish literature exists as a dual entity. It was composed in two languages. The changing emphases between one language and the other reflect changing circumstances through the centuries'.[3] These shifting circumstances are of course directly related to power, to the imposition of the English language and British culture on Ireland and the resultant marginalization and displacement of Irish. Although this Guide deals with Irish literature in English we will retain an awareness of this fractious, gapped tradition and we will consider the appropriations of the English language by a range of Irish writers. Hence, as asserted by Seamus Deane (born 1940), we will retain a sense that 'Irish culture tends to dwell on the medium in which it is written because it is difficult not to be self-conscious about a language which has become simultaneously native and foreign.'[4] In the first chapter, we will address the complications and enablements of this dual tradition and this critical relation to English and to literary form. We can view the Revival as an effort to repair the rupture in Irish history and tradition caused by British occupation and the imposition of British culture on Ireland, thereby striving to achieve a new national reconciliation and unitary communal tradition. However, while most of the key constituencies who comprise the Revival made a claim to ownership of an authentic Irishness, they were often at odds with one another over whose claims had primacy. This is particularly evident in the schism between Anglo-Irish, Protestant writers and Catholic, 'Irish Ireland' ones, though we will also outline in the opening chapter how not all literature and criticism may be lumped into this dichotomy.

The first chapter will begin with a discussion of Yeats's critical work and literary programme. Certainly, Yeats could never be accused of a lack of engagement. In addition to his writings, Yeats founded the Irish Literary Theatre with his patron Lady Augusta Gregory (1852–1932) and literary colleague Edward Martyn (1859–1923). The Irish Literary Theatre performed its first play in 1899 and the Abbey Theatre which became its national platform opened in Dublin in 1899. We will begin the first chapter by looking at Yeats's essay 'The Celtic Element in Literature' (1897) which embodies his core ideas for the Revival and for Irish literature. However, this article is also a useful means of anticipating the

'Irish Ireland' challenges to his work and his Anglo-Irish status since it is written in direct dialogue with the English Victorian writer and scholar Matthew Arnold (1822–95) and his theories about the Celts. The ambiguous origins of Yeats's theories of Celtic culture are precisely the aspects of his work that are contested by others. In addition to Arnold's Celticism, the first chapter will also address the cultural inheritance which Yeats acquires from the work of Anglo-Irish writers such as Thomas Davis (1814–45), Standish O'Grady (1832–1915) and Douglas Hyde (1860–1949). Due attention will also be given to other Anglo-Irish colleagues or critics of Yeats in this period such as Lady Gregory, John Millington Synge (1871–1909) and George Bernard Shaw (1856–1950).

Additionally, Chapter One covers the 'Irish Ireland' ideal most commonly associated with D. P. Moran (1869–1936). Moran's antipathy to Anglo-Irish versions of the nation will be evaluated in the terms of his own effort to purify Irishness through a specifically Catholic nationalist set of strictures. However, Joyce's critical work is assessed with regard to his dissent from his own Catholic background, his hostility to the assumptions of Irish Ireland, and equally his lampooning of the Anglo-Irish Literary Revival. The first chapter concludes by outlining the attitudes to national literature of the 1916 revolutionaries MacDonagh and Pearse.

Chapter Two deals with the impact of partition upon literature and criticism, especially in the context of the ideological premises of the Irish Free State (which was renamed Éire in the 1937 Constitution and became the Republic of Ireland in 1949) and the Northern Irish State. The permeation of Irish Ireland thinking in official cultural discourse in the Free State is considered in relation to the work of Daniel Corkery (1878–1964). In contrast to Corkery's writings, the literary criticism of figures such as Seán O'Faoláin (1900–91), Frank O'Connor (1903–66) and Patrick Kavanagh (1904–67) is analyzed as granting, by turns, creative opposition to or exasperated contempt for the prevailing ideological norms of the Free State and subsequent Irish Republic. With regard to the North, a comparable critical lineage of dissent from the stultifying Unionist hegemony which controlled the State is traced in the work of writers such as John Hewitt (1907–87), Sam Hanna Bell (1909–90) and Louis MacNeice (1907–63). The second chapter concludes with a discussion of the increasing international interest in Irish literature in the second half of the twentieth century. In particular, the influence of the interpretative school of New Criticism upon the development of a more formalized and institutional Irish literary criticism is appraised in relation to the formative work from the 1950s onwards of scholars such as Denis Donoghue (born 1928), Donald Davie (1922–95), Vivian Mercier (1919–89), Richard Ellmann (1918–87) and Hugh Kenner (1923–2003). While these critics helped to pave the way for the emergence of Irish

Studies as an academic discipline from the late 1970s to the present, it is also notable that a number of key thinkers within that developing Irish literary criticism also took issue with the notions of Irishness and literature set in place by their forbearers such as Mercier, Ellmann or Kenner.

Therefore, Chapter Three unfolds the core debates and competing interpretative schools of contemporary Irish Studies. Specific reference is made to Revisionism, a critical impulse to revise the mythology of official Irish Nationalist versions of history and literature, and, contrastingly, to the Field Day project and to criticism engaging with post-colonial theory, both of which, while also wishing to re-think existing paradigms, are opposed to Revisionism and, to a degree, seek to reart-iculate national or indeed nationalist interpretations. The key debates and antagonisms within contemporary Irish literary criticism are related to social change and upheaval in both the Republic and the North of Ireland. The chapter is also grounded in the differing accounts of the Revival period offered by contemporary Irish Studies in order to tease out the motivations behind current critical approaches and their attitudes to literature, history, nation and society. Revisionist tendencies are discussed with regard to key figures such as Edna Longley (born 1940) and Roy Foster (born 1949). The central tenets of the Field Day project are addressed most particularly through the work of Seamus Deane, and postcolonial interpretations in relation to scholars such as Declan Kiberd (born 1951) and David Lloyd (born 1955). Subsequently, Chapter Four continues our assessment of contemporary Irish Studies by illustrating the competing re-examinations of literature and culture produced in the aftermath of partition. Specifically, this chapter finds, in today's differing re-readings of literature and criticism in the early decades of the Northern and Southern states, a deeper understanding of the origins of present disputes about the role of literature and the aesthetic, about social diversity and difference, about the politics of literary form and the pressures placed upon the critical impulse in times of ideological conformism or conflict.

Chapter Five affirms that gender politics are central not only to debates about the nation and the imaginations of nationalism but also to issues of literary and aesthetic form, the tasks of criticism and Irish society and its discontents. With reference to controversies surrounding the work of Synge and Sean O'Casey (1880–1964), this chapter examines how Ireland, from the Revival to the present, is often personified as female, yet women remain merely ciphers or symbolic objects through which male writers construct their personal and national identities. The emergence of an Irish feminism across the twentieth century is addressed from the activism of women such as Hanna Sheehy-Skeffington (1877–1946), Constance Markievicz (1868–1927) or Maud Gonne (1865–1953), through the ground-breaking literary scholarship of B. G. MacCarthy (1904–93), to the poetry and criticism of contemporary figures such as Eavan Boland (born 1940). Feminist interventions in the politics of literary form, voice and register are demonstrated through a discussion of the work of Kate O'Brien (1897–1974), Elizabeth Bowen (1899–1973) and Mary Lavin (1912–96). Chapter Five also stresses that it is not only women who write about gender and that masculinity should not be allowed to achieve a normative transparency in literary debate. Consequently, this chapter also appraises the often troubled, uncertain or fluid masculinities in Irish writing from the Revival period through to the fiction of John McGahern (1934–2006). Furthermore, Chapter Five details both affinities and disputes between feminist and postcolonial approaches to Irish literature.

Contemporary writing in the Irish Republic and the North of Ireland is investigated in Chapter Six, which builds upon our sense of how literature and criticism are embedded in social change across the twentieth century. Affirmative responses to transformations in the Republic are addressed alongside much more circumspect or pessimistic articulations of ongoing inequalities with reference, for example, to the fiction of John Banville (born 1945), Patrick McCabe (born 1955), Colm Tóibín (born 1955), Edna O'Brien (born 1932) and Emma Donoghue (born 1969); the poetry of Boland, Brendan Kennelly (born 1936) and Paul Durcan (born 1944); and the drama of Tom Murphy (born 1935). With regard to the North, the intense social pressures which led to the onset of the Troubles and a concomitant literary flourishing in the mid-1960s are assessed in the thoughtful but contentious response of Seamus Heaney (born 1939). Heaney's effort to find mythic patterns through which to understand political violence in the North is contrasted with the poetry of Derek Mahon (born 1941), Paul Muldoon (born 1951), Ciaran Carson (born 1948) and Medbh McGuckian (born 1950). Heaney's work is also related to the Field Day project together with the drama of Brian Friel (born 1929). Contrasting attitudes to identity politics, language and place are covered in an analysis of the plays of Stewart Parker (1941–98) and Frank McGuinness (born 1953). Contemporary fiction is evaluated in terms of the city, pluralism and postmodernism with reference to Dermot Bolger (born 1959) and Roddy Doyle (born 1958) in the Republic and to Glenn Patterson (born 1961), Robert McLiam Wilson (born 1964) and Frances Molloy (1947–91) in the North. The conclusion picks up on live debates within Irish Studies concerning multiculturalism, race, diversity and pluralism. From the 1980s onwards the economic boom of the Celtic Tiger (so named as an Irish version of the Tiger economies of Asia and their free-market, deregulating ethos) has made the Republic an increasingly globalized space.[5] So too the Peace Process, which built upon the IRA ceasefires of 1994 and 1998, led to the Good Friday Agreement of 1998, and involved the British, Irish and US governments, and the current era of political devolution has increasingly opened the North to a globalized world economy. The conclusion addresses both the possibilities and problems of these new dispensations in the context established by our account of contemporary writing in Chapter Six.

For now, we will anticipate the discussion of the Revival in Chapter One. The chapter that follows will begin with Yeats's essay 'The Celtic Element' as a means of unfolding the main facets of his vision of a national rebirth. By way of setting Yeats's essay in context and of indicating the contentious inheritances which comprise his project, we will conclude this introduction by clarifying the key ideas which Yeats gleaned from Matthew Arnold. As a scholar, Arnold gave a series of lectures in 1866 arguing for the establishment of the first ever chair in Celtic Studies at Oxford University in what is a testament to his intense interest in Celtic cultures.[6] Arnold's work was itself directly influenced by his reading of *Poésie des Races Celtiques* or *The Poetry of the Celtic Races* (1860) by the French philosopher Ernest Renan (1823–92) This was a formative work in the European race theory that developed in the nineteenth century and which, as a sprawling range of pseudo-scientific, pseudo-anthropological and philological discourses, went on to have such hideous consequences in the twentieth century. This is not to say that Renan or nineteenth-century race theorists such as he are directly responsible for the racial extermination programmes of the twentieth century but a naïve or innocent reading of such theories stands as one of the many things obliterated by the concentration camps of Nazi Europe. In Renan's own work, he sought to complement emerging theories of the Teutonic or Anglo-Saxon races as the primary and most developed of human cultures and societies with a validation of the Celtic peoples.[7] In terms that would echo not only through Arnold and Yeats but also down through a vast body of thinking about Irish identity and culture thereafter, Renan claimed that the Celts were an extremely emotional and melancholy bunch. As he famously put it: even when the Celtic race appears to be happy 'a tear is not slow to glisten behind its smile'.[8] And, in an equally important presumption, he averred that the Celts were 'an essentially feminine race'.[9]

Arnold reiterates these terms and regards the Celts as spiritual, emotional and poetic but his apparent praise has an ulterior purpose. He felt that his own Victorian English society had become too materialistic and philistine. So the Celts could be offered as an antidote to this spiritual lack, but not on their own terms, for they were to be annexed into a fully integrated Britain. And while the spiritual, emotional, feminine Celts provide the local colouring and the poetry, they cannot be entrusted to undertake any of the governing of this united Britain.

For the Celt, as Arnold puts it, is 'always ready to react against the despotism of fact'.[10] Indeed, Arnold denies any living present or purpose to Celtic cultures and considers them merely archival curios or museum pieces by which an overly materialistic England may spiritually re-enrich itself. So, according to the perversity of Arnold's Celticism, Celtic cultures are to be collected paradoxically as repositories of their own demise, as, in turn, he as their celebrant is also their undertaker. The chapter that follows will assess how Yeats critically takes up Arnold's and Renan's terms.

CHAPTER ONE

Irish Literature and Criticism in the Revival

Anglo-Irish Irelands: Yeats and his inheritances

Given the political impetus behind Arnold's Celticism, its desire to endorse and galvanize a settled and homogeneous British nation, it may seem odd that the Irish nationalist Yeats should take up Arnold's template in his own essay 'The Celtic Element in Literature'. But it does need to be acknowledged that where Arnold saw the different races as complementing one another in a unified British State, Yeats seeks to turn Arnold's model against its own putative logic. Yeats argues that if Saxon and Celt are so racially, historically and culturally distinct in their identities and values, then this necessitates political separatism and an Ireland unfettered by British domination and materialism. Nonetheless – as will be discussed in due course with regard to those critical paradigms opposed to Yeats's project – while his political intentions are radically different from Arnold's, Yeats does broadly accept the racial designations and assumptions of Arnold's lectures. Yeats is eager, however, to stress his deeper and more profound attachment to Celtic culture than Arnold, in a manner that helps explain the reasons for his own and Lady Gregory's systematic effort to collect, recuperate and rewrite a disparate array of Irish folk cultural sources into a literary tradition, such as in *Representative Irish Tales* (1891). Yeats claims:

> ■ When Matthew Arnold wrote, it was not as easy to know as much as we know now of folk-song and folk-belief, and I do not think he understood that our 'natural magic' is but the ancient religion of the world, the ancient worship of Nature and that troubled ecstasy before her, that certainty of all beautiful places being haunted, which it brought into men's minds.[1] □

Yeats is here trying to establish an organic connection with that folk culture, which, in turn, itself provides a direct bond with nature. Yeats contrasts this Celtic union with the natural world with the alienation from, and indeed loss of, nature in even the very best of

Western European literature and its pastoral modes, so that he writes of the ancient Roman poet Virgil (70–19 BC), William Shakespeare (1564–1616) and the Romantic poet John Keats (1795–1821):

> ■ They looked at nature in the modern way, the way of people who are poetical, but are more interested in one another than in a nature which has faded to be but friendly and pleasant, the way of people who have forgotten the ancient religion.[2] □

Thus, for Yeats, 'all folk literature, and all literature that keeps the folk tradition, delights in unbounded and immortal things'.[3] So where Arnold sought to petrify Celtic culture, Yeats endeavours to claim it as a timeless resource which is able to offer him access to a people, a collective tradition, untrammelled by the limitations of his contemporary society. To that end, he rewords Arnold's theories about the Celts' reaction against the 'despotism of fact' and thorough melancholy, which, he argues, stem from

> ■ that melancholy which made all ancient peoples delight in tales that end in death and parting, as modern peoples delight in tales that end in marriage bells; and made all ancient peoples, who, like the old Irish, had a nature more lyrical than dramatic, delight in wild and beautiful lamentations.[4] □

We can discern here the implacable anti-modernity that is given directly political shape in a play such as Yeats's *Cathleen ni Houlihan* (1902), wherein Michael Gillane is required to renounce the material world of money, possessions and marriage in order to answer the lament of his nation personified as Mother Ireland or Cathleen. What is truly Irish, it is implied, is either that which has been uncontaminated by the material world, or that which is once more prepared to renounce the petty concerns of that world. Hence, what Ireland needs to restore to itself is not to be found in Dublin or Belfast for example, but in a realm where the artist may commune with a rural, peasant people themselves at one with nature.

It can be pointed out that the melancholy attributed to the Celtic peasant not only by Yeats but also by Arnold and Renan before him is particularly disingenuous, to put it mildly, in an Irish context, given the Famine (which directly impinges on Arnold's lectures) and a broader history of dispossession, poverty and suffering. The social and historical conditions producing a vast Irish folk and ballad tradition of loss and lament are thus recoded and decontextualized as an immemorial metaphysical disposition. Yeats's sense, in the above passage, that it is he and the urban intelligentsia who suffer 'penury', inverts the reality of social inequality in assembling a model of spiritual debasement designed to transfigure the rural poor into keepers of cultural riches. A Yeats poem such as 'The Fisherman' is creatively charged by its attempt to construct an ideal rural peasant to whom Yeats's work may be dedicated in the face of an acknowledgement that such a figure does not exist, that realities may be very different. It is Yeats's intention, however, that art is to have a transformative role, that it may redeem a society lost to materialism and philistinism. His use of the peasantry as a point of access to an 'ancient' world also discloses that part of Yeats's revival mission was to repair a rupture in Irish history and tradition caused by Ireland's subjugation and the imposition of the British culture that he sees as the vehicle of modern, materialist corruption. While the marginalization of the Irish language and the fragmentation of Irish culture prevent any sense of cultural continuity, Yeats endeavours to restore and recuperate out of that discontinuity, if not a unitary tradition, then a unity of purpose that may finally make Irish culture whole again in the present. So the lessons and achievements of antiquity that have been preserved in however disparate and fragmentary a form, the remaining repositories of Irish culture, may speak once more and assume their full meaning in the present and in the transformation of Irish national life.

Equally, Yeats's effort to reassert a sense of Irish cultural tradition entails a rejection of the contemporary British supplanting and inferiorization of it. Part of the point of Yeats's association of his own project and the folk culture which supports it with the ancient past is to proclaim that Ireland *does* have a worthy and noble culture with a history and an authority of its own. It is not merely a regional or provincial variant of British culture, nor indeed a cultural dead-end that has served its limited aims and been eclipsed by the achievements and advancements of England. The linking of the present to the ancient past seeks to circumvent the Anglicization and disruption of Irish cultural tradition, and it jointly serves to aggrandize Irish literature as being one of the formative sources of the great literary traditions of the Western world (before its contamination by Britishness). Yeats also approvingly reiterates Renan's claim that the Lough Derg purgatory had a key influence on *The Divine Comedy* of Dante (1265–1321). Yeats goes on to link 'The Celtic Movement' with a pan-European Symbolist which includes the German composer Richard Wagner (1813–83), the English Pre-Raphaelite painters and poets such as Dante Gabriel Rossetti (1828–82), the French poets Villiers de l'Isle Adam (1840–89) and Stéphane Mallarmé (1842–98), the Belgian poet and playwright Maurice Maeterlinck (1862–1949), the Norwegian dramatist Henrik Ibsen (1828–1906) and the Italian poet, playwright and novelist Gabriele D'Annunzio (1863–1938). For Yeats, all great literatures must create 'a sacred book'.[5] Yeats's own art similarly strives to produce such a 'sacred book', an epic Irish text to inspire and redeem the nation. His reclamation of the heroic myth of Cuchulainn in a play like *On Baile's Strand* (1904), or of the many heroes of both ancient legend and more recent Irish literature and politics who people his poetry, are all enlisted to shake the foundations of a complacent, materialist society through an eruption of the sacral, restorative intoxication and power of art. Such art, Yeats intended, would reconstitute the Irish nation according to its own heroic ideals, and behind such epic idealism stands Yeats himself as the supreme artistic hero. Indeed, Yeats carefully dates the prefatory note to his *Autobiographies* as 25 December 1914 so that the book of his life is brought into being on Christmas Day and thereby (somewhat mischievously, perhaps) positions Yeats as the new Messiah. Though adept at self-promotion, Yeats did also more selflessly commit himself to collective projects like the Irish Literary Theatre and its commitment to advancing the work of a whole gamut of writers.

In another essay, 'The Theatre' (1900), Yeats outlined the goals of that national drama:

■ We must make a theatre for ourselves and our friends, and for a few simple people who understand from sheer simplicity what we understand from scholarship and thought. We have planned the Irish Literary Theatre with this hospitable emotion, and that the right people may find out about us, we hope to act a play or two in the spring of every year; and that the right people may escape the stupefying memory of the theatre of commerce that clings even to them, our plays will be for the most part remote, spiritual and ideal.[6] □

In this excerpt there is the familiar effort to connect Yeats's own intellectual ambitions and reading of Irish culture with a (somewhat condescendingly defined) 'simple' popular audience in an authentic bond that once more resists the depredations of commerce and modern life. But it is in this endeavour that Yeats builds upon the work of a number of figures in the second half of the nineteenth century who similarly sought to reconcile the intellectual and the people in the reclamation of heroic forms. The historiography of Standish O'Grady had sought to retrieve the 'heroic period' of Irish history, which encapsulated 'the spirit of a whole nation', since 'those heroes and heroines were the ideals of our ancestors, their conduct and character were to them a religion, the bardic literature was their Bible [...] The same human heart beat in their breasts as beats amongst us today. All the great permanent relations of life are the same'.[7] And, in terms that are echoed in Yeats, this timeless transmission of these essential Irish heroic virtues is made more exigent by the sprawling corruption of the modern world, of what O'Grady terms 'the vastness and populousness of this age'.[8] So, as with Yeats, there is in such sentiment a deeply ingrained fear of modern society and the modern masses and a hope that the return of heroic forms will give shape and meaning to what is perceived as chaos.

The essay 'The Necessity for De-Anglicizing Ireland' (1892) by Douglas Hyde comparably wills the salvation of a shapeless Irish society. Hyde felt that the British occupation of Ireland had disrupted the continuity of Irish history and that the Anglicization of Ireland had ruined the autonomy and integrity of Irishness as an identity of its own. Consequently, Hyde argued, Ireland was in a 'half-way house', neither one thing nor the other, since people had turned their backs on the language and culture of their true Irish heritage and had instead sought to copy and emulate English culture. For Hyde, this was a doomed servility since the Irish were not English and their second-order 'approximation of Anglicized culture left Ireland in its present 'anomalous position'. The political and social upheavals and failures of nineteenth-century Ireland, Hyde averred, were directly attributable to 'the race diverging during this century from the right path, and ceasing to be Irish without becoming English'.[9] In particular, it was the revival of the Irish language, and more generally Irish culture itself, which were vital weapons in defeating the 'West Britonism' – the mimicking of British culture – that had contaminated Ireland. So, in Hyde's model, both Irish culture and nationality are ideally defined in terms of racial purity:

■ On racial lines, then, we shall best develop, following the bent of our own natures, and, in order to do this, we must create a strong feeling against West-Britonism [...] upon Irish lines alone can the Irish race once more become what it was of yore – one of the most original, artistic, literary, and charming peoples of Europe.[10] □

In this essay, Hyde also called for copies of the work of Thomas Moore (1779–1852) and Thomas Davis to be kept and read in every Irish household. Indeed, Davis too had forcefully stated the case for the rescue of the Irish language in 1843: 'A people without a language of its own is only half a nation. A nation should guard its language more than its territories – 'tis a surer barrier, and more important frontier, than fortress or river'.[11] It is noteworthy that over half a century before Ferdinand de Saussure (1857–1913), or the twentieth-century development of structuralism out of his ideas, which sought to demystify the notion that language had a natural or direct connection to the reality it supposedly represents and to conceive it instead as merely an arbitrary system of signifiers and signifieds, Davis conceives of the English language as comprising 'arbitrary signs'. This adumbration of de Saussure and structuralism *avant la lettre* as a direct result of what Davis regarded as the imposition of the English language on Ireland raises important questions about the experimentations of Irish writers in the twentieth century. Are they due to a more generalized European and Western collapse of faith in humanism, in a widespread falling away of the belief that language and representation adequately map the world – which can be characterized as a move through modernism into postmodernism and through structuralism into post-structuralism or deconstruction – or are they due to a more specific causal context in the sundering of the Irish language and Irish culture by British domination (and precisely these issues will be addressed in relation to Joyce and Beckett in due course)?

Nevertheless, before Davis is unduly transformed into a straightforward proto-structuralist, it is vital to bear in mind that his own motive for highlighting the arbitrariness of the English language, its ill-fitting unsuitability for representing Ireland, was to position the Irish language as avowedly natural, even biologically so. And just as the Irish language organically emanates from the very body of its speakers, so too is it naturally embedded in Ireland's landscape. In Davis's mind, the Irish language offers a kind of cultural inoculation that wards off the infection of English encroachment. Given this kind of assertion of both racial and linguistic purism, such an argument is made intensely ironic, and ultimately untenable, by the fact that much of the archival retrieval of traditional Irish ballads and songs by the likes of Moore, Davis or Hyde involves translation and an uneasy Anglo-Irish admixture. So the advocacy of the Irish language and the national rebirth it represents remain anticipations of a purer future rather than a reality since the hybrid form of these translated ballads and songs defeats the very purity they are intended to confirm. Likewise, the fact that many of the literary figures engaged in the revival of folk ballads and songs were socially Anglo-Irish also caused them problems, and their inheritance was roundly mistrusted by the Catholic, Irish Ireland thinkers such as D. P. Moran and Daniel Corkery (for an amalgam of reasons that we will discuss shortly).

But with regard to Yeats, the work of Moore, Davis, Hyde and O'Grady was important in emboldening his own revivalist mission, and in his essay 'Irish National Literature' (1895) Yeats writes of sensing for the first time in his life the emergence of 'a school of men of letters united by a common purpose' to which he is a contributor. Yeats states that it is their collective desire 'to fashion out of the world about us, and the things that our fathers have told us, a new ritual for the builders of peoples, the imperishable moods'.[12] Though clearly not an admirer of their literary abilities, Yeats was willing to praise the laudable purpose of Hyde's and Moore's translations: 'Despite their constant clumsiness and crudity, they brought into the elaborate literature of the modern world the bold vehemence, and the avid definiteness, the tumultuous movement, the immeasurable dreaming of the Gaelic literature'.[13]

In another piece, 'Nationality and Literature' (1893), Yeats also sought to promote the work of Davis and O'Grady, as well as of Sir Samuel Ferguson (1810–86) and James Clarence Mangan (1803–49). Using both Greek and English literature as his template, Yeats identified three key formal movements in the development of a nation's literature: narrative or epic poetry, a dramatic period and finally lyric poetry. Ireland, since its full national character remained unexpressed, was for Yeats in the first, formative, epic or ballad period of building national self-consciousness. To Yeats, the best Irish writers – Ferguson, Mangan, Davis and O'Grady – are epic or ballad writers whose work has the value of giving heroic form to a renewed and unitary Irish identity: 'Our poetry is still a poetry of the people in the main, for it still deals with the tales and thoughts of the people'.[14] A comparable national unity and consciousness whereby artists and intellectuals may shape, elevate and synthesize the untainted pre-modern simplicities of the Irish peasant is to be found in Yeats's 'The Literary Movement in Ireland' (1901).[15] The task of art in an era of material debasement, according to Yeats, is to provide 'a voice of the idealism of the common people'.[16] However, Yeats's ideal of an art reconciled with its people and a people reconciled with its art has been highly problematic for his critics and detractors. His assertion that the foundation of Irish literature is 'fixed in legend rather than in history' has, for his opponents, less to do with the national revival of an immemorial Irishness deprived of its immediate continuity by British impingement and more to do with constructing a consolatory myth for the Anglo-Irish Ascendancy in the face of the reality of their imminent demise.[17]

It is notable that Yeats desires, to appropriate one of his own terms, a unity of culture between artist and common people, but that unity is a highly selective one. The social basis of the Ireland which Yeats wished to reawaken has a clear three-tier structure:

■ Three types of men have made all beautiful things. Aristocracies have made beautiful manners, because their place in the world puts them above the fear of life, and the countrymen have made beautiful stories and beliefs, because they have nothing to lose and so do not fear, and the artists have made all the rest, because Providence has filled them with recklessness.[18] □

So Yeats's ideal organic Ireland comprises aristocrats, the rural peasantry and artists. The significant omissions are obviously the middle and working classes. It is a vision of society that is strictly hierarchical and fixed, and which is constructed in scorn of the convulsions of modern, industrializing and urbanizing society. In a sense, Yeats's three-tier rural alliance may offer a necessary and laudable antithesis to the deprivations of modern capitalism and materialism. However, for all its horrors and world wars, the twentieth century was also the onset of democratization and the full emancipation of women and the working class, and in this context Yeats's hierarchical ideal appears much more sinister. In fact, the adjectives employed in one of Yeats's key polemics against the modern world are highly instructive:

■ All our scientific, democratic, fact-accumulating, heterogeneous civilisation [...] prepares not the continuance of itself but the revelation as in a lightning flash, though in a flash that will not strike only in one place, and will for a time be constantly repeated, of the civilisation that must slowly take its place.[19] □

The 'scientific' and the 'fact-accumulating' may be understood in terms of his anti-rationalism, his emotional Celticism, yet the disparagement of the 'democratic' and the 'heterogeneous' betrays how Yeats's ideal Celt underpins a highly reactionary yearning for social hierarchy and the protection of racial purity and homogeneity. The above passage is also spurred by a portent that the historical continuity of modern society is about to be utterly effaced. In the context of the Irish Literary Revival, Yeats's recourse to the ancient Celtic past always sought an epic return of former glories, a messianic interruption of the banality of modern society.

However, Yeats's messianism is always ready to turn into apocalypticism. Poems such as 'Leda and the Swan' and 'The Second Coming' crystallize Yeats's version of history, according to which history moves in gyres or huge cyclical patterns that are predetermined rather than being a process of progress and development or a continuum in which people may intervene and change its outcomes. 'Leda and the Swan' for instance is fundamentally non-democratic in its annunciation of a new age in that it insists that knowledge and awakening are to be forced upon people rather than learned. Indeed, the English writer George Orwell (1903–50) wrote after Yeats's death that

■ Translated into political terms, Yeats's tendency is Fascist [...] the theory that civilization moves in recurring cycles is one way out for people who hate the concept of human equality [...] It does not matter if the lower orders are getting above themselves, for, after all, we shall soon be returning to an age of tyranny.[20] □

Orwell is suggesting that Yeats's gyring, cyclical version of history precludes social reform or emancipation. Indeed democratization, or any attempt to change society, is pointless in these terms since history's cycles of civilization and barbarism bring great epochs into being and then obliterate them with the same inexorable certainty. So why bother, Orwell intimates, trying to change something that is already determined and which will be erased in any case by the next turn of the gyre. With regard to Orwell's accusation of Fascism, Yeats did late in his life flirt with the Blueshirts, the Irish Fascist movement modelled on the Italian Fascists of Benito Mussolini (1883–1945). In his letters, Yeats remarked of Gavin O'Duffy (1892–1944), the leader of the Blueshirts: 'Politics are growing heroic [...] I do not think him a great man though a pleasant one, but one never knows, his face may harden or clarify'.[21] Given Yeats's cultural privileging of the epic and heroic as suitable models for Ireland to renew its sense of itself as a great nation, it is telling that he sees politics becoming similarly 'heroic' with the emergence of an Irish Fascist movement.

As indicated in the samples of Yeats's criticism that we have surveyed, his ideal Irish society was always hierarchical and harked back to a fixed pre-modern simplicity. Yeats appears to have found in Fascism, however briefly, a framework in which to realize that hierarchical vision. While Fascism is obviously a modern political ideology that seeks to mobilize the masses of industrialized, capitalist societies, it does so according to a paradigm of pre-modern purity and security through which its people may be reordered and redeemed. Yeats's Fascism is indefensible and should be recognized as such. However, it should also be pointed out that he very rapidly withdrew his support for Fascism – though not so much on ethical grounds as strategic ones. He feared the return of O'Duffy's Fascists from the Spanish Civil War (1936–9) for he came to regard them as a part of his enemies who had marginalized his revival project and its good intentions for Ireland: 'I am convinced that if the Spanish war goes on, or if it ceases and O'Duffy's volunteers return heroes, my "pagan" institutions, the Theatre, the Academy, will be fighting for their lives against combined Catholic and Gaelic bigotry'.[22]

Anglo-Irish Irelands: Synge, Lady Gregory Shaw

In trying to understand how the Romantic nationalism of Yeats's work in the late nineteenth century and early twentieth century became so isolated and embittered in his later life, we will turn in due course towards his contemporary critics, particularly D. P. Moran, who had opposed his project from the outset, before returning to his work and the more recent critical paradigms that have assembled themselves around it in Chapter Three. For now, we can observe that Yeats was not the only Anglo-Irish writer to incur the wrath of a specific kind of Irish Catholic Nationalism and its own claims to Irishness and to the ultimate meaning and direction of the Revival. The work of the dramatist John Millington Synge caused controversy, most notably when the Dublin performance of his play *The Playboy of the Western World* was disrupted by rioting in 1907. As Lady Gregory reported to Yeats in her famous telegram: 'Audience broke up in disorder at the word shift'.[23] (The word 'shift' is a term for a woman's undergarment and we will return to its significance in Chapter Three.) The Irish Nationalists in the theatre who revolted had been scandalized by the play's representation of Irish peasant life since its tale of murder, earthy sexual dealings and rough manners directly contravened their own idealization of rural existence. It is clear that Synge, like Yeats, was contesting ownership of peasant life as a repository of the 'real' Ireland with this metropolitan, middle-class Catholic Nationalism. Indeed, Synge's preface to the play, dated 21 January 1907, refers to 'those of us who know the people', and combines a Yeatsian claim to hold an authentic connection to peasant culture with an equally Yeatsian and implacable anti-modernity:

> ■ In writing *The Playboy of the Western World*, as in my other plays, I have used one or two words only, that I have not heard among the country people of Ireland, or spoken in my own nursery before I could read the newspapers [...] in countries where the imagination of the people, and the language they use, is rich and living, it is possible for a writer to be rich and copious in his words, and at the same time to give the reality which is the root of all poetry, in a comprehensive and natural form. In the modern literature of towns, however, richness is found only in sonnets, or prose poems, or in one or two elaborate books that are far away from the profound and common interests of life [...] In Ireland, for a few years more, we have a popular imagination that is fiery and magnificent, and tender; so that those of us who wish to write start with a chance that is not given to writers in places where the springtime of the local life has been forgotten, and the harvest is a memory only, and the straw has been turned into bricks.[24] □

In this passage there is a demonstrable hostility to the city and the spaces of modern, urban life, and a simultaneous lament for and celebration of the rural world that is being obliterated by the encroachment of modernity. Significantly, Synge claims that both the language and imagination of his work emanate directly from a popular, rural source. Additionally, his definition of a properly authentic and vibrant national literature insists upon a connection with that peasant origin, in contrast to the literatures of the urban world, which, however polished or formally honed, lack the organic depth of his own work.

Synge was particularly vexed by the reaction to *Playboy* given that the rioters were not peasants but the urban, Catholic middle class in Dublin:

> ■ the scurrility and ignorance and treachery of some of the attacks upon me have rather disgusted me with the middle-class Irish Catholic. As you know I

have the wildest admiration for the Irish Peasants, and for Irish men of known or unknown genius – do you bow? – but between the two there's an ungodly ruck of fat-faced, sweaty-headed swine.[25] □

Here Synge distils a fundamental tension between the different constituencies who comprised the Revival. For he, like Yeats, contests ownership of the putatively 'real', authentic or organic Ireland and its peasant keepers with the emergent Catholic, metropolitan middle class. And just as Yeats had constructed his ideal, three-tiered hierarchy of aristocrats, artists and peasants, so Synge seeks an intimate communion between writer and peasant undisturbed by the intrusion of the middle class (or the working class for that matter).

Lady Gregory correspondingly attempted to assert an Irishness bound by an organic connection that would transcend political fraction in both her own work and her collaborations with Yeats. However, her *Our Irish Theatre* (1913) is also instructive in exhibiting a growing frustration with the reaction to her and Yeats's institutional efforts in developing a National Theatre and their archival accumulation of folklore and tradition. *Our Irish Theatre* quotes the founding statement of the Literary Theatre and its desire for a dignified, cultural resurgence of Irishness and a concomitant urge that this redeemed Irishness would set aside political divisions:

■ We hope to find in Ireland an uncorrupted and imaginative audience trained to listen by its passion for oratory [...] We are confident of the support of all Irish people, who are weary of misrepresentation, in carrying out a work that is outside all the political questions that divide us.[26] □

But the yearning of Gregory's hopes turns markedly to disdain and despair in the wake of the *Playboy* riots. She writes: 'It was a definite fight for freedom from mob censorship'.[27] So while Yeats, Synge and Gregory sought to restore an organic relation between artist and society– especially through their intended bond with a rural popular subject and tradition – they increasingly found themselves haranguing what they saw as a crass, philistine populism. Across the work of all three writers, there is a prevailing feeling as the twentieth century moved on that they are being overtaken by energies in the Revival period which they cannot control and which are unamenable and unresponsive to their ideal organic unities.

The exiled George Bernard Shaw also tends to fare badly with recent nationalist critical paradigms. His play *John Bull's Other Island* (1904) was a direct and avowedly ecumenical intervention in the debates we have already discussed about the Revival, Ireland, Britain and interlocking stereotypes. For his own part, Shaw intended the play as a critique of the Revival in words that echo the intent behind Joyce's *Dubliners* (which we will discuss shortly): '*John Bull's Other Island* was uncongenial to the whole spirit of the neo-Gaelic movement, which is bent on creating a new Ireland after its own ideal, whereas my play is a very uncompromising presentment of the real old Ireland'.[28] In the play, Shaw launches an attack on an obsessive Irish recourse to 'imagination' which he views as pandering to British stereotypes of the dreaming Celt. One of the primary targets of Shaw's cynicism was Yeats's *Cathleen Ni Houlihan* and its recourse to the 1798 rebellion. However, Yeats – despite some misgivings about the exilic perspective of Shaw – was generous enough to praise the play's diagnostic vision:

■ You have said things in this play that are entirely true about Ireland, things which nobody has ever said before, and these are the very things that are most part of the action. It astonishes me that you should have been so long in London and yet have remembered so much.[29] □

In addition to undermining Revivalist stereotypes, Shaw also sought to dismantle British assumptions and received wisdoms, in particular turning the stereotypes of Arnoldian Celticism back against the English:

■ Blackguard, bully, drunkard, liar, foulmouth, flatterer, beggar, backbiter, venal functionary, corrupt judge, envious friend, vindictive opponent, unparalleled political traitor: all these your Irishman may easily be, just as he may be a gentleman [...] but he is never quite the hysterical, nonsense-crammed, fact-proof, truth-terrified, unballasted sport of all the bogey panics and all the silly enthusiasm that now calls itself 'God's Englishman'.[30] □

However, the apparent even-handedness of Shaw's satire was not appreciated by the proponents of Irish Ireland, of a nation unsullied by both British and Anglo-Irish influence. We will now appraise the leading advocate of this Irish Ireland philosophy, D. P. Moran.

Irish Ireland: D. P. Moran

Moran was one of the most vociferous and implacable opponents of the endeavours of Yeats and other Anglo-Irish writers, and projects such as the Irish Literary Theatre. Moran harangued Yeats from the pages of the magazine *The Leader* and he most famously published *The Philosophy of Irish Ireland* (1905). Moran's thought is also reactivated in the criticism of Daniel Corkery, who would become the quasi-official intellectual of the new Irish Free State and to whom we shall turn in

Chapter Two. As the apparently tautological nature of his term suggests, D. P. Moran's 'Irish Ireland' was a highly rigidified and attenuated definition of Irishness. We noted that Anglo-Irish writers such as Yeats or Hyde were engaged in a project to de-Anglicize Ireland, to reclaim its cultural and racial purity and identity in a rigorously separatist manner. However, these Protestant, Anglo-Irish intellectuals then became the victims of that same exclusivist and purifying logic which was turned against them by the Irish Ireland movement personified by Moran. The Irish nation was and is a Catholic nation, according to Moran, and the Anglo-Irish thus fail his even more circumscribed litmus test of national belonging. In fact, the Anglo-Irish were themselves mongrels, exactly the problem rather than the solution to the ills which Moran identified in Irish society. So while the grammar of Moran's argument seems comparable to that of Hyde or Yeats, his ultimate goal is to exclude what he saw as all that is non-Catholic and non-indigenous in order to regain a true, pure Irishness (and thus the Protestant, hyphenated Anglo-Irish had to be expurgated as an unnecessary complication):

> ■ Even if the Anglo-Saxon race [...] the English-speaking race stopped where it is we could not keep on in our present way without disaster. But the English speaking race, in the meshes of which we are interwoven by a thousand material and immaterial ties, is making the pace and we must either stand up to it – which I fear we cannot; isolate ourselves from its influence – which we largely can do; or else get trodden on and be swallowed up – which, it appears to me, is, if we keep on as we are going, inevitable.[31] □

In an echo of Davis and Hyde, Moran's own late discovery of the Irish language offered the means to alter the Irish character and purify the nation since they would otherwise be lost forever: 'We must be original Irish, and not imitation English. Above all we must relearn our language, and become a bi-lingual people. For the great connecting link between us and the real Ireland, which few of us know anything about, is the Gaelic tongue'.[32] So the 'real' Ireland may utilize language to protect and separate itself finally from Britishness: 'A distinct language is the great weapon by which we can ward off undue foreign influence and keep ourselves surrounded by a racy Irish atmosphere'.[33] The 'racy' nature of this anticipated Irish future discloses not only the dynamic nature of the society Moran felt he was anticipating but also puns on race and reminds us of the ethnic and biological exclusions of his ideal nation. One major issue that vexed Moran was that mass emigration, especially since the Famine, resulted in the Irish nation abroad sending part of its income home to relieve the plight of family members who had been left behind. To Moran, this subsidizing was blighting economic activity and motivation at home and it is interesting that for all his Catholicism and his sense of a fixed Irish destiny and identity, his musings on the state of Ireland are informed by a ruthless social Darwinism:

■ The more we struggle amongst ourselves and compete against one another the better for the commonweal [...] there will be an apparent waste of energy at which a shallow mind will be dismayed [...] the net benefit to the Gaelic Revival of all this energy let loose in free fields will be comparatively enormous. Uniformity is soul destroying, and leaves more than half the faculties of a man dormant. It is in strife of all kinds that men are drawn out for all they are worth, and free play for strife and competition is an essential condition if we are to get the greatest net amount of energy out of any community.[34] □

Thus, in Moran's work there is an uneasy tension between a yearning for purity and homogeneity in the sphere of race and culture and a simultaneous advocacy of market-driven innovation in the realm of economics. As we will analyze in the next chapter, the Irish Free State and the Irish Republic that superseded it found it extremely difficult to reconcile precisely these tensions.

In the meantime, we will scrutinize Joyce, in part to indicate that though there are profound differences between him and Yeats there are also some important commonalities. Some of the more recent critical paradigms that we will survey in this Guide tend to polarize Yeats and Joyce and, in doing so, to construct their own agendas around this dichotomized template that perhaps says much more about the different schools of Irish Studies today than it does about the writers in question. What Joyce did share with Yeats was an assertion of art and the aesthetic and an imaginative space entirely at odds with mainstream Irish society and politics. The Catholic Joyce was just as fierce an opponent of the narrow Catholic nationalism represented by Moran as was Yeats and so too his work was just as vehemently indicted by that nationalism as Yeats's. We will focus on two important Joyce essays: 'The Day of the Rabblement' (1901) and 'Ireland, Island of Saints and Sages' (1907).

Irish Ireland and its critics: Joyce

'The Day of the Rabblement' is a polemical piece directed specifically at the Irish Literary Theatre and its founders, Yeats, Lady Gregory and Edward Martyn. In terms of Joyce's own work, the essay considers the relationship between art and its audience, in this case, between the writer and what Joyce deems the 'rabblement' – the mob, the rabble. This essay, written early in Joyce's career and rejected for publication by University College Dublin journal *St Stephen's* (primarily on the basis of a reference to an Italian novel that had been placed on the list of the Vatican's Index of Prohibited Books), neatly distils Joyce's changing attitude to the Irish Literary Theatre and the Revival it sought to encourage. Initially, Joyce had supported the Theatre more generally, its aim of producing European drama as well as Irish work, and in particular its first production, *The Countess Cathleen* (1892), which had incurred the hostility of Moran's Irish Ireland movement (on the basis of his objection to the Anglo-Irish intrusion upon the canon of Irishness) and of the Catholic Church (on the grounds of its supposed heresy). Famously, Joyce refused to sign a student petition condemning the play. Indeed, Joyce also looked favourably on the Irish Literary Theatre's second play, Martyn's *The Heather Field* (1899), and he would later produce a version of it in Zurich in 1919.

However, 'The Day of the Rabblement' signals a very abrupt change of Joyce's opinion in regard to the overall direction of the Irish Literary Theatre in 1901. For the year in which Joyce (hastily) wrote his polemic saw the Theatre produce Douglas Hyde's *Casadh an tSúgáin* (*The Twisting of the Rope*, 1901) and *Diarmuid and Gráinne* (1900) by Yeats and George Moore (1852–1933). To Joyce, the production of these plays indicated that the Irish Literary Theatre had been intimidated by the controversies surrounding its initial work and had capitulated to the demands of what he regarded as a crass, populist nationalism. Such a retreat, for Joyce, betrayed the original intention of the Irish Literary Theatre to produce work not only by Irish dramatists but also by the great European playwrights such as Joyce's hero Ibsen: 'the Irish Literary Theatre must now be considered the property of the rabblement of the most belated race in Europe'.[35] So, according to Joyce, both the Irish Literary Theatre and populist nationalism hold each other in a mutually destructive embrace. Notably, Joyce recognizes 'a time of crisis' for literature and art at the onset of the twentieth century, and therefore a concomitant need to defend and sustain art's integrity against decay in a convulsively changing modern world – a sentiment he in fact thus shares with the founders of the Irish Literary Theatre. Nonetheless, Joyce evidently feels the frustration of an opportunity missed, that the Irish Literary Theatre backtracked after the bad press surrounding its formative productions and surrendered the opportunity to establish what Joyce would have considered a more European and international theatre and concomitant intellectual crosscurrent of ideas. Hence, provincial, populist acceptance becomes the bargaining chip by which the Irish Literary Theatre relinquishes its artistic integrity and its more cosmopolitan mission statement. Joyce was particularly frustrated by the fact that Ibsen's *Ghosts* (1881) and *The Power of Darkness* (1886) by Leo Tolstoy (1828–1910) were plays that were both banned in England by the British government but could have been performed in Ireland had the Irish Literary Theatre had either the courage or conviction to do so.[36]

Having also attacked the quality of work written by Moore and Martyn, Joyce concludes his essay by alluding to his hero Ibsen dying in Oslo and also Gerhart Hauptmann (1862–1946), the author of *Michael Kramer* (1900), whom Joyce places as Ibsen's successor. Additionally though, Joyce positions himself as the third artist in this great lineage, as the young master in waiting standing expectantly and portentously by the door – this image itself is an allusion to Ibsen's *The Master Builder* (1892).[37] Joyce's advocacy of the heroic artist standing scornfully out-with the multitude and the will of popular consensus would appear to find its full realization in Stephen Dedalus's wilfully removed God of Creation in *A Portrait of the Artist as a Young Man* (1916). Nonetheless, it is worth considering to what extent Dedalus's character can be taken as Joyce's self-portrait. For though Dedalus spends much of his young adulthood expounding his aesthetic and artistic theories – in both *Portrait* and *Ulysses* (1922) – he never actually produces any work of note himself and there is a strong sense that there is a parodic dimension to Joyce's creation. Joyce's attack on art that is merely the mouthpiece of the rabblement, his rejection of populism, should not then be read simply as an assertion of a disengaged or indeed escapist art. To that end, it is notable that although the 'paralysis' of *Dubliners* signals the deadening, unimaginative entrapment of a community in stasis, so too Dedalus is imprisoned rather than liberated by his enclosed artistic withdrawal and dislocation. To a large degree, if *Dubliners* depicts the debilitating effects of a community without an artist, then *Portrait* also castigates the limitations of an artist without a community. The parallel perspectives of Dedalus and Bloom in *Ulysses* can then be interpreted as Joyce's own effort to resolve this fissure between the artistic and the popular, to embed his own aesthetic in the ordinariness of the everyday.

'Ireland, Island of Saints and Sages' helps to distinguish Joyce's perspective from the racial purities hankered after by his contemporaries such as Yeats and Hyde. But specifically, Joyce is clearly and diametrically opposed to the narrow Catholicism of Irish Ireland's canon of nationality which, Joyce observes, is contradicted by history. He happily lists the many Protestants or migrants who have been involved in Fenian, Nationalist and Republican struggles and uprisings. Joyce's litany is explicitly a counterpoint to the rewriting of Irish history in Catholic terms by Irish Ireland. More broadly, Joyce continues that

■ Our civilization is a vast fabric, in which the most diverse elements are mingled [...] Nationality (if it really is not a convenient fiction like so many others to which the scalpels of present day science have given the coup de grace) must find its reason for being rooted in something that surpasses and transcends and informs changing things like blood and the human word.[38] □

Joyce here very eloquently undermines two key elements that inform the mainstream Revival's guarantors of Irishness: 'blood' or biological race, and 'the human word' or language. Both are rendered fluid and contingent rather than fixed and unyielding. In his early critical writings such as 'Ireland, Island of Saints and Sages' we can trace the origins of the 'Cyclops' chapter in *Ulysses* wherein The Citizen, based on Michael Cusack (1847–1906), the founder of the Gaelic Athletic Association, represents a monocular, limited and one-dimensional view of Ireland and the world at large that typifies Irish Ireland. Bloom's definition of a nation being the same people living in the same place at the same time is, by contrast, more generous and open-ended and facilitates a more heterogeneous Irish identity.

Nonetheless, Joyce is seeking to redefine Irish identity rather than avoid it completely – a fact that was largely lost on literary criticism until the development of Irish Studies in the last three decades of the twentieth century. While Joyce ponders whether nationality is 'a convenient fiction', he is also passionately concerned about the state of Ireland, and his antipathy to mainstream Irish Nationalism should therefore not be misread as apathy. The ambivalence of the exilic Joyce's relationship to a national literary endeavour is tellingly condensed in two verbs near the close of *A Portrait*. As part of Dedalus's *non serviam* (I will not serve), he declares: 'When the soul of a man is born in this country there are nets flung at it to hold it back from flight. You talk to me of nationality, language, religion. I shall try to fly by those nets'.[39] Here 'fly by' can obviously mean to avoid, to transcend and to produce an art that flouts such concerns. However, the phrase can also mean, 'to fly with the aid of', and it can also imply that it is precisely such social pressures that enable Joyce's writing, that they will provide him with the means to fly. Similarly, in his concluding diary entries, Stephen writes as he prepares to leave Ireland: 'I go to encounter for the millionth time more or less the reality of experience and to forge in the smithy of my soul the uncreated conscience of my race'.[40] In this passage the verb 'forge' simultaneously articulates Dedalus's aim of becoming the first writer to create or produce his nation's defining literary instrument and defeats it as another 'convenient fiction' by carrying with it 'forge' in the sense of 'to fake or dubiously copy'.

As to the causes of Ireland's misfortunes, 'Ireland, Island of Saints and Sages' exhibits a stringent critique of British rule in Ireland, which Joyce defines in terms of imperial or colonial occupation that are contentious and which we will examine in the critical debates around his work. Joyce indicts the British administration as a destructive colonial presence which he compares to the actions of Belgian imperialism in the Congo. He continues his polemic by stating of the ordinary Irish person that

■ the economic and intellectual conditions that prevail in his own country do not permit the development of individuality. The soul of the country is weakened by centuries of useless struggle and broken treaties, and individual initiative is paralysed by the influence and admonitions of the church, while its body is manacled by the police, the tax office, and the garrison [...] I do not see what good it does to fulminate against the English tyranny while the Roman tyranny occupies the palace of the soul.[41] □

It is readily apparent in Joyce's indictment of the Ireland that he grew up in that the individual is shackled not only by British imperialism but also by the grip of the Catholic Church and by the failings of mainstream nationalism. It is therefore no accident, perhaps, that in *Ulysses* the entrapped Stephen feels there are three nooses around his neck: by implication, an ever-tightening authoritarian complicity between the British administration, the hegemony of the Catholic Church and a repressive, bourgeois Irish Nationalism. To that end, in a famous letter to his lover and future wife Nora Barnacle (1884–1951) on 29 August 1904 that was etched in his rage (and personal guilt) at his mother's premature death due to what Joyce saw as her mistreatment by a repressive, uncaring patriarchal social order, Joyce launches an absolute, systemic condemnation of society:

■ My mind rejects the whole present social order and Christianity – home, the recognised virtues, classes of life, and religious doctrines. How could I like the idea of home? My home was simply a middle-class affair ruined by spendthrift habits which I have inherited. My mother was slowly killed, I think, by my father's ill-treatment, by years of trouble, and by my cynical frankness of conduct. When I looked upon her face as she lay in her coffin – a face grey and wasted with cancer – I understood that I was looking on the face of a victim and I cursed the system which had made her a victim.[42] □

As to how Joyce's own art would confront that society, 'Ireland, Island of Saints and Sages' also grants a useful insight into the form and technique of his writing. Whereas many Revivalists sought to resurrect a range of idealized, older fragments of Irish culture and shape them into a harmonized, live tradition in the present, Joyce realized, years before Yeats's 'September 1913' or Yeats's later work, that romantic Ireland was indeed long dead and gone:

■ The old national soul that spoke during the centuries through the mouths of fabulous seers, wandering minstrels, and Jacobite poets disappeared from

the world with the death of James Clarence Mangan. With him, the long tradition of the triple order of the old Celtic bards ended; and today other bards,
animated by other ideas, have the cry. One thing alone seems clear to me.
It is well past time for Ireland to have done once and for all with failure. If she
is truly capable of reviving, let her awake, or let her cover up her head and lie
down decently in her grave forever.[43] □

If Joyce's own aesthetic is to take on and to pass judgement on
society, then what he regarded as either the dismal nostalgia or wilful
escapism of the main Revival writers will not suffice. He sought to justify his uncompromising and uncompromised vision in *Dubliners* in this
letter to his publisher:

■ My intention was to write a chapter of the moral history of my country and
I chose Dublin for the scene because that city seemed to me the centre of
paralysis. I have tried to present it to the indifferent public under four of its
aspects: childhood, adolescence, maturity and public life. The stories are
arranged in this order. I have written it for the most part in a style of scrupulous meanness and with the conviction that he is a very bold man who dares
to alter in the presentment, still more to deform, whatever he has seen and
heard. I cannot do more than this. I cannot alter what I have written.[44] □

The excoriating precision of Joyce's 'scrupulous meanness' in
Dubliners helps explain why the work had to struggle for almost a decade
to be published in 1914 – and indeed why sections of it were destroyed
by printers unhappy with its content (as would happen to *Ulysses*). The
very first line of *Dubliners* echoes the inscription above the entrance
to Hell in Dante's *Inferno*, suggesting to readers that they must make
their own infernal journey through this work. Its absolute negativity
is certainly of a very different order from the Celtic melancholy formu-
lated by Arnold or Yeats. Indeed, the stories 'A Mother' and 'A Little
Cloud' directly accuse the Revivalists of pandering to British stereotypes
of Ireland and the Celts, and of doing so, in spite of all the pious rhetoric
about spirituality and emotion, for reasons entirely consisting of material self-advancement and meretricious bourgeois cynicism. The following excerpt from Joyce's critical writing specifically distances his own
work from what he adjudges the mythologizing, folkloric nostalgia of
Yeats and others: 'Life we must accept as we see it before our eyes, men
and women as we meet them in the real world, not as we apprehend
them in the world of faery'.[45]

What Joyce did share with Yeats and other Revivalists, however, was
an acute concern with how to use the English language in expressing
Irish experience, and Joyce, in his own way, reinforces Yeats's resistance
to Irish literature being swallowed up as a mere regional variation of
English literature. Joyce has a shrewd grasp of British cultural hegemony

and its capacity to appropriate and rewrite Irish literature in its own dominant terms:

■ Ireland is a great country. They call it the Emerald Isle. The Metropolitan Government, after so many so many centuries of holding it by the throat, has reduced it to a specter. Now it is a briar patch. They sowed it with famine, syphilis, superstition, and alcoholism. Up sprouted Puritans, Jesuits, and bigots [...] Ireland, however, is still the brain of the United Kingdom. The foresighted and ponderous English provide humanity's swollen belly with the perfect instrument of comfort: the Water Closet. The Irish doomed to express themselves in a language that is not their own, have stamped it with their genius and compete for glory with other civilized countries. This is called 'English Literature'.[46] □

This dilemma of having to write in a language not one's own is most clearly reflected in the discussion that Stephen has with his English Dean of Studies in *A Portrait*:

■ The language in which we are speaking is his before it is mine. How different are the words *home*, *Christ*, *ale*, *master*, on his lips and on mine! I cannot speak or write these words without unrest of spirit. His language, so familiar and so foreign, will always be for me an acquired speech. I have not made or accepted its words. My voice holds them at bay. My soul frets in the shadow of his language.[47] □

Here we have a reverberation of Thomas Davis's feeling of being dispossessed within the arbitrary set of signs that he regards as the English language. The fretting of Stephen in what he considers to be the language of his master also helps explain the utter linguistic breakdown in *Dubliners*, a text that is riven by broken sentences, unfinished thoughts and conversations, paralysed expression. Nevertheless, it transpires in Stephen's discussion with his Dean of Studies that it is the young Dedalus who knows the correct etymology of the word *tundish*. The implication, then, is that he knows the language better than this Englishman, better than his master. So although this medium, which is at once 'familiar' and 'foreign', is evidently a disempowerment, it can also become an enabling condition, a highly subversive means by which the language of his master may be turned against his master.

Joyce's ability to inhabit the English language, to take full possession of it, shape it, distort it, is enacted in *Ulysses* (especially 'Oxen of the Sun', which proffers a consummate historical sweep of the contingency of English) and in *Finnegans Wake* (1939). Joyce therefore differs from a Davis or a Hyde in that he does not seek to return to the Irish language as the befitting medium of Irish experience but instead subverts the

English language. His reasons for this choice, together with a key insight into the politics of language in his work, are foregrounded by his essay 'Ireland at the Bar' (1907), which deals with another Joyce – though not a family relative – Myles Joyce, who was executed for a crime which he did not commit: the Maamtrasna murders of 1882. Myles Joyce spoke little or no English though he had to learn a bit for the purposes of being judged by an Anglophone British court. For Joyce, Myles Joyce and his misrepresented and eventual conviction by the British court assume a national significance:

> ■ The figure of this bewildered old man, left over from a culture that is not ours, a deaf-mute before his judge, is a symbol of the Irish nation at the bar of public opinion. Like him, Ireland cannot appeal to the modern conscience of England or other countries.[48] □

Taking Myles Joyce as an emblem of an Ireland unable to articulate itself and the injustices it has suffered to the wider world, Joyce thus conveys that the English language must be his medium. He is certainly aware of the power relations that have induced this situation but he takes the marginalization of the Irish language in his own moment in history (rightly or wrongly) as a *fait accompli* and as a consequence resolves to write in an English that is antagonistic to, and subversive of, that very medium.

'Ireland at the Bar' can be read as prefiguring the first chapter of *Ulysses* in which it is the Englishman Haines who speaks Irish and whose Irish is mistaken for French by the old milkwoman. Symbolically here Joyce is dispensing with the idea that the Irish language would connect him to some authentic, popular Irish audience. So, in a way, this scene in the first chapter of *Ulysses* offers a different take on the problems of an audience for Irish literature in English that are also rehearsed in Yeats's 'The Fisherman' wherein Yeats's ideal reader (a rural peasant) does not exist in actuality: there is no literate, English-reading peasantry nor can his work spring from an Irish-speaking community. It is worth reiterating though that Joyce, in signalling the depleted state of the Irish language, attends directly to issues of culture and power. It is highly significant that the first English presence in *Ulysses* is not Privates Carr or Compton – figures of military domination who appear in the 'Circe' chapter of the novel – but Haines the cultural imperialist for whom the Irish language becomes another of his accumulated cultural treasures while simultaneously being denied any living currency among Irish people themselves. Joyce is careful, however, to frame the action of the first chapter in the Martello Tower, a former British military garrison built to protect the occupation from French attack or invasion, so that Haines's Matthew Arnold-type cultural appropriation and pseudo-anthropology are seen as directly connected to military power and vice versa. So Joyce deploys the English language strategically and he does so as part of his internationalist perspective, in performing his task of voicing Ireland's plight not only to itself but also to the world. However, his internationalist perspective and his exilic status led to his attack by the Irish Ireland movement, who opposed him just as forcibly as they did Anglo-Irish, Protestant writers.

A revolutionary criticism? MacDonagh and Pearse

There is a certain affinity between Joyce's pragmatic, inventive relation to the politics of language and the work of Thomas MacDonagh. Mac-Donagh produced one of the foundational texts of Irish literary criticism, *Literature and Ireland: Studies Irish and Anglo-Irish* (1916). This work was published posthumously after MacDonagh's execution by the British authorities for his part in the Easter 1916 Rising. Indeed, MacDonagh, who was a lecturer at University College Dublin, was famously working on the final drafts of the book while participating in the uprising. As with Joyce's advocacy of an enabling, critical distance from the medium of English, MacDonagh writes: 'We have now so well mastered this language of our adoption that we use it with a freshness and power that the English of these days rarely have'.[49] Most importantly, MacDonagh, like Joyce, sought to resist racial definitions and delimitations of Irish literature:

■ I have little sympathy with the criticism that marks off subtle qualities in literature as altogether racial, that refuses to admit natural exceptions in such a naturally exceptional thing as high literature, attributing only the central body to the national genius, the marginal positions to this alien strain or that.[50] □

Thus, MacDonagh refuses to enthrone one nominally pure Irish form of writing above all others. His rejection of a notional Irish essence overturns the terminology of Yeats, and by extension Arnold's Celticism, as well as resisting the strictures of Moran's Irish Ireland. Instead MacDonagh proposes to replace the idea of the Celtic Note (based on essential, racial demarcations) with what he terms the Irish Mode (a much more culturally and critically acquired discourse). The Irish Mode proposed a form of Irish writing in English that preserved Irish cadences and patterns, and which took possession of English and shaped it to the needs of Irish experience and culture. MacDonagh argues that he advances his Irish Mode in order to avoid the vague racial longings of the term Celtic and 'to fix certain standards, to define certain terms. I trust that as a result the Irish Mode will be better understood and appreciated than the Celtic Note for which I substitute it'.[51] MacDonagh helps us to understand that the 1916 Rising and the Revival period itself contained many divergent constituencies. While willing to fight and ultimately die for Ireland, MacDonagh's conception of Irish literature was distinctively and generously open-ended since his Irish Mode proposed not an exclusive, racially and linguistically pure Irish canon in the manner of Irish Ireland. Rather, it was a critical invitation for many forms of Irish writing in English to be considered in all the tension, precariousness and possibility of their dual linguistic and cultural inheritance.

MacDonagh was commemorated in Yeats's 'Easter 1916' along with other luminaries such as Connolly and Pádraic Pearse, and it was Pearse whom Irish Nationalist posterity would celebrate above all of the martyrs. Nevertheless, Pearse's own thoughts on literature are more complex than standard accounts of his unflinching, idealized nationalism would allow. Certainly, unlike Joyce or MacDonagh, Pearse did yearn for an Irish essence to be distilled in literature and language:

> ■ The spiritual thing which is the essential thing in nationality would seem to reside chiefly in language (if by language we understand literature and folklore as well as sounds and idioms), and to be preserved chiefly by language; but it reveals itself in all the arts, all the institutions, all the inner life, all the actions and goings forth of the nation.[52] □

Here the full realization of this Irish essence is not only obtained through literature and language but also institutionally in an anticipation of an independent Ireland. In addition to chiming with both the sentiment and intent of Moran's Irish Ireland, there are also the traces of Yeatsian and Arnoldian desires in this essentialism. Despite his interest in folklore, however, Pearse was very keen to distinguish himself from an Anglo-Irish archive of popular materials. Notably, Lady Gregory had been moved, when she collected folklore at a Galway workhouse, by 'the contrast between the poverty of the tellers and the splendours of the tales'.[53] Here there is a palpable idealization of the at once quaint and noble quality of the stories which transcends the degradations of the social conditions of the poor. Pearse – who is often accused of embodying only a backward-looking idealism – calls for a new, fully modern Irish literature. This demand is illustrated by his attitude to the folk tale. Pearse argues that

> ■ its time and place are the winter fireside, or the spring sowing time, or the country road at any season. Thus we lay down the proposition that a living literature cannot (and if it could, should not) be built up on the folk tale. The folk tale is an echo of old mythologies: literature is a deliberate criticism of

actual life [...] This is the twentieth century; and no literature can take root in the twentieth century which is not of the twentieth century. We want no Gothic revival.[54] □

In other words, he calls for an Irish literature that seeks not to escape reality but to confront it, to shape itself to the challenges of modernity (unlike, the reference to a Gothic revival implies, the Anglo-Irish tradition of folklore collation). The execution of both Pearse and MacDonagh prevents us from knowing whether their attitudes to literature would have changed after the War of Independence and the partition of Ireland. In the next chapter, we will trace the development of literary criticism and literature in the two new States brought into being by partition. We will begin with Daniel Corkery, whose work most closely articulates the official discourse of the Irish Free State, before moving on to consider more dissenting interventions of literature and criticism.

CHAPTER TWO

Irish Literature and Criticism after Partition

Criticism and the Free State: Daniel Corkery

This chapter details core details about Irish literature in the wake of the War of Independence and partition and follows those debates through to the 1970s. We will first examine how the energies of the Revival's national re-imagining continue in the work of certain writers and critics in an effort to shape the specifically Irish and nationalist credentials of the new Free State. In turn though, we will address the abatement of those nationalist dynamics in literary criticism which either was or became fundamentally opposed to the official doctrine of the new Ireland. The response of literature and criticism to the Northern Irish state and its ideological strictures will also be analyzed in due course, before we address an increasing interest in Irish literature by an array of international critics in the post-Second World War period. But we will commence with an examination of Daniel Corkery's criticism and its close alignment to the official nationalism of the Irish Free State in order to enable us to sense the dominant cultural and social climate of the period.

Corkery's *The Hidden Ireland* (1924), which was his homage to eighteenth-century poets in rural Munster, is an act of historical recovery and national archiving which continues the Revivalist desire to reconstruct a sense of an Irish tradition. Thus authentic, 'hidden' Ireland is proposed as the 'real' Ireland uncorrupted by British rule and Anglicization. Corkery asserts that in order to find the unchanging, hidden Ireland we must 'leave cities and towns behind'.[1] We will discuss below his antipathy to Anglo-Irish Revivalists such as Yeats, but we can also stress here a similar anti-urban, anti-modern effort to reclaim a national essence or to connect with a popular, rural subject that characterizes the enterprises of Yeats, Lady Gregory or Synge. In addition to attacking Anglo-Irish literature, Corkery also rails against any writer who appears ambivalent or uncertain on the national question, as well as the many Irish literary exiles – the most prominent of which was Joyce. Much as

Corkery fulminates against Joyce, the contradictions in some of his arguments actually serve to endorse Joyce's pragmatic and strategic use of
the English language. For all Corkery's loathing of the what he saw as
the betraying ambiguity of a writer like Joyce, he himself was a lifelong
enthusiast of the Irish language who nonetheless wrote in English and
was Professor of English at University College Cork for 16 years.

In his work *Synge and Anglo-Irish Literature* (1931), Corkery develops D. P. Moran's thesis of an Ireland unsure of its identity, race and
culture: 'Everywhere in the mentality of the Irish people are flux and
uncertainty. Our national consciousness may be described, in a native
phrase, as a quaking sod. It gives no footing. It is not English, nor Irish,
nor Anglo-Irish'.[2] So we can immediately contrast Joyce's fluid identities
in *Ulysses*, wherein flux and uncertainty are in fact creative conditions,
with Corkery's desire for sure-footed, grounded fixity. For Corkery, the
writer has a very specific purpose and literature has a most secure origin in a culture: 'Is the writer not the people's voice? Has there ever
been, can there ever be, a distinctive literature that is not a national
literature? A national literature is written primarily for its own people'.[3]
Corkery is keen to assail expatriate and exilic writers such as Joyce,
Austin Clarke (1896–1974), George Bernard Shaw or Patrick MacGill
(1891–1963), whom he dubs 'those wild geese of the pen', while at
the same time condemning Anglo-Irish, Protestant writers as 'spiritual
exiles'.[4] In the movement from Moran to Corkery we can trace the
increasing solidification and dominance of the Irish Ireland doctrine in
the political ideology of the Irish Free State. Certainly Corkery's assault
on Anglo-Irish literature for not being 'a homogenous thing' is familiar enough from our discussion of Moran's criticism, and he labels the
work of Yeats, Gregory and Martyn at the Abbey theatre as 'freakish'
and 'written under the domination of English literary fashions […] It
may be that it is no more than an exotic branch of English literature'.[5]
Such writing, Corkery maintains, is not truly Irish or indigenous and
lacks any authentic connection to the Irish people: it is not informed
by Irish culture but is rather produced and shaped by 'colonial moulds':
'This colonial literature was written to explain the quaintness of the
humankind of this land, especially the native humankind, to another
humankind that was not quaint, that was standard, normal. All over the
world is not that the note of colonial literature?'[6] Thus, the perspective
is very much that of an outsider, an interloper, whose mission is not to
represent the Irish faithfully but to exoticize and petrify them in the
stereotypical forms expected by a foreign (largely British) audience.

All of this kind of sentiment does echo Moran but the impact of
the development of the Irish Free State and the bolstering it gives to
Irish Ireland can be illustrated in the encroaching criteria of normality in Corkery's terms of reference. Corkery judges literature through

the mutually defining lenses of normality and nationality. It is the task of a nation and its literature to become normal – and these codes of normalcy are typically employed to dismiss the claims of belonging of the hyphenated Anglo-Irish: 'If this literature then be not a normal literature it is not a national literature, for normal and national literature are synonymous in literary criticism [...] a normal literature is written within the confines of the country which names it'.[7] But where Irish Ireland has previously been part of a cultural nationalist project that was itself a facet of a larger nationalist campaign against the British occupation and administration of Ireland, the formation of the Irish Free State, whose institutions and state ideology gave concrete form to the ideas of Irish Ireland, affords legal and cultural authority to a project that can no longer be couched in oppositional or revolutionary terms. And the key trope in Corkery's effort to imagine a literature befitting an Irish Free State that now has its own political institutions, its bureaucracy, its police force and army, in short control over its own affairs, is this assertion of being normal. But what precisely constitutes a 'normal' Ireland with autonomous control of its own state and culture?

Ironically, given the fierce separatism of the Irish Ireland endeavour, the Irish State's becoming normal involves it becoming like any other European state. And, despite haranguing Anglo-Irish writers for employing 'colonial moulds' in representing Ireland, Corkery turns to English culture for his model of how Irish literature may be national and normal. For instance, he picks 'The Soldier' (1915) by Rupert Brooke (1887–1915) as an example of how English writers are '100 per cent English', and urges Irish writing to follow suit in its national endeavours. Most importantly, Corkery's yearning for a normal, national culture is both jarred and stirred when watching Gaelic Games. In the following quotation, he refers to a range of Anglo-Irish writers: Yeats; the poet, playwright and painter George William Russell (1867–1935), known as 'A.E.'; the poet and novelist James Stephens (1882–1950); the playwright, novelist and fantasy and myth writer Lord Dunsany (1878–1957); Thomas Moore; and the playwright Lennox Robinson (1886–1958). Corkery contrasts these with a number of English writers: the novelists John Galsworthy (1867–1933), Arnold Bennett (1867–1931) and H. G. Wells (1866–1946), and the poet, novelist and playwright John Masefield (1878–1967):

■ I recall being in Thurles at a hurling match for the championship of Ireland. There were 30,000 onlookers. They were as typical of this nation as any of the great crowds that assemble of Saturday afternoons in England to witness Association football matches are typical of the English nation. It was while I looked around on that great crowd I first became acutely conscious that as a nation we were without self-expression in literary form. The life of this people

I looked upon – there were all sorts of individuals present, from bishops to tramps off the road – was not being explored in a natural way by any except one or two writers of any standing. And even of the one or two, I was not certain, their efforts being from the start so handicapped. It was impossible to feel that one could pose such Anglo-Irish writers as the world knows of against that multitude [...] One could not see Yeats, A.E., Stephens, Dunsany, Moore, Robinson, standing out from that gathering as natural and indigenous interpreters of it. On the other hand there seems to be no difficulty in posing Galsworthy, Masefield, Bennett, Wells, against any corresponding assemblies in England. Those writers do belong. They give the crowd a new significance: through them we may look with better eyes at the massed people of England. The crowd equally deepens the significance of the written word.[8] ☐

Therefore, Corkery's version of a normal society and culture seeks 'typical' and customary social practices that are to be formally rendered into literary types. Most pertinently, individuals assume collective typicality in this symbolic ordering process. But just as we highlighted the significant absences in Yeats's three-tier vision of Ireland – aristocrats, artists and peasants – so Corkery's own effort to bring high and low together in social unity makes a place for bishops, the artist and tramps. Again both the middle and working classes are omitted from the organic harmony. The 'crowd' which is to be given a 'significance' in this model is thus not the urban masses but a carefully selected hierarchy of types. Similarly, Yeats's effort to naturalize the relationship between the artist, culture and society is repeatedly directly in the above passage. But the overriding contradiction for a homogenizing, separatist Irish Ireland paradigm is that Corkery turns to England and English writers for his concept of a normal society and literature. Put simply, the argument runs along the lines of: in order to be exclusively ourselves, we need to be more like them.

In the next chapter on Irish Studies paradigms, we will directly address challenges posed to Corkery by David Lloyd and Seamus Deane who argue that the cultural nationalism of the new Irish Free State and finally the Irish Republic shared important, repressive and stifling similarities to the British colonial administration which preceded it. But for our purposes here, the problems of Corkery's sense of what constitutes normality anticipate and disclose that when Ireland – or at least 26 counties of it – gained its own autonomous state, it became increasingly difficult if not impossible to lend Irish nationalism and its culture a straightforwardly emancipatory or radical hue. The new Free State which sharpens Corkery's desire for normality, for homogeneity, for a settled and naturalized legitimacy of both national institutions and culture is significantly repressed in Corkery's threefold definition of Irishness: 'The three great forces which, working for long in the Irish national being, have made it so different from the English national being, are: (1) The Religious Consciousness of the People; (2) Irish Nationalism; and (3) The Land'.[9] It is precisely what Corkery absents – the State – which holds together his key constituencies of the Catholic Church, the nation and its territorial legitimacy and propriety. We can read Corkery's omission as an effort to forestall an acknowledgement of Irish Ireland's petrifaction into a repressive state formation whose empty rhetoric and idealism, as we shall detail below, was refracted back upon it by a generation of writers utterly disillusioned with the post-independence state.

Firstly, let us outline some of the main legislative building blocks of the new State. Article 1 of the 1922 Constitution of the Irish Free State (Saorstát Éireann) established Ireland as a 'co-equal' member of the British Commonwealth, thereby anticipating eventual full independence and the formation of the Republic in 1937. Institutionally an apparent move to freedom and national liberation, there was at the same time a more repressive climate emerging within Ireland. Film censorship was instituted in 1923, followed in 1929 by the legislative provision for the censorship of literature and the press. Additionally, the legal right to divorce, which had been inherited from the British parliament, was revoked in 1925 and the importation and sale of contraceptives was banned in 1935.[10] Subsequently, the 1937 Constitution consolidated the more repressive dynamics of Irish society. It was enacted 'In the Name of the Most Holy Trinity, from Whom is all authority', and while it acknowledged other faiths it also advanced the 'special position' of the Catholic Church. Article 41 of the Constitution pledged to guard the institution of Marriage, as part of its overarching defence of the Family, and it effectively banned divorce. A lot of important literature and criticism did perform a dissenting role in this new dispensation, as well as, at times, voicing despair or resignation.

A succinct way to indicate a shift in literary and critical response to the emerging Free State is offered by George Russell's time – from 1923 to 1930 – as editor of the journal the *Irish Statesman*. As a key associate of Yeats, Russell had believed the Literary Revival had been crucial to a new broader awakening in Irish life in which the nation had been spiritually and intellectually improved. Subsequently, Russell used his editorial position at the *Irish Statesman* to inspire support for the new Free State government led by William Cosgrove (1880–1965, President of the Executive 1922–32). His belief was that, in turn, Cosgrove's government would support literature and the arts in order to continue the cultural and intellectual well-being and development of the nation. But the introduction of the Censorship Bill in 1928 and its eventual passing into law a year later sundered Russell's faith in the new state's commitment to literature and artistic freedom. In the following attack on government policy there is a stark irony in the fact that a

Revivalist like Russell, whose career was dedicated to reawakening the nation, fears that Irish national consciousness will in fact be killed off once more by the very state ushered in by the nationalist upsurge in the Revival period:

■ If we destroy in Ireland our National Gallery, our Abbey Theatre, our Feis Ceoil [music festival], and our poetic and imaginative literature, the agencies by which the mysterious element of beauty filters into national consciousness, we are certain that in fifty years the nation would be corrupt or dead.[11] □

Moreover, George Bernard Shaw also used the pages of the *Irish Statesman* to castigate the new Free State government. For Shaw, the censorship issue crystallized his larger concern that the Ireland instigated by the War of Independence would become an increasingly insular backwater. Having overturned British rule, Shaw identified an odd coalition between Catholic and Protestant conservatism on social matters and expresses his fears that if Ireland

■ slips back into the Atlantic as a little patch of grass in which a few million moral cowards are not allowed to call their souls their own by a handful of morbid Catholics, mad with heresyphobia, unnaturally combining with a handful of Calvinists mad with sexphobia [...] then the world will let 'these Irish' go their own way into insignificance without the slightest concern.[12] □

So there developed a clear discrepancy between the rhetoric of the Literary Revival and the conservative, censorious and economically isolated society that emerged after 1922. In terms of literature, there was the self-imposed exile in continental Europe of famed writers such as Joyce, Samuel Beckett and Sean O'Casey. Indeed, O'Casey's *The Plough and the Stars* (1926), which looked back upon the Easter Rising, caused rioting upon its performance in Dublin (we will discuss this in depth in Chapter Four). There were also increasing numbers of indigenous writers and critics who effectively became internal exiles so at odds were they with the prevailing climate in the Free State and subsequent Irish Republic. A generation of writers that includes Patrick Kavanagh, Austin Clarke and Flann O'Brien (1911–66) all used satire to undermine the idealism of official rhetoric with what they deemed the mundane realities of the new state. The Republic's official self-image is neatly distilled in the famous or notorious – depending on your point of view – St Patrick's Day radio broadcast in 1943 by Eamon de Valera (1882–1975, Taoiseach [Prime Minister] of Ireland 1932–48, 1957–9; President 1959–73):

■ The Ireland which we dreamed of would be the home of a people who valued material wealth only as a basis of right living, of a people who were satisfied with frugal comfort and devoted their leisure to the things of the spirit; a land whose countryside would be bright with cosy homesteads, whose fields and villages would be joyous with sounds of industry, the romping of sturdy children, the contests of athletic youths, the laughter of comely maidens; whose fire-sides would be the forums of the wisdom of serene old age. It would, in a word, be the home of a people living the life that God desires that men should live.[13] □

This idyllic dream of rural peasant sanctity would not be out of place in the work of some of the Anglo-Irish Revivalists whom we have already covered, yet the crucial change is that it is the Catholic bourgeoisie and the state they control who have become the guarantors and keepers of this delusory dream rather than the Protestant Ascendancy they displaced.

Criticism and the Free State: O'Faoláin, O'Connor and Kavanagh

In opposition to official doctrine, Seán O'Faoláin argued that by the late 1930s there was a 'wholesale flight from the fields' as people sought to escape the deprived reality of rural Ireland.[14] In addition to his critical work, O'Faoláin's fiction also demonstrates an implacable disillusionment with the new Irish state. Daniel Corkery produced his short story 'Seumas' during the War of Independence and its exalted revolutionary fervour was designed to inspire actively romanticized heroism in others.[15] By contrast, O'Faoláin's story 'The Patriot', although seeking to pay tribute to the combatants in the struggle, ultimately discloses a failed quest that bespeaks a disillusionment with the establishment of the Irish Free State and the Civil War.[16] Ultimately, in O'Faoláin's stories – or indeed those of Frank O'Connor – the sentimental connection between romantic heroism and the people breaks down or is exposed as untenable. Where once a perceived patriotic quest sought to supplant an acknowledgement of other issues concerning society, class, gender, morality and religion, it is precisely those issues that rupture a nationalist longing for unity in the romantic tale and imbue such stories with a post-war melancholy and despair. While Corkery's nationalist idealism continued unabated – and, in literary terms, we have discussed how his *Synge and Anglo-Irish Literature* offers a highly attenuated canon of Irishness – there is a shift in literary style in the work of O'Faoláin and O'Connor away from the romantic structure to naturalism and a thorough demythologizing of both violence and state ideology.[17]

Notably, both O'Faoláin and O'Connor had been mentored by Corkery and their turning away from his literary and critical positions is illustrative of their increasing discontent politically and artistically. Their disillusionment was perhaps sharpened by their political commitment prior to the foundation of the state, O'Faoláin having fought as an IRA (Irish Republican Army) member in the War of Independence while his fellow Republican O'Connor went on to fight with the Anti-Treaty rebels in the Civil War and was arrested and imprisoned in 1923 for doing so. In a key essay, 'The Future of Irish Literature' (1942), O'Connor viewed post-Revival culture as symptomatic of a wider social failure as the energy, imagination and purpose of the Revival dissipated into philistinism and fracture:

■ Irish society began to revert to type. All the forces that had made for national dignity, that had united Catholic and Protestant, aristocrats like Constance Markievicz, Labour revolutionaries like Connolly and writers like AE, began to disintegrate rapidly, and Ireland became more than ever sectarian, utilitarian (the two nearly always go together), vulgar and provincial.[18] □

Moreover, O'Connor would later look back on the Civil War as ultimately futile because it ushered in such a conservative state. And one of the most significant casualties of the repressive nature of the state, for O'Connor, was the imagination:

■ What neither group saw was that every word we said, every act we committed, was a destruction of the improvisation and what we were brining about was a new establishment of Church and State in which imagination would play no part, and young men and women would emigrate to the ends of the earth, not because the country was poor, but because it was mediocre.[19] □

Hence, O'Connor believed that the dynamism and ideas generated by the cultural resurgence prior to independence had been usurped by a deadening stasis which was stifling literature. Indeed, he described the 1940s and 1950s as 'the death-in-life of the Nationalist Catholic establishment'.[20]

Similarly, O'Faoláin's career as a writer and critic signals a deepening alienation and burgeoning dissent with the direction taken by the Free State and then the Republic. Having been away from Ireland between 1926 and 1933 (including time spent at Harvard University), one of O'Faoláin's most important contributions to Irish literary and social critique was his editorship of the journal *The Bell*.[21] O'Faoláin edited *The Bell* from 1940 to 1946 and in many ways it filled the cultural and critical void left by the demise of Russell's *Irish Statesman* in 1930. The very title of *The Bell* illustrates O'Faoláin's thinking at the time. In his introductory contribution to the first issue O'Faoláin outlines why this sparse name with its minimum of associations was given to the journal. His explanation directly dismisses a litany of heroes, heroines and icons in the mythology of Irish Nationalism:

■ If you begin to think of alternatives you will see why we could not have used any of the old symbolic words. They are as dead as Brian Boru, Granuaile, the Shan Van Vocht, Banba, Roisin Dubh, Fodhla, Cathleen ni Houlihan, the swords of light and the risings of the moon. These belong to the time when we growled in defeat and dreamed of the future. That future has arrived and, with its arrival, killed them. All our symbols have to be created afresh, and the only way to create a living symbol is to take a naked thing and clothe it with new life, new association, new meaning, with all the vigour of the life in the Here and Now. We refused to use the word Irish, or Ireland, in the title. We said, 'It will plainly be that by being alive.'[22] □

In this passage there is a palpable desire to think things anew and a corresponding assertion that the old iconography and terms of reference of the national imagination are no longer suited to the new dispensation. So here we confront the paradox that the national symbols and consciousness resurrected by the Revival are deemed by dissenters such as O'Faoláin to be moribund once more in the dominant cultural and political conditions of the society instigated by that very same Revival period. As with O'Connor's sense of the death-in-life of the Catholic, Nationalist establishment, O'Faoláin saw literature and criticism as the necessary means by which the dead remnants of repeated attempts to revive old forms could be finally dispensed with. In a sense, O'Faoláin pitched himself as the undertaker tasked with burying such dead dreams. The official neutrality of the Republic in the Second World War certainly sharpened O'Faoláin's assertion that life was being effaced with lifelessness and this stagnation must be surmounted: 'Life is so isolated now that it is no longer being pollinated by germinating ideas wind-borne from anywhere'.[23]

In terms of literary genre, both O'Faoláin and O'Connor used the short story to indict what they deemed the pervasive stasis of society. And both writers offer insightful and provocative accounts of the social import of this cultural form that has been used extensively by an array of Irish writers. Most succinctly, O'Connor defined the short story as the primary mode of expression for 'submerged population groups'.[24] In other words, people who were at the margins of society or those excluded from dominant forms of representation. O'Connor's model was based on his account of the short story's role in literature in the United States. In America, he claimed, there were, due to continual waves of immigration and settlement, a whole range of divergent ethnic

groups and ghettos. To employ his own term, many 'submerged population groups' were articulating their experiences on the social margins while attempting to enter a mainstream that was itself constantly
being transformed and which had no overarching, consensual unity.
In O'Connor's eyes, the short story is suited to confronting a shifting,
fragmentary society based on uneasy tensions between folk and cosmopolitan traditions, between old and new. By updating folktales, short
stories, for O'Connor, are 'drastic adaptations of a primitive art to modern conditions.'[25]

If we accept this model, wherein short stories are particularly suited
to articulating fragmentary societies and marginalized social groups,
it should perhaps be pointed out that we are also implicitly accepting
another proposition. Namely, that the novel is, by contrast, the primary
form of unitary or even 'normal' societies. To provide a clear sense of
the wider importance of these issues, we can briefly turn to the most
canonical proposal of the novel's formative cultural role in cementing
the development of cohesive, modern nations: Benedict Anderson's
Imagined Communities: Reflections on the Origin and Spread of Nationalism
(1991).[26] Anderson regards the novel as emerging historically with the
rise of the bourgeois nation state and he contends that it grants a cultural means by which individuals in such nations can imagine themselves as part of a united national community that stands in the place of
older regional divisions. Central to this process, according to Anderson, is
the development of print technology, a literate population and indeed
a standardized national language through which this new unity may
be expressed. One danger of Anderson's model is that it tends to construct a narrative of development in which, by implication, properly
matured and normative societies produce novels while those which are
seen as abnormal or backward produce the more fractious short story
form.[27] Additionally, it can be suggested that this wedding of the novel
to the development of the nation state underplays the extent to which
the purported unity of these new 'imagined communities' is in fact
a coercive one. That is, part of the point of the conventional novel and
its standard language is to assert the primacy of that standard language
and in doing so to repress, or at best relegate to an inferior formal position, regional dialects or working-class vernaculars.

With these qualifications in mind, however, we can interpret
O'Connor's model of the short story's appropriateness for the experiences
of submerged population groups as emerging from of a particularly Irish
literary encumbrance. We can regard the preponderance of the short
story form in Irish writing as a sign of the impact and legacy of the
imposition of British rule in Ireland, and with that the imposition of
British culture and the English language. That is to say, Irish society, the

Irish language and Irish culture were denied the opportunity to develop as other nation states because of the disruption of British occupation. As a result, the short story form comes to prominence precisely because it articulates the fragmentary nature of Irish society: the uneven clash of indigenous and colonial cultures, the marginalization of the Irish language, and the banishment of the Irish from the political administration of their own country. So the consensual, unitary vantage point necessary for the production of the novel is impossible in the Irish case where society is ravaged by ongoing processes of domination and resistance. There is no already agreed language and culture in which to imagine a unitary society, nor, for that matter, an already agreed society in which to produce a unitary language and culture.

Certainly, O'Faoláin and O'Connor's former mentor Corkery could conceive of the short story as a form of anti-colonial resistance, as the literary means through which the dispossessed and marginalized Irish could voice their exclusion. Furthermore, in the passage from Corkery we have already examined, in which his experiences at Thurles impelled him to call for Irish writers to imagine national forms that finally express an Irish nation, he tellingly wished to model such efforts on what he deemed a normal English situation. Hence, the premise is that English culture and society are already normal; Irish culture and society must therefore become so. Yet what is notable about O'Connor's and O'Faoláin's literary usage and critical understanding of the short story long after partition is that both writers are still employing it to represent 'submerged population groups' who are forgotten, marginalized or isolated by an Irish administration. One way to explain this, of course, is to argue that the ravages of British rule are not undone overnight and that literature and society in the Free State and Republic were engaged in an ongoing process of overturning that legacy. But equally, the short stories and critical work of both O'Connor and O'Faoláin suggest that the Irish state produced its own 'submerged population groups'. O'Connor deems short story protagonists 'outlawed figures wandering about the fringes of society'[28] and his own work cogently demonstrates his sense of how new generations of outlaws and fringe-figures were brought into being by the narrow strictures of the post-independence state and its institutions. In this case, therefore, the short story is less the form of anti-colonial resistance and more a refusal to be co-opted by the new Irish state. Hence, O'Connor writes of the individual: 'there is no longer a society to absorb him, and [...] he is compelled to exist as it were by his own inner light'.[29] So rather than seeking a national form through which to project an imagined Irish social unity and cohesion, O'Connor instead protests with 'the short story writer's morality of the lonely individual soul'.[30]

Similarly, in his important, polemical article, 'The Dilemma of Irish Letters' (1949), O'Faoláin pitches his own grasp of the social resonance of the short story as follows:

■ The life now known, or knowable to any modern Irish writer is either the traditional, entirely simple life of the farm (simple intellectually speaking); or the groping, ambiguous, rather artless urban life of these same farmer's sons and daughters who have, this last twenty-five years, been taking over the cities and towns from the Anglo-Irish [...] In such an unshaped society there are many subjects for little pieces, that is for the short-story writer; the novelist or the dramatist loses himself in the general amorphism, unthinkingness, brainlessness, egalitarianism and general unsophistication.[31] □

So, for O'Faoláin, the short story in the Free State and Republic is vital as much for what it does not say as what it does. Its focus on marginalia, on isolated and fragmentary bits and pieces, indicts the larger social milieu which has caused that fractiousness and exclusion in the first place. Mainstream Irish society and culture, O'Faoláin maintains, consist merely of the outmoded remnants of tradition and the vacuous aspirations of the emergently dominant Irish middle class.

In addition to O'Connor and O'Faoláin, Patrick Kavanagh's work proffers a searing indictment of the official self-image of the Free State and early Republic, particularly given his dual sense of the Monaghan countryside of his upbringing and the Dublin literary scene which he encountered as a writer. Indeed, Kavanagh's writing offers perhaps the most direct means of undermining de Valera's rural idyll by pursuing a concentrated portrayal of rural poverty in Monaghan. In his critical work, Kavanagh became highly attuned to how a metropolitan Dublin intelligentsia and British audience expectantly wished to receive his own work in stereotyped pastoral forms. Kavanagh writes about the Revival:

■ In those days in Dublin the big thing besides being Irish was peasant quality. They were all trying to be peasants. They had been at it for years but I hadn't heard. And I was installed as the authentic peasant ... I would say now that that so-called Irish Literary Movement which purported to be frightfully Irish and racy of the Celtic soil was a thoroughgoing English-bred lie.[32] □

Kavanagh was critical of his own early writing which he felt pandered to such stereotypes. His radical rejection of what he felt were outworn exotic modes necessitated a different kind of engagement with his own terrain. Most notably, in terms that would later be continued in the parish of Seamus Heaney's work, Kavanagh sought to affirm the importance of his own locality as the true ground of the universals of experience. Kavanagh employed the term 'parochialism' to denote this negotiation between local particularity and universal resonance. He contrasts his affirmative parochialism with what he deems an attenuated provincialism as follows:

> ■ Parochialism and Provincialism are opposites. The provincial has no mind of his own; he does not trust what his eyes see until he has heard what the metropolis – towards which his eyes are turned – has to say on any topic [...] The parochial mentality on the other hand is never in any doubt about the social and artistic validity of his parish [...] Parochialism is universal; it deals with the fundamentals.[33] □

So while parochialism is habitually seen as a pejorative designation, Kavanagh sought to redeem its meaning. In so doing he contrasted it with what he calls provincialism, which, for him, was the prevailing Irish cultural mindset of narrow-mindedness, imaginative cowardice and debased exoticism. So metropolitan national life cast itself as outward-looking, sophisticated, internationally informed and relevant, when, to Kavanagh, it was instead merely regurgitating the same hackneyed, delimitative stereotypes about Ireland for equally closed-minded audiences in both Ireland and abroad.

Kavanagh's effort to reclaim his parish imaginatively sought to indict both the cultural idealism foisted upon it and the poverty and deprivation it endured at the hand of the new state, and it resulted in poetry such as *The Great Hunger* (1942). Apart from his literary output, Kavanagh was also responsible for the short-lived and highly polemical journal *Kavanagh's Weekly*, which appeared in 13 issues between 12 April and 5 July 1952. Following on from O'Connor and O'Faoláin's meditations on a stagnant death-in-life under the new Irish state, Kavanagh declared in the very first issue of *Kavanagh's Weekly* that 'The country is dead or dying of its false materialism'.[34] So Kavanagh's primary targets were the social and economic conditions which produced the rural poverty that he sought to bewail in his work and, at the same time, the Revivalist and metropolitan use of peasants as idealized symbols of national spirituality and simplicity that he adjudged to be wilfully ignoring that deprivation. However, a large part of Kavanagh's ire emerged from the fact that he too – as with the Revivalists or the pastoral idealists – was making a claim for authenticity. Where we discussed how the liberal intent of the very title of O'Faoláin's *The Bell* was attempting to forgo the effort to specify some essential or authentic Irishness, Kavanagh was still endeavouring to assert a true Irishness. So while hostile to the neglectful idealism of official state discourse, Kavanagh was also scathing in his reading of Anglo-Irish efforts to annex peasant life. Notably, he used the pages of *Kavanagh's Weekly* to launch an attack on Synge and his Anglo-Irish legacy as 'bitterly non-Irish' despite all the fumbling for authenticity:

> ■ His peasants are picturesque conventions; the language he invented for them did a disservice to letters in this country by drawing our attention away from the common speech whose delightfulness comes from its very ordinariness. One phrase of Joyce is worth all Synge as far as giving us the cadence of Irish speech [...] Synge provided Irish Protestants who are worried about being 'Irish' with an artificial country.[35] □

Such sentiments were shared with Kavanagh by his contemporary Austin Clarke. Clarke had lost his job as an assistant lecturer at University College Dublin in 1921 where he had been appointed to replace Thomas MacDonagh, simply because he had married in a civil ceremony rather than in a Catholic wedding mass. In spite of this, Clarke's hostility to the new state was less because of its coercive repression and much more because he felt its petty materialism had corrupted the national purity it was meant to embody. Like Kavanagh, Clarke intended to express an authentic or true Irishness. Consequently, he attacked Sean O'Casey's *The Plough and the Stars* as an example of the mock Irishness that his own writing and generation would usurp: 'several writers of the new Irish school believe that Mr O'Casey's work is a crude exploitation of our poorer people in an Anglo-Irish tradition that is now moribund'.[36]

Nevertheless, in terms of religion or sectarian division, Kavanagh's writing is also highly instructive in how it troubles the major division of the post-Revival period: partition itself. Monaghan was politically in the Free State and the Republic yet geographically in the North, being one of the three overwhelmingly Catholic provinces of Ulster that was not included in the state of Northern Ireland. The precarious position of Kavanagh's Monaghan and parish in terms of official boundaries also serves to remind us that the Free State was not the only state instigated by partition which enabled the hegemony of a dominant majority to go unchecked.

Criticism and Northern Ireland

If the Irish Free State and the Irish Republic which superseded it enshrined an exclusive political and religious outlook in institutional form then so too the Northern Irish State, which was legislated into being with the Free State by the Government of Ireland Act of 1920, sought to shore up a monolithic and unremitting ideology. Where de Valera's St Patrick's Day radio broadcast sought to imagine the Republic displaced as a pastoral dream, Sir James Craig (1871–1940, Prime Minister of Northern Ireland 1921–40), expressed the official version of Northern Ireland in terms unashamedly tied to state power and control when telling the Stormont Parliament on 24 April 1934: 'I have always said I am an Orangeman first and a politician and Member of this Parliament afterwards [...] in the South they boasted of a Catholic State. They still boast of Southern Ireland being a Catholic State. All I boast is that we are a Protestant Parliament and Protestant State'.[37]

The Northern Irish State was deliberately constructed as a political entity with a Protestant majority that guaranteed its ongoing existence. Discrimination against the Catholic minority bounded by the Northern State was institutionalized, with varying degrees of formality, in terms of voting rights, and access to employment and housing. In a process known as gerrymandering, parliamentary constituencies were manipulated to ensure Protestant majorities within each – though this was more difficult in the west of the Northern State. The Unionist MP E. C. Ferguson's comments about Fermanagh straightforwardly illustrate the tactics behind gerrymandering:

■ The Nationalist majority in the county, notwithstanding a reduction of 336 in the year, stands at 3,684. We must ultimately reduce and liquidate that majority. This county, I think it can be safely said, is a Unionist county. The atmosphere is Unionist. The Boards and properties are nearly all controlled by Unionists. But there is still this millstone around our necks.[38] □

This description of the Catholic population as a 'millstone around our necks' discloses both the attitudes and the problems of the Northern State since it was supposedly a democratic answer to the War of Independence that ensured Unionists in the North could freely remain British yet its existence relied upon suppressing and indeed repressing the sizeable Catholic minority within its borders. Furthermore, E. C. Ferguson's wish to 'liquidate' the Catholic majority in Fermanagh is highly troubling and, at the very least, it indicates that the Unionist establishment made no effort to try and secure the consent of the Catholic population. Rather it hoped they would be expurgated. So, from the outset, Northern Ireland was a democracy so long as you were a Protestant, its apparent freely expressed right to remain British a somewhat forced political machination that ensured decades of unfreedom for its Catholic population.

With the social change of the 1960s and the Civil Rights movement, there were efforts to make the North more representative or liberal in its outlook but the following comments at the end of the 1960s by Terence O'Neill (1914–90, Prime Minister of Northern Ireland 1963–9), the reformist Unionist Prime Minister, demonstrate how his attempt to include Catholics in the civic life of Northern Ireland was based on them living like Protestants, behaving as the already accepted citizens do (the inverse image of which is perhaps official nationalism in the Irish Republic readily accepting Protestants into its canon so long as they are good nationalists):

> ■ It is frightfully hard to explain to Protestants that if you give Roman Catholics a good job and a good house they will live like Protestants because they will see neighbours with cars and television sets; they will refuse to have eighteen children. But if a Roman Catholic is jobless, and lives in the most ghastly hovel, he will rear eighteen children on National Assistance. If you treat Roman Catholics with due consideration and kindness, they will live like Protestants in spite of the authoritative nature of their Church.[39] □

Despite his liberal intentions, O'Neill's views highlight how the Unionist State accepted its own identity, power and hegemony as normative and, in particular, as requiring no justification other than the tautological fact of its own power.

Nonetheless, the competing names which designate the territory encompassed by the Northern Irish State – Northern Ireland, the North, Ulster and the Six Counties – disclose an uncertainty and instability of definition with which Unionist ideology has struggled in its desire for homogeneity and historical continuity. One of the most controversial aspects of the Irish Republic's constitution is Article 2, which makes a territorial claim over 'the whole island of Ireland' (including the Six Counties which comprise Northern Ireland), while it is not often acknowledged that the Unionist use of the term Ulster to denote Northern Ireland also makes a territorial claim beyond its constitutional confines. In this case, however, it is an odd territorial claim, or perhaps more properly a semantic claim to the term Ulster which simultaneously tries to repress the territorial implications of the possession of the term. For of course Ulster actually designates the nine-country province of Ulster, three counties of which were not included in Northern Ireland due to their large Catholic populations so as to ensure a Protestant majority overall in the six-county 'Ulster' constituted by the Northern Irish State.

A key writer, critic and cultural activist who grappled with the problems of the sectarian divisions which cleaved the North socially and institutionally was John Hewitt. His means of trying to overcome Protestant and Catholic or British and Irish schisms was to advocate a regionalism that would, he hoped, unite the people of the North in a shared local identity. Hewitt's regionalist programme is most succinctly expressed in his article 'Regionalism: The Last Chance' (1947). The following passage indicates that his regionalism was not only an effort to address religious and sectarian divides in the North but also a response to what he deemed the dislocations of the modern world more broadly:

■ Threatened by over-centralisation, already half-subsumed by a century of increasing standardisation in material things, rapidly losing his individual responses in the hurricanes of propaganda, political, commercial, ideological, western man gropes instinctively for the security of a sheltering rock. Many in these islands seek among the rubble of once valid religions for that shelter [...] One other approach remains [...] one which, although it begins with the individual, must immediately pass beyond the individual and react upon the community – another word which to live must become flesh. This word is regionalism.[40] □

In Chapter Four we will discuss how Hewitt's regional model and its legacy are contested entities as there has remained, for some critics at least, a suspicion that his regionalist programme was merely a cultural effort to shore up consent for the continued existence of the Northern State. But it should also be registered that Unionist politicians intervened to prevent Hewitt from becoming director of the Ulster Museum due to his supposed 'Communist' sympathies. To that end, Hewitt's Methodist school teacher father admired the socialists James Larkin (1876–1947) and Keir Hardie (1856–1915) and introduced his son to the radical English writer William Morris (1834–96). With regard to his cultural activism, Hewitt co-founded the *Lagan* magazine in 1943, notably along with the playwright and prose writer John Boyd (1912–2002) and Sam Hanna Bell. Boyd summed up the ethos behind the magazine in his editorial introduction to its first issue: 'It must be realized by writers that now is the time to take new bearings, to try new paths, to explore new terrain; that the central problem is to interpret the complex spiritual life of this province'.[41]

Moreover, *Lagan* did importantly cross-fertilize ideas with O'Faoláin's *The Bell* in the Republic. So too *The Bell* published Hewitt, MacNeice, Hanna Bell and the Belfast shipyards poet and playwright Thomas Carnduff (1886–1956). Indeed, O'Faoláin dedicated two issues of *The Bell* to Ulster writing. In introducing the first of these, O'Faoláin proclaimed: 'I begin to feel now that in this new Ulster of ours there *is* Humanity and there *is* the Artist. They are solving our dichotomies'.[42] So Hewitt was certainly a part of literary movements on both sides of the border which tasked themselves with thinking anew. The task for Hewitt was to try and reconcile his regionalism and desire for a local identity with this other aim of rethinking old polarities. Hewitt's inter-est in the Rhyming Weavers – eighteenth-century Ulster pre-industrial workers who wrote poetry in their own Northern vernacular voice – undoubtedly helped to merge his socialism and regionalism. On the question of rootedness, and in particular Hewitt's attempt to balance his regional agenda with his effort to reconfigure traditional divisions, he stated that he was not averring that 'a writer ought to live and die in the house of his fathers' but equally, he insisted, a writer must have 'ancestors': 'Not just of the blood, but of the emotions, of the quality and slant of the mind. He must know where he comes from and where he is: otherwise how can he tell where he wishes to go?'[43]

Hence, taking the Rhyming Weavers as his own literary ancestors, Hewitt's work strived to voice a specifically Ulster voice or poetic register as well as thematically and imaginatively recovering his own territory. So where we discussed how the Revival and Southern writing wrestled with the problems of the marginalization of the Irish language and the concomitant necessity of shaping the English language in one's own terms, Hewitt's use of English had this different though parallel concern with trying to infuse it with Ulster vernacular words and patterns. In his essay 'The Bitter Gourd: Some Problems of the Ulster Writer' (1945), Hewitt states that of course he writes in English but yet: 'The writer must be a rooted man, must carry the native tang of his idiom like the native dust on his sleeve; otherwise he is an airy internationalist, this-tledown, a twig in a stream'.[44] Interestingly, Hewitt's example here of a vacuous internationalism is Joyce's *Finnegans Wake*. With regard to Hewitt's own sense of the grounding of his work, he turns to Scottish literature and its tradition of writing in Doric or Scots vernacular. In praising Scottish Letters, Hewitt postulates contrastingly that in Ulster 'we have no such literary heritage, no such ancient language'.[45] Hewitt therefore places himself as a figure who must instigate such a heritage in his regional idiom. The fact that he turns to Scotland, in anticipating his own Ulster–Scots vernacular, is part of the problem of his regionalism for critics hostile to the Northern Irish State in that his apparently shared local identity is also a British one.

Another crucial writer, who continues the Ulster–Scotland confluence, is Glasgow-born Sam Hanna Bell. As with the antipathy in Hewitt's regionalism to the increasing disjuncture of modern society, Hanna Bell similarly sought to recover and retain an ancestral tradition: 'The old ways of our community are vanishing rapidly'.[46] Equally though, Hanna Bell shared the desire to redefine old paradigms rather than merely repeat them. In contrast to O'Faoláin's feeling of isolation during the Second World War in the neutral Irish Republic, Hanna Bell believed that the encroachment of international events on the North helped in some way to open up possibilities in the stagnant Northern State – particularly as demonstrated by the flowering of cultural activity which occurred in the 1940s: 'Perhaps it was a sudden sense of interrupted isolation, of being cast from the fringe of Europe into portentous happenings'.[47] In Hanna Bell's dual commitment to preserve custom and to be sensitive to the flux of the world, he seeks to place the writer as someone who is engaged with society without being driven by its whims:

■ Not for him the music, the dancing banners, the operatic halberds. His duty is to herald the great procession to its destination. Clearly he must not canter ahead and decapitate the procession, nor meander so slowly that far behind thousands of perplexed and sweating brethren mark time [...] If he suffers from any trepidation he must conceal it. His position is not an enviable one.[48] □

Through his metaphor of a procession, Hanna Bell styles the unenviable position of the writer as a precarious mission to give the imaginative lead without resorting to elitist detachment and to connect with people without populism. In a similar vein, Louis MacNeice, whose poetry addressed social inequality and sectarian division in Ireland, as well as the rise of Fascism in Europe, the Spanish Civil War and World War Two, declared that: 'The writer today should be not so much the mouthpiece of a community [...] as its conscience, its critical faculty, its generous instinct'.[49] There is no finer embodiment of MacNeice's dictum than his own work *Autumn Journal* (1939), which indicted with equal measure world political events, contemporary materialism and sectarian polarity in Ireland through a generously poised yet fiercely unremitting poetic imagination.

Internationalizing Irish literary criticism

But in terms of the internationalism which, by turns, galvanized or troubled the critical impulse of the writers we have covered thus far in this chapter, it is noteworthy how Hewitt in particular singles out Joyce's *Finnegans Wake* as his example of a literary work that is so experimentally self-referential and wide-ranging in its scope that it has paradoxically lost its connectedness to the world. Although we observed how Hewitt was striving to re-energize Northern culture, his own means of doing so insisted on a regionalist programme that had of necessity to be rooted in locality. The shifting languages and forms of *Finnegans Wake* clearly flout such regionalist demands. By way of anticipating a more internationalist criticism that developed through the course of the twentieth century and which focused on key Irish writers from Modernist and postmodernist perspectives, *Finnegans Wake* – while still under its provisional title *Work In Progress* – elicited a series of responses from Joyce's fellow exile Samuel Beckett and others entitled *Our Exagmination Round His Factification For Incamination Of Work In Progress* (1929). Beckett used his introductory essay to denounce any literary criticism which sought to reduce literature to preconceived paradigms or national and political demarcations: 'Must we wring the neck of a certain system in order to stuff it into a contemporary pigeon-hole, or modify the dimensions of that pigeon-hole for the satisfaction of analogymongers? Literary criticism is not book-keeping'.[50] For Beckett, Joyce's work and literature more generally 'is not *about* something; *it is that something itself*'.[51] That is, if literature refers to anything it is ultimately to itself, its own language, its own form and textual medium. Concomitantly, another contributor to the same collection, Eugene Jolas (1894–1952), asserted that Joyce's work demonstrated that 'the real metaphysical problem today is the word. The epoch when the writer photographed the life about him with the mechanics of words redolent of the daguerreotype, is happily drawing to its close. The new artist of the word has recognized the autonomy of language'.[52]

So although published as early as 1929, Beckett's collection on Joyce adumbrates the development of structuralism, post-structuralism and deconstruction in the latter part of the twentieth century. All of these practices treated language as a system with its own governing structures which, in the cases of post-structuralism and deconstruction, could be made to fall apart and collapse in play and contradiction. But, to return to the 1920s, there also emerged a slightly different approach that became known as New Criticism and which treated the literary work as an object in itself. The New Criticism's emphasis was on the coherence and integration of the formal features of the literary work – and the kind of literary work most privileged by this movement was the poem.[53] New Criticism was not, however, pure formalism as it also posited that the formal unity and empirically discerned structures of the literary work would express or crystallize the emotional and metaphysical complexities of life and experience. The idea that the literary work formed an object in itself was an effort to wrestle the text from, firstly, approaches which privileged the role of the author or the reader in making meaning, and, secondly, criticism which took into account the social, historical or political contexts of literature. For our purposes, New Criticism is central to the interest of a number of important international (largely Anglo-American) critics in Irish literature and most particularly in engendering a series of debates in the journal *Studies* in 1955 and 1956. The interventions helped to sow the seeds of the institutional development of Irish Studies as an academic discipline in its own right, in addition to following the critics we have covered in this chapter thus far in their respective attempts think Irish literature anew.

The debates in *Studies* were conducted between Denis Donoghue, Donald Davie and Vivian Mercier. Donoghue's article 'Notes Towards A Critical Method: Language As Order' (1955) asserts that 'poems are made out of the poet's desire to create forms, entities, things of order with which to oppose the continued flux, change, transience of life'.[54] Donoghue is articulating the New Criticism creed of the literary object as offering order in the face of chaos. But the main point here is that Donoghue's own grasp of New Criticism and its literary empiricism equipped him with a sense of being a proper critic himself. In turn, by looking around the Irish literary scene, he feels that there is no established or substantial critical tradition and movement in Ireland. The English poet and critic Davie wrote 'Reflections of an English Writer in Ireland' (1955) as a reply but his intended rebuttal actually served to justify Donoghue's contention: 'nothing is more striking in the Anglo-Irish literary tradition than the absence of any true critic at all, certainly of any critical tradition'.[55] The writers and critics whom we have covered in this Guide up to this point obviously serve to refute this assertion; but we can also note that this is not the first time that a critic or indeed a group of critics have set themselves up as bearers of a new, necessary criticism seeking to redress the void which they have putatively inherited from others. Nevertheless, the main point of the *Studies* responses was to call for a newly professionalized, specialized and institutionalized critical framework. In particular, this challenge is taken up by Mercier's contribution 'An Irish School of Criticism?' (1956). Firstly, Mercier welcomes Donoghue's New Criticism as 'a natural and healthy reaction against the over-emphasis of Marxists and others on the political and social content of literature as well as on the political and social conditions in which it was produced'.[56] In addition, according to Mercier, New Criticism's empirical emphasis on the literary object provides a specialized method of analysis by which an entire professional, institutional development of Irish literary criticism may proceed:

> ■ The gulf between scholarship and criticism seems even wider and deeper in Ireland than in other countries. Those who criticize don't know – those who know don't criticize. In other words, our critics are too unscholarly, our scholars too uncritical or too indifferent to the common reader.[57] □

There is perhaps a tension in the effort to establish an Irish critical tradition based on New Criticism given that Irishness – as context, as social and historical material – would have to be discarded in the concentration on the literary object. Indeed, writing elsewhere with David Greene, Mercier tried to account for the interest in writers from the Revival period such as Yeats, Joyce, Synge and O'Casey by international scholars in the following way:

> ■ The literary movement which these forces and these writers produced is unique, if only for the fact that it achieved two things which could easily

have cancelled each other. It made articulate the ideals of a people who were in the process of achieving political independence and of re-establishing their national identity, and at the same time it produced a literature capable of commanding respect independently of its geographical and political orientation.[58] □

In other words, Mercier and Greene try to admit the political and social conditions in which the Revival was embedded but yet retain an insistence that the greatness of the work not only transcends but also is, in fact, independent of those same contextual pressures. As we will consider in the next chapter, this tension between text and context will characterize some of the core debates within Irish Studies as an institutional discipline from the 1970s to the present. But for now, credit is undoubtedly due to Mercier since his own critical work did prefigure some of the main aspects of Irish Studies in the academy. One of Mercier's most brilliant engagements is *The Irish Comic Tradition* (1962). Therein Mercier traces a comic tradition from the ninth century onwards with reference to both popular and literary culture, from popular ballads to *Finnegans Wake*. Most significantly, Mercier retained a sense of Ireland's double linguistic and cultural inheritance by insisting of the Irish language that 'contemporary Anglo-Irish literature cannot be fully understood and appreciated without some knowledge of that tradition'.[59] Mercier also produced exemplary work on Beckett (he did in fact attend the same grammar school as Beckett attended – Portora Royal in Enniskillen, Northern Ireland). Mercier's famous reading of *Waiting For Godot* (1953 in French; 1955 in English) – as a 'play in which nothing happens, *twice*'[60] – insightfully distils in a single phrase the creative nothings which characterize Beckett's entire oeuvre, his capacity to produce artistic positives from existential negatives in acts of enabling despair.

In terms of pain and suffering, Beckett's difficult, and, paradoxically, at once direct and oblique work has had an enormous resonance across Western culture, especially in the aftermath of the Second World War, during which he helped the French Resistance – an experience which appeared to humble his more lofty versions of himself and his work. We can note briefly here in this context, that one of the most famous accounts of Beckett's work, specifically *Endgame* (1957 in French; 1958 in English), is offered by the German philosopher Theodor W. Adorno (1903–69): 'Understanding it can mean nothing other than understanding its incomprehensibility, or concretely reconstructing its meaning structure – that is has none'.[61] Aptly enough for a strongly dialectical thinker, Adorno posits in *Negative Dialectics* (1973) that if the meaning of Beckett's work is that there is no meaning, then that meaninglessness itself has meaning in a world after the horrors of the Holocaust. And though Beckett never refers to concentration camps by name, Adorno regards *Endgame* as the only fitting reaction to them:

■ To Beckett [...] the created world is radically evil, and its negation is the chance of another world that is not yet. As long as the world is as it is, all pictures of reconciliation, peace, and quiet resemble the picture of death [...] The true nihilists are the ones who oppose nihilism with their more and more faded positives, the ones who are thus conspiring with all extant malice, and eventually with the destructive principle itself. Thought honours itself by defending what is damned as nihilism.[62] □

Hence for Adorno, the real nihilists are those who perpetuate the horror of history, of things as they are, whose naïve view of history as progress has a constitutive hollowness at its core after events such as the Holocaust. As such, Beckett's writing is less a resigned capitulation to the world and more an absolute negation of the deathly naivety of progressive thought.

To return to New Criticism and an Anglo-American interest in Irish literature, two influential international critics who wrote consistently about Irish writers before the institutional emergence of Irish Studies are Richard Ellmann and Hugh Kenner. Despite being a New Critic, Ellmann's 1959 biography of Joyce in a sense took the author's life as itself a kind of literary object. He notably began with the proclamation: 'We are still learning to be James Joyce's contemporaries'.[63] That is, Ellmann regards Joyce as in a High Modernist framework where the artist forms part of a cultural vanguard in scorn of the rest of society and whose elevated insights require a great deal of catching up from the masses. So here there is the familiar New Critical and High Modernist credo of artistic integrity and order against social fragmentation and degradation. Ellmann does at times find Joyce's ego a difficult proposition but there remains an intimation of a master more educated than his own and future generations. However, in his later work Ellmann does alter his perspective and discerns in Joyce a more humane generosity. It can be observed that Ellmann's own experiences in the Second World War, in which he served in the US Army and confronted the horrors of the Holocaust first hand, engendered in him a humanistic outlook. Most especially, *The Consciousness of Joyce* (1977) traces a compassionate rather than elitist Joyce. Ellmann explains how *Ulysses* was structured by *The Odyssey* because of Joyce's interest in Odysseus whose name is derived from the combination of two Greek works – *Od* from *outis* meaning nobody, and Zeus the supreme deity – so that Odysseus is 'the divine nobody, at once unique and nondescript'.[64] So there is a shift in Ellmann's work from a vantage point of elitist artistic withdrawal to read in Joyce a more political or empathetic effort to reconcile the lofty and the lowly, to piece together an encompassing vision from a fragmented society rather than merely dismiss it.

Kenner's critical work provides a sustained and focused appraisal of aesthetic style and technique in the authors he covers. As with Beckett's 1929 collection on Joyce, Kenner proposes in *Dublin's Joyce* (1955) that Joyce's writing is 'about words, the complexity is there, in the way people talk, and Joyce copes with it by making it impossible for us to ignore the word on the page'.[65] In contrast to Ellmann's earlier interpretation of Joyce's creed of artistic heroism, *Dublin's Joyce* also averred for the first time that Stephen's character was in fact a parodic figure rather than a semi-autobiographical aggrandisement: 'Our impulse on being confronted with the final edition of Stephen Dedalus is to laugh'.[66] Additionally, Kenner's *Joyce's Voices* (1978) was exemplary is shaping what is now a critical commonplace about free indirect style in Modernist fiction: that is, the ability of an author to withdraw from the style of his or her narrative and to allow a character's consciousness to colour the tone and shape of what is still ostensibly a third person perspective. Kenner uses a passage involving the character Uncle Charles in *A Portrait* to illustrate this thesis: 'the normally neutral narrative vocabulary pervaded is by a little cloud of idioms which a character might use if he were managing the narrative'.[67]

By using Beckett as his model, Kenner was also able to identify formative influences on the Protestant or Anglo-Irish imagination. Kenner pinpoints two spiritual traditions 'by which history has shaped the specifically Protestant character: the personal testimony and the issueless confrontation with conscience'.[68] As we will shortly discuss, a much less well received attempt to interpret prevailing themes in Irish culture is *A Colder Eye: The Modern Irish Writers* (1983). Here Kenner scrutinizes what he terms 'Irish facts' which, he claims, are 'definable as anything they will tell you in Ireland, where you get told a great deal'.[69] Kenner continues: 'No Irishman apparently addresses pen to paper with any intent save to produce a good yarn [...] any such form of words as "They will tell you in Ireland" means that the next statement though enlightening, is better not trusted'.[70] Which is to say, the Irish are a garrulous and mischievous nation whose facts are fictions and who are a peculiarly distinctive hoard of storytellers.

The emergence of Irish Studies introduced a generation of Irish critics who took issue with such ongoing pronouncements about the Irish (there is a touch of Matthew Arnold in Kenner's claims) but their dispute was with more than just this kind of purveying of mock Irishness. More substantively, critics such as Seamus Deane, Declan Kiberd and David Lloyd believed that the New Criticism, High Modernist and international accounts of major Irish writers treated the Irish context of such literature as at best an encumbrance and at worst an irrelevance to understanding their work. These Irish Studies scholars suspected that the New Critical and Modernist paradigms proposed ultimately that Irishness was something to be transcended for Irish writers to be considered truly great. For Deane, Kenner's *A Colder Eye* 'exploits the whimsical Irishness of the writers in a particularly inane and offensive manner. The point is not simply that the Irish are different. It is that they are absurdly different because of the disabling, if fascinating, separation between their notion of reality and that of everybody else'.[71] So too, Kiberd, despite being supervised as a student at Oxford by Ellmann, accused him and other 'humanist critics' of being too quick to see Irish Nationalism purely as chauvinism in the work of Joyce and others. Specifically, such critics misunderstand or ignore the dynamics of Irish writing, its socio-historical context, its political conflicts and the power relations it confronts. So in fact, Kiberd asserts, nationalism and the Irish dimension to writers like Joyce are not restrictive but affiliated with many non-Western cultures across the world: 'their range of reference is not Eurocentric, but far wider than that of most humanists themselves. The law, which seems established to many Anglo-American readers of *Ulysses*, did not appear as such to Joyce, being merely a tyranny based on official terror'.[72]

In other words, Kiberd is affiliating Irish literature with postcolonial situations rather than European cultural traditions. Postcolonialism, which is most canonically associated with writers and critics such as Frantz Fanon (1925–61), Edward Said and Ngũgĩ wa Thiong'o (born 1938), developed out of the struggles for independence of peoples under colonial domination. The fact that this movement is termed *post*-colonialism alerts us that the processes of decolonization endure after independence or apparent national liberation have been achieved. One of they key assertions of postcolonial criticism is that imperialism was not only about the military, economic and political domination of other peoples but was also embedded in culture, in the effort to supplant and destroy indigenous languages and cultures through the imposition of the language and culture of the imperial state. The task of postcolonial criticism, therefore, is, in Ngũgĩ's phrase, to 'decolonize the mind'.[73] So contemporary Irish Studies critics such as Kiberd, Deane or David Lloyd conceived of Ireland and Irish culture in these postcolonial terms. As we have already discussed this kind of interpretation is broadly nothing new – Joyce, we observed, compared British rule in Ireland to the Belgian colonial presence in the Congo, while critics such as Moran or Corkery, along with much Irish Nationalism more generally, viewed the resistance to British occupation as an anti-colonial dynamic.

However, as we will outline in the next chapter, these recent Irish Studies invocations of postcolonialism coincide with the upsurge in political violence in the North of Ireland. And some of the most heated debates that we will discuss, hinge on competing attitudes to that conflict. Equally, we will address the emergence of Revisionism in Irish Studies, of an effort to deflate the rhetoric of nationalism and the founding of the Irish Republic – and again, this is not necessarily a new departure as a number of the critics we cover regard themselves as heirs to writers such as O'Faoláin or, in some cases, Yeats and others. The institutional development of Irish Studies as an academic discipline is not by any means reducible to a simple postcolonial-Revisionist debate and we will cover a range of critical voices. But we will also explain why postcolonial and revisionist approaches to literature take place in the terms that they do. In order to assess precisely how and why these contemporary critical paradigms interpret literature in their respective manners, we will assess in the next chapter their competing versions of the ultimate meaning of the Literary Revival and key writers therein.

CHAPTER THREE

The Development of Irish Studies: Contesting the Revival

Revisionism, postcolonialism, Field Day

In order to understand the motivations and intentions behind the key critical approaches in contemporary Irish Studies, we will ground our account of such critics in this chapter in their reading of the Revival period. Where the Revival witnessed an energetic array of contesting attempts to re-imagine Irish cultures and identities, so too contemporary Irish Studies undertakes a similar mission. Hence, we will appraise the critical interventions of Irish Studies through the lens of their own reassessment of that earlier period of national re-conception. Just as debates about literature were either harnessed to, or resistant to, national paradigms in the Revival, the important recent critical interventions in the work of Yeats, Joyce and the Revival have also been, by turns, galvanized or hindered by debates about and within Ireland. Most particularly, social change in the Irish Republic from the 1960s onwards and the onset of political violence in the North (itself coupled with social change) have all given an urgency, at times a vitriol, yet also a clarity, to the evaluation of the Revival, its writers and its fractious legacy. Obviously we will address such issues directly in the chapters on the North and the Republic but we will also bear in mind how such pressures impinge on the critical paradigms surrounding the Revival. The major critical fracture is often characterized as a confrontation between, on the one hand, Revisionism, and, on the other, a reworked Irish Nationalism (at least, according to Revisionists) that is most commonly associated with the Field Day project.

Although it would be entirely misleading to portion all critical debate into two neatly dichotomized camps, Revisionism and Field Day, as general and admittedly imperfect groupings, are indicative of a major antagonism that has sought to contest the meanings of the Revival. So, without wishing to homogenize Revisionism as an intellectual school, it broadly seeks, in its own terms, to demythologize Irish Nationalist versions of history, to contrast an idealized iconography of political struggle with the reality of historical events and the state of Irish society. George Boyce and Alan O'Day offer a good summary of the loose assemblages of cultural and historiographical activity that are thought to coalesce under the rubric of Revisionism:

■ 'Revisionism' has been dated variously to a revulsion from the officially propagated histories of the post-1922 Irish Free State and of Northern Ireland culminating in the founding of *Irish Historical Studies* in the late 1930s to the disillusionment with the failure of the Republic to deliver the promised economic and cultural goods by the 1960s generation of Irish who looked to America and swinging London as their talismans, to the 'Troubles' in Northern Ireland that laid claim to a tradition of Republican violence, and to the whole Island's entry into the European Union, a decision nullifying fundamental tenets of nationalism and Unionism.[1] □

Francis Shaw's 'The Canon of Irish History – A Challenge', for example, was published posthumously in 1972 having been rejected for publication during his lifetime, and it controverts the view that 'In 1916, half-a-dozen men decided what the nation should want'.[2] Shaw's ultimate aim was to demythologize a whole host of Irish Republican and Nationalist icons such as Wolfe Tone and Pearse. We could also invoke Roy Foster who proposes that 'we are all revisionists now': 'In a country that has come of age, history need no longer be a matter of guarding sacred mysteries. And to say "revisionist" should just be another way of saying historian'.[3] In other words, Revisionism does not seek to glorify or consecrate events to fit the needs of a heroic nationalist narrative of Irish history. Hence, for Foster, all critical activity worthy of the name 'criticism' should have this revisionary eye. However, Revisionism does not have a monopoly on the claim to being exigently engaged in a rethinking of outmoded paradigms of Irish history and culture – this is exactly what the founders of Field Day state of their own project.

Field Day began as a theatre company founded in 1980 by the actor Stephen Rea (born 1946), and the playwright Brian Friel. Quickly, four other fellow directors of Field Day were recruited: Seamus Deane, Seamus Heaney, David Hammond (born 1928) and Tom Paulin (born 1949). In addition to theatrical productions, Field Day also issued a pamphlet series that included work by key figures in Irish Studies such as Deane and Declan Kiberd, as well as in 1988 a set of pamphlets featuring Edward Said, Fredric Jameson and Terry Eagleton (born 1943). Most ambitiously, Field Day undertook the compilation of *The Field Day Anthology of Irish Writing*, a far-reaching and comprehensive assemblage of hundreds of years of Irish writing (the motives for which, as will be detailed below, are contentious). Seamus Deane states very clearly that Field Day was not about regurgitating existing nationalist paradigms and pieties: 'its origin does not lie in the "soul" of an embryonic nation. But it is given to the [...] idea of renovation, of adventure, of going out from the established to a new consciousness'.[4] Nonetheless, Stephen Rea's definition of the project is couched in terms of a national undertaking that echoes the Revivalist agenda: 'we want to give some kind of expression in dramatic form to the Irish people'.[5] But Deane markedly distinguishes the Company's aims from the Revival theatre of Yeats and Lady Gregory by asserting that Field Day is 'like the Abbey in its origin in that it has within it the idea of a culture which has not yet come to be in political terms. It is unlike the Abbey in that it can no longer subscribe to any simple nationalism for the basis of its existence'.[6] To a degree, a part of this rejection of 'simple nationalism' was a new theoretical engagement with Irish Literature – most specifically with postcolonial theory – that was galvanized by the contributions to the pamphlet series not only from Deane but also from Said, the exiled Palestinian intellectual and leading figure in postcolonialism, Jameson the renowned American Marxist, and Eagleton the key British Marxist critic. In introducing the republication of the series of pamphlets by Eagleton, Said and Jameson in book form, Deane wrote:

> ■ Ireland is the only Western European country that has had both an early and a late colonial experience. Out of that, Ireland produced, in the first three decades of this century, a remarkable literature in which the attempt to overcome and replace the colonial experience by something other, something that would be 'native' and yet not provincial, was a dynamic and central energy. The ultimate failure of that attempt to imagine a truly liberating cultural alternative is as well known as the brilliance of the initial effort. Now that the established system has again been called into question, even to the point where it must seriously alter or collapse [...] Field Day's analysis of the situation derives from the conviction that it is, above all, a colonial crisis.[7] □

On the other hand, Roy Foster has voiced his suspicions about this theoretical turn in Irish Studies and argues that it offers a means of renewing old stereotypes: 'it is curious how old-fashioned the conclusions of modernism tend to be: as cultural commentators turn their attention to history, perfidious Albion and betrayed Hibernia take the stage once more.'[8] Edna Longley, as will be analyzed later, also senses that Field Day and the work of a critic like David Lloyd are merely cloaking the 'simple nationalism' dismissed by Deane in a theoretical guise, and that ultimately the interpretation of the situation in the North of Ireland as a 'colonial crisis' is a means of legitimizing the Irish Republican armed struggle. For his own part, Deane believes that one of the effects of Ireland's colonial crisis is an ongoing dislocation and dispossession so that the Field Day Company's broader mission, and the

Field Day Anthology specifically, may be viewed as 'an act of repossession' from colonial appropriation.[9] The purpose of the anthology, Deane maintains in its introduction, is to affirm that despite the disruption of Irish history and culture by British domination: 'There *is* a story here, a meta-narrative, which is, we believe, hospitable to all the micro-narratives that, from time to time, have achieved prominence as the official version of the true history, political and literary, of the island's past and present.'[10]

Contesting Yeats

In this highly charged critical environment, Yeats's work is often a target. Declan Kiberd castigates Yeats for having fully ingested Matthew Arnold's stereotyping of the wild Celt: 'Yeats's search has long been recognized as a quest for a mode of expression, which would preclude any truth it might express [...] This was nothing other than the search for a national style and, as such, the purest Celticism'.[11] Deane also attacks what he regards as a romantic version of Irish literature, of which Yeats is one of the culprits, a romanticization which constitutes the Irish writer as a 'licensed barbarian – a sort of wild Irish native performing in an English court'.[12]

In addition to allegations of pandering to an English audience and its stereotypical expectations of Irish culture, Yeats's mythic Ireland and his ancient vision are equally regarded by some key critics as having another function: namely, to aggrandize the cause of the Protestant Ascendancy and to disavow the historical reality of the relative social decline of that class. Thus, Tom Paulin asserts that Yeats's 'mature verse combines muscle-flexing Protestant triumphalism with an elitist dedication'.[13] W. J. McCormack observes: 'I take Protestant Ascendancy to be the central assumption of Yeats's meditation of his own inheritance. By it he measured the politics of the Irish Free State'.[14] Gerry Smyth too interprets Yeats's work as an effort, however forlorn, of seeking to shore up the hegemony of the Anglo-Irish Ascendancy in a continuation of the Protestant Sir Samuel Ferguson's work in the nineteenth century to retain a key Anglo-Irish dimension to both history and literature:

■ As self-appointed spokesman for the dwindling Anglo-Irish Protestant population of Ireland, Yeats's task (following Ferguson's example) was to invent a history and an identity which would guarantee Anglo-Irish inclusion in, if not domination of, a restored Irish nation.[15] □

Moreover, the dismissal by Conor Cruise O'Brien (born 1917) continues the objections that George Orwell raised about the hierarchic nature of Yeats's politics, in this instance through Cruise O'Brien's sense of Yeats's admiration for Kevin O'Higgins (1892–1927), the 'strong man' of Irish politics of the time, and Yeats's equation of such political will in Ireland with the rise of Fascism in Europe: 'Yeats was trying to create a movement in Ireland which would be overtly Fascist in language, costume, behaviour and intent'.[16]

In our account of Yeats's critical work in Chapter One, we noted how his effort to revive and mobilize Ireland was indeed highly stratified and there is an elitist disdain in his creative writing as well. 'No Second Troy', that testy testament to his unrequited love for Maud Gonne, castigates the ignorance of the crowd, while 'To A Shade' elegizes the fallen hero Charles Stuart Parnell (1846–91) who was thwarted by a populist sentiment. However, the Parnell elegy also instructs that Yeats sought to salvage in his own artistic aesthetic imaginative and cultural potentials that were denied by mainstream politics, crass demagoguery and what he regarded as the staid, habituated consensus of modern life. Hence, 'To A Wealthy Man' indicts just about all of Dublin society, including the Protestant Ascendancy class, for their philistine refusal to appreciate and endorse art.

Nonetheless, 'September 1913' is much more specific in venting its spleen against the materialism of the urban middle and working classes – compounded in the poem by the pun on 'save' where the heroes of the past who seek the salvation of their nation's soul – including John O'Leary (1830–1907) who had an enormous influence on the young Yeats – are contrasted with the self-serving, petty concerns of the Dubliners interested only in saving money. But 'September 1913' also reinforces Yeats's commitment to the restorative power of art and the complexity of his own aesthetic for while the content of the poem is unrelentingly pessimistic about contemporary Ireland, the poem's form, its repeated refrain about a dead and gone romantic Ireland, retains, commemorates and redeems what the poetic voice claims has been set aside. The poem turns on the word 'yet' and there is a strong sense, embedded in the very form of 'September 1913', that it is through art that a heroic Ireland is recuperated and still made possible. Despite Yeats's search for appropriately heroic and epic forms, with which to inspire Ireland, however, much of the criticism of his work centres on how this ideal – of an Ireland renewed – does not tally with the contempt for vast swathes of Ireland also contained therein.

A really concentrated and illustrative reading of both Yeats and the Revival, more generally, is provided in George Watson's *Irish Identity and the Literary Revival: Synge, Yeats, Joyce and O'Casey* (1994). Watson discerns a crucial opposition between the Yeatsian hero indifferent to public or social concerns, and the popular hero who embodies merely the stereotypical aspirations of the crowd. Watson reads Yeats's idea of heroism as one of 'reckless, uncalculating idealism'.[17] For example, Watson interprets Yeats's elegies for Lady Gregory's son, Robert Gregory (1881–1918), who was killed in the First World War, such as 'In Memory of Major Robert Gregory' and 'An Irish Airman', as using Robert Gregory as a complete symbol of the Yeatsian heroic type: the poems deal not with the political or social context of the Great War but instead isolate in Gregory 'a disengaged free spirit committed only to the lonely and extravagant gesture, whose self-realisation occurs in a moment of burning intensity'.[18] Hence, Watson asserts, in 'Easter 1916' the Rising is seen as a spontaneous, self-contained gesture, a heroic act cutting across history rather than being its culmination. The Rising is an irruption of heroism in a context of utter mundanity.

As events turned out, through the War of Independence and the Civil War, to the consolidation of the Irish Free State and the ascent of a Catholic, bourgeois control of the state, it is not difficult to understand how Yeats's earlier high-minded, aristocratic, solitary, heroic acts become transmuted into a withdrawn, elitist disapproval. Watson observes a shift in Yeats's later poetry wherein the bravado and the swagger of heroic defeat and failure are gone. Instead there is a direct confrontation with historical experience in which Yeats, Watson posits, channels his former celebration of doomed things into elegiac power and beauty.[19] Thus, the acknowledgement in 'Upon a House Shaken' of the political activism of the Land League and a politicized peasantry who wished to reclaim their land, and the impact of the Land Act of 1909 in which Anglo-Irish estates such as Lady Gregory's began to be redistributed, is echoed with darker resonance in later poems like 'Coole Park, 1929' and 'Coole and Ballylee, 1931' that directly attest to the break up of the Anglo-Irish estates and the entire social class and hegemony which they embody.

To that end, Seamus Deane's *Celtic Revivals* (1985) asserts that 'perhaps the most seductive of all Yeats's historical fictions is his gift of dignity and coherence to the Irish Protestant Ascendancy tradition'.[20] Deane couches the tensions of Yeats's epic national imagining in the following way: 'Yeats began his career by inventing an Ireland amenable to his imagination. He ended by finding an Ireland recalcitrant to it'.[21] Perhaps the most sustained and negative critique of Yeats's work is provided by David Lloyd's *Anomalous States* (1993). Lloyd reads 'Coole Park and Ballylee, 1931' as symptomatic of Yeats's high-minded arrogance by stressing that the actual geography of the landscape does not tally with the imaginative topography constructed by Yeats. The Ballylee's river does not actually emerge as a lake in Coole Park but it does so, according to Lloyd, in Yeats's mind in order to produce a symbolic continuity not present in reality. Lloyd also argues that the poem's reference to the swan which paradoxically appears in the moment of its vanishing is instructive of how the real or the actual is rewritten by hyperbolic, imaginative allegory in Yeats. For Lloyd, the basis of Yeats's poetic emanates from his effort to found a tradition around Lady Gregory's estate and the Anglo-Irish Ascendancy class she represents in the very moment of the historical demise of that same class. Additionally, in the phrase, 'All is changed', Lloyd discerns an allusion to 'Easter 1916' that is deeply reso-nant since the actions of those involved in the Easter Rising trouble and usurp Yeats's own desire as a self-proclaimed national poet to identify the nation completely within the symbols and terms of reference of his own poetry:

■ At the very moment where Yeats in 'Coole Park and Ballylee, 1931' seeks to retrieve a poetic tradition from its demise, he dares reference to the poem in his canon which most thoroughly explores the poet's marginalization or redundancy.[22] □

So Lloyd posits that Yeats's own envisaged role as a national poet is usurped by the rebels of 1916 whose actual violence displaces Yeats's codes of heroism framed in epic literary form for the emulation of a future Ireland yet to be. So we could again read Yeats's work in terms of a mythic, idealized heroism confuted by reality and the agency of others which jointly undermine his desire to order events in his own terms. Moreover, the actions of the 1916 rebels become nationally symbolic, they are trans-formed in their actions into symbols of a new Irish nation, but this sym-bolic transfiguration occurs, Lloyd avers, at the moment of their death. And he finds an irreconcilable tension of double or competing meanings in the bringing into being of a newly constituted Ireland that has entered his-tory and asserted its continuity, identity and futurity on an act of rupture.

We can clarify this complex account another way. While Lloyd clearly strives to indict Yeats's cultural politics, he nevertheless also grasps Yeats's poetry as offering insight into the limitations of the Irish Free State, and latterly the Irish Republic, and the cultural nationalism that serves to legitimize each. To Lloyd, the nation state offers itself as the organic expression of its people and their history yet its apparent narrative continuity and legitimacy is founded on an act of violence whose martyred participants are dead. Erased from the actual nation they must, nonetheless, be continually remembered symbolically but this aesthetic recoding cannot finally disguise the constitutive violence that it tries to replace with organic unity and institutional legitimacy. So where Lloyd dissects how Yeats's later work tries to found an Anglo-Irish, Ascendancy tradition in the moment of its own isolated demise, he also finds the directly inverse tension of the Irish State being born in the death of its founders. While critical of the politics of Yeats's later work, Lloyd believes that the aesthetic tensions of these poems also serve to expose and impugn the limitations of supposedly representative democracy, wherein the state's representation of its own organic conti-nuity is, in fact, based on violence, exclusion and erasure.

Seamus Deane's Field Day pamphlet, *Heroic Styles: The Tradition of An Idea* (1984), similarly impugns Yeats and it undertakes its criticism in concert with an appraisal of Joyce through which Deane seeks to undermine two dominant ways of reading Irish literature and history (that are ascribed to Yeats and Joyce, respectively):

■ One is 'Romantic', a mode of reading which takes pleasure in the notion that Ireland is a culture enriched by the ambiguity of its relationship to an anachronistic and a modernised present. The other is a mode of reading which denies the glamour of this ambiguity and seeks to escape from it into a pluralism of the present. The authors who represent these modes most powerfully are Yeats and Joyce respectively. The problem which is rendered insoluble by them is that of the North. In a basic sense the crisis we are passing through is stylistic. That is to say, it is a crisis of language – the ways in which we write it and the ways in which we read it.[23] □

So the most immediate motivation for Deane's need to disrupt these established paradigms is the Northern conflict and the exhaustion of established thinking that it represents for him. Deane is particularly exercised by what he regards as a literary unionism in Yeats and other Protestant writers masquerading as cultural nationalism, the effect of which is to petrify Irishness into defensive and outworn stereotypes that ultimately served (and serve) a British cultural and political agenda. Deane finds that in Yeats's last writings the romantic, mythic national paradigm he represents is finally unmasked as the debilitating annexation, appropriation and attenuation of Irishness by the Anglo-Irish intellectual. For example, in 'A General Introduction for my Work' (1937), Yeats aligns himself to an English tradition stretching from Shakespeare, Edmund Spenser (?1522–99), Blake, to William Morris, as opposed to what he deems a self-destructive Irish disposition, in order to claim 'everything I love has come to me through English'. On this point, Deane comments wryly: 'The pathology of literary unionism has never been better defined'.[24] Thus, Deane identifies in Yeats's work an unhelpful romantic paradigm of Irishness and he goes further to task the Field Day project with the urgent necessary of dissolving that mystique: 'Everything, including our politics and our literature, has to be rewritten – i.e. re-read. That will enable new writing, new politics, unblemished by Irishness, but securely Irish'.[25]

However, Paul Scott Stanfield offers a more sympathetic appraisal of Yeats's later isolation:

■ In the 1930s his solitude increased. The ascendancy of de Valera made the Anglo-Irish tradition of independent nationalism a virtually untenable faith. Most of those with whom Yeats had at one time or another made common cause – John O'Leary, John Synge, Lady Gregory, Kevin O'Higgins, George Russell, were dead.[26] □

Edna Longley's *The Living Stream: Literature and Revisionism in Ireland* (1994) also provides a reading of Yeats that is fundamentally opposed to the interpretations of Deane, Field Day more broadly, and David Lloyd. Longley's Yeats is not merely an elitist but also the man who used his position in the Irish Senate to speak out against the ban on divorce by the Irish Free State and against a wider repressiveness by a new bourgeois, Catholic hegemony. As to the motivations of Field Day, Longley regards its Anthology as 'a directive encyclopaedia, an interpretive centre packaged and signposted', especially for consumption abroad since, as Longley notes, over half the first print-run was destined for the USA.[27] She also points to the contradictions of Deane's desire for a writing that is 'unblemished by Irishness, but securely Irish': 'By inviting readers on to purely textual ground, and loading the text, Deane tries to have his Nationalist history and eat it, to deconstruct and canonise in the same gesture'.[28] Additionally, Longley highlights the irony at the core of the Field Day reading of Yeats for while most of the Irish critics in its coalition sought to dismantle his Irish and national credentials, Edward Said, the leading postcolonial critic invited to produce a pamphlet on Yeats, actually endorses him. Said writes:

■ despite Yeats's obvious and, I would say, settled presence in Ireland, in British culture and literature, and in European modernism, he does present another fascinating aspect: that of the indisputably great *national* poet who articulates the experiences, the aspirations, and the vision of a people suffering under the domination of an offshore power. From this perspective Yeats is a poet who belongs to a tradition not usually considered his, that of the colonial world ruled by European imperialism now – that is, during the late nineteenth and early twentieth centuries – bringing to a climactic insurrectionary stage, the massive upheaval of anti-imperialist resistance in the colonies, and of metropolitan anti-imperialist opposition that has been called the age of decolonization.[29] □

Indeed, here we could also mention John Wilson Foster's account of the almost Oedipal struggle that generations of Irish Nationalist critics have had with Yeats, seeing him, as it were, as the father they do not want, or at least the father who stands in the way of their own full communion with the nation and with nationalism, the figure whose authority must be supplanted for their bond with Mother Ireland to be enacted.[30] Even though Said's interpretation of Yeats is a positive one, Longley feels that it is just as misinformed and ideologically motivated as the dismissals. There is, for Longley, no real grasp of Yeats's class position, or his religious background, of the historical complexities with which he dealt. Both Said's and Terry Eagleton's Field Day pamphlets, according to Longley, assume 'a homogeneous, unproblematic Irish people'.[31] Moreover, just as Longley accuses Field Day of dressing up old nationalist doctrines in new terms, so too she suspects that Lloyd's *Anomalous States* 'cloaks familiar Marxist-Republican doctrines in theoretical euphemism [...] one glimpses once again a sinister purity'.[32]

To Longley, the later isolation of Yeats is a direct result of the exclusive and repressive nature of the Free State and the canons of Irishness established by the likes of Corkery. In this interpretation, Yeats had to reconsider his Protestant literary predecessors, as in a poem like 'Blood and the Moon', precisely because of this increasing marginalization of his position in the new state and the direction taken by that state. It is notable that in an early essay, 'Irish National Literature' (1895), the young romantic nationalist Yeats had criticized the Victorian critic Edward Dowden (1843–1913) for including in his Irish literary canon the Protestants James Usher (1581–1656, scholar, Archbishop of Armagh and Primate of the Anglican Church in Ireland 1625–56), Laurence Sterne (1713–68, novelist), Jonathan Swift (1667–1745, satirist and poet) and George Berkeley (1680–1753, philosopher, Bishop of Cloyne 1734–52): 'Some of my countrymen include among national writers all writers born in Ireland, but I prefer, though it greatly takes from the importance of our literature, to include only those who have written under Irish influence and of Irish subjects'.[33] Even here, however, there is a nagging doubt about the 'importance' of other aspects of literature that are being repressed in the exclusive nationalist canon that Yeats himself constructs. Equally, in the later essays cited by Deane in his condemnation of Yeats's literary unionism, it should be recognized that Yeats does apologize for the solely Protestant, Anglo-Irish composition of his reworked national tradition though he argues, rightly or wrongly, that he has no alternative. Hence, for Longley, 'Blood and the Moon', the Coole Park poems, and his final works represent the rhetorical defiance of an imagination under siege: 'Marginalised groups assert their presence in territorial and genealogical terms [...] Yeats opted for "Anglo-Irish solitude", thus making a virtue of necessity'.[34]

Just as Longley's readings of Yeats's later ancestral and marginalized broodings differ from Lloyd's or Deane's, her sense of 'Easter 1916' stresses a more open-ended, generously spirited complexity that is ultimately central to her own literary criticism and to the Revisionist undertaking more generally. In particular, Longley picks up on the poem's contrast between the 'stone' of ideological or political fixity and the 'living stream' as a symbol of the flux of life and history:

■ Today, Yeats's living stream might represent the last seventy-five years and Southern revisionism, while his 'stone' might represent either Northern

Republicanism or neo-Pearsean efforts to 'Reclaim the Spirit of 1916'. 'Easter 1916' is, in fact, the first work of revisionist poetry, revisionist history, revisionist literary criticism. But the poem involves a double revisionism, a revisionist double-take, successive 'changes' in perspective.[35] □

Longley, therefore, certainly finds in Yeats a number of key tensions and problematics, but also, just as importantly, the seeds of revisionism, a refusal of ideological or political fixity and a concomitant commitment that criticism is always an ongoing, self-critical undertaking whose task should ultimately be the affirmation of the fluidity and complexity of art, history and life.[36]

Additionally, Marjorie Howes's *Yeats's Nations: Gender, Class, and Irishness* (1996) is a highly informed resource which refutes the idea that Yeats was solely an authoritarian figure. Howes highlights how Yeats's entire vision was formed out of a faith that the world and the imagination exist through the interpenetration of opposites. Hence, it is not so much that Yeats regarded authority as preferable to democracy as that he harnessed both as inexorable, mutually engaging contraries: 'Yeats accepts both democracy and authority, individual and race, equally, as the necessary and interdependent faces of an important historical and political antinomy [...] Yeats affirmed that each contrary was no less true because its opposite was also true'.[37]

Contesting Joyce

Where Yeats represents the distillation of a romantic, mythic Irishness in *Heroic Styles*, Deane posits that Joyce embodies a different but no less restrictive and reiterative paradigm of detached, modern pluralism. Specifically, Deane mistrusts what he claims is this consumerist pick-and-mix aspect to Joyce's plural, interchangeable identities and languages:

■ The pluralism of his styles and languages, the absorbent nature of his controlling myths and systems, finally gives a certain harmony to varied experience. But, it could be argued, it is the harmony of indifference, one in which everything is a version of something else, where sameness rules over diversity, where contradiction is finally and disquietingly written out.[38] □

So, for Deane, Yeats and Joyce represent mutually sustaining (and mutually destructive) paradigms that must be circumvented: the archaic, mythic model and the disengaged, dislocated modern one – both of which, Deane insists, blight any meaningful breakthrough in the Northern Irish political crisis. Deane's *Strange Country: Modernity and Nationhood in Irish Writing* (1997) also offers a reading of Irish culture that regards it as trapped in restrictive stereotypes which are just as capable of being produced by Irish as British or other writers. This effort to produce a unitary Irish character and culture that is transhistorical actually has the effect of producing a paradigm which is historically mired and doomed to be continually repeated. Hence, Irish culture becomes a repetitive, self-perpetuating monotony, a deadening re-iteration of the same models:

■ Essentialism is coercive because it always insists on the necessity of reconciling difference with sameness, discontinuity with continuity, arguing, for instance, that the same Irish spirit prevailed time and time again, despite the refusal by its oppressors to acknowledge its legitimate claims. This is not an impossible position but it is a repetitive one. It is productive of monotony, because it orders miscellaneous materials into repetitive, typifying narratives.[39] □

So paradoxically when this essentialism believes that it is most fully speaking for Ireland, representing Ireland, it is actually doing the direct opposite and entombing the differences of Ireland in a restrictive model which allows merely established stereotypes to speak rather than the more complex reality of Ireland.

Another highly important critical work that enables us to consider how Irish writers (or critics for that matter) are sometimes complicit in representational modes constructed to contain Ireland is Joep Leerssen's *Remembrance and Imagination* (1996). Leerssen argues that the purpose of colonial stereotypes was to exoticize Ireland, to make it strange and otherworldly. He postulates that since the Act of Union in 1801 the *destinataire*, that is, the intended or target audience for Irish writers, was in England as there was not enough of a literate middle class in Ireland itself. He argues that Irish writers engaged in what he calls *auto-exoticism*: that is, they exoticized themselves due to the inexorable power of colonial stereotyping:

■ Ireland as a *representandum*, as subject matter, does not speak in its own voice but is spoken for; the author speaks, not as an Irish person, but as an intermediary on behalf of Irish people, adopts a (purportedly neutral) mid-way point between readership (English) and topic (Irish).[40] □

In other words, where such a vast, dominant set of discourses exists – stretching back hundreds of years – which represents Irishness in fixed, habituated forms, it can be consciously tempting, unconsciously programmed or hegemonically inevitable, that some Irish writing will reactivate and sustain those stereotypes. We could consider the representation of the peasant in the Revival, the melancholy soul of Celticism, the influence of Renan and Arnold in Yeats's work, right through to the present and a character like Father Jack in the Channel Four comedy *Father Ted* (1995–8), which is written by the Irishmen Arthur Matthews (born 1959) and Graham Linehan (born 1968). Ultimately, Leerssen defines *auto-exoticism* as 'a mode of seeing, presenting and representing oneself in one's otherness (in this case: one's non-Englishness) [...] Ireland is made exotic by the selfsame descriptions which purport to represent or explain Ireland'.[41]

If Leerssen's work offers a means by which we can interpret some Irish writing as actually voicing someone else's constructions of itself in the same mistaken moment that it believes it has achieved its fullest self-expression, then David Lloyd's book *Nationalism and Minor Literature: James Clarence Mangan* (1987) provides a different and inverse set of issues. Although Lloyd analyzes the nineteenth-century poet Mangan, he considers how the Irish use of the English language is not only a sign of defeat or assent to a dominant culture in an engaging survey that has direct relevance to much twentieth-century literature as well. Where Leerssen's *auto-exoticism* enables us to understand literature in which apparent Irish essence is really proprietary British discursive structure, Lloyd elucidates writing wherein seeming conformity to the hegemony of English literary convention is instead subversive minority appropriation. Lloyd makes use of the theory of minor literature developed by Gilles Deleuze (1925–95) and Felix Guattari (1930–92) in relation to the work of Franz Kafka (1883–1924). Deleuze and Guattari state: 'A minor literature doesn't come from a minor language; it is rather that which a minority constructs within a major language [...] in it language is affected with a high coefficient of deterritorialization'.[42] Deleuze and Guattari use Kafka, a Czech Jew who wrote in German, to establish this theory that writing from minority cultures or groups within a dominant or major language can tend to subvert radically, or in their own terms deterritorialize, that major language, its structural foundations and its cultural assumptions.

Indeed, while their study focuses on Kafka, Deleuze and Guattari suggest that minority discourse is appropriate to a whole range of literature where minor writers emerge from positions that are displaced by or within a more dominant culture and they include Joyce and Beckett in their examples. The off-kilter relationship to the norms and standards of the major language, Deleuze and Guattari insist, facilitates a highly politically charged space of writing that effaces the supposed transparency or objectivity of the process of representation: 'In major literatures [...] the individual concerns join with other no less individual concerns, the social milieu serving as a mere environment or a background [...] Minor literature is completely different, its cramped space forces each individual intrigue to connect immediately to politics'.[43]

Deleuze and Guattari's insight into how language is tasked with becoming the terrain of the collision between movements of reterritorialization and deterritorialization, between the strictures of power and the resistance of dissent, is taken up by Lloyd in relation to Irish culture. He sets out the main tenets of the normalizing, reterritorializing codes of major literature as geared towards the production of an autonomous ethical identity for the subject, as in the *Bildungsroman* and its carefully plotted development of the self. We could therefore point to the parody and subversion of this form in the fiction of Joyce, Beckett or Flann O'Brien, for example. Lloyd posits that minor literature countermands the production of narratives of ethical identity:

> ■ Minor modes of writing, as the utterance of those excluded from representation, tend to undermine the priority given to distinctive individual voice in canonical criticism [...] and in doing so commence the questioning of the founding principles of canonical aesthetic judgements.[44] □

In thinking about the applicability of Lloyd's theory across twentieth-century Irish writing, we could not only include the more explicitly experimental forms of Joyce, Beckett or Flann O'Brien, but equally the parodic, mimicking and ultimately disruptive voices in the fiction of, say, Patrick McCabe, or the seemingly straightforward yet odd, off-kilter narratives of William Trevor (born 1928), the curious and rhetorical formality of his prose that is almost realism but not quite. A Trevor novel like *Miss Gomez and the Brethren* (1971) appears eager to copy the major literature forms of Kingsley Amis (1922–95) and English middle-class writing yet the result is a kind of flat, prosaic surrealism that also simultaneously bespeaks another inheritance through Joyce and Beckett and which can be read as precisely the kind of deterritorialization intended by Deleuze and Guattari's model. With regard to the Revival, Lloyd insists that mainstream Irish nationalism failed to question the idealism of identarian thinking and became as such an instrument of bourgeois hegemony for the Irish Free State and latterly the Republic, so that it engages in a reterritorialization rather than a deterritorialization of identity.

To return to Joyce, Lloyd's work also usefully offers a different means of reading Joycean aesthetics from Deane's consumerist, indifferent pluralism. Indeed, in *Celtic Revivals*, Deane also attacks what he terms Joyce's creed of artistic freedom from a different perspective – as a depoliticized compensation and retreat from intractable historical complexity: 'since history could not yield a politics, it was compelled to yield an aesthetic'.[45] However, Lloyd analyzes the form and aesthetics of Joyce's writing as deeply political and subversive with regard to the mainstream cultural nationalist project that Lloyd's own criticism seeks to attack.

Lloyd contrasts Joyce's work with the efforts to recover Irish cultural history in Thomas Davis's Young Ireland movement or latterly in Douglas Hyde's translations. In particular, Lloyd identifies a fundamental contradiction in these efforts to repair and resume a pure Irish popular tradition uncontaminated by Anglicization. For all the antipathy to hybridity, to an Ireland caught between Irish and British culture, the collection and translation of folk songs and poetry by Davis and Hyde attests not to continuity but to gaps, rupture, and most importantly, to impurity, to cultural forms that are now contingent, hybrid and heterogeneous. According to Lloyd, not only contradiction but also a deep irony is compounded by the fact that the main influence on these apparently purely Irish endeavours to recover a genuine, untainted and essential national character from an immemorial popular source is offered by the Wordsworthian 'common language' paradigm of British Romanticism.

Most insightfully, Lloyd contrasts Hyde's effort to redeem a notionally 'pure' version of the folk song 'Mo bhrón ar an bhfarraige' (Oh my grief on the sea!'), with the same song's appearances in *Ulysses* in continually shifting, hybrid forms. Lloyd uses this hybridization – and deploys his own trope of *adulteration* – to make a broader point about the form and technique of Joyce's novel:

> ■ Joyce's, or Stephen's, version of this love song of Connacht rather insists on its heterogeneity in the course of an essentially 'inconsequential' mediation or miscegenates it with an entirely different – but no less 'Irish' – tradition of Gothic vampire tales [...] Accordingly, where the principal organizing metaphor of Irish nationalism is that of a proper paternity, of restoring the lineage of the fathers in order to repossess the motherland, Joyce's procedures are dictated by adulteration.[46] □

Lloyd, therefore, directly contrasts Joyce's adulteration with the singular, patriarchal vision of mainstream Irish Nationalism that is most vividly represented by the Citizen in the 'Cyclops' chapter of *Ulysses*. Despite the Citizen's hostility to the adulteration or hybridization of Irish culture and his desire for Irishness to have a singular unitary character, Lloyd observes how the 'Cyclops' chapter is set in Barney Kiernan's pub which is at the heart of Dublin, but also located in Little Britain Street. The pub is also in the vicinity of the Linenhall, the law courts and the Barracks, and across the river from Dublin Castle, the centre of British administration. Equally, many of the characters who pass through the bar (itself a parodic form of the legal bar in that Kiernan's pub functions as a site of censure and debate) are connected in one way or another with these institutions. Hence, for Lloyd, despite the desire of the Citizen's singular outlook for a pure, purportedly normative Irish perspective from which others are seen to deviate, *Ulysses* makes clear the already adulterated and hybrid fabric of the nation and society. Lloyd finds that adulteration in the very form and style of *Ulysses* since the novel continually refuses the enthronement of any one, privileged representational mode through its shifting modulations in form and style through not only 'Cyclops' but also the novel as a whole.[47]

Vincent J. Cheng's *Joyce, Race and Empire* (1995) is another critical work that reads formal difference and multiplicity in Joyce's work, not as depoliticized pluralism, but as being directly engaged in undermining the prevailing ideologies and discourses of nation, identity and cultural formation. Cheng argues that Joyce's fiction demonstrates

■ his understanding that peoples and populations depend not on static essences and absolute differences but rather contain pluralistic and heterogeneous characteristics (of both individual and cultural difference) that cannot be so conveniently named and essentialized. While Joyce's writings are arguably 'nationalist' in intention, they repeatedly remind us to be vigilant about forms of national consciousness that simply reproduce the same binary, essentialist hierarchies inherited from Anglo-Saxonist racism.[48] □

In addition, Declan Kiberd's *Inventing Ireland* (1995) proposes a reading of Joyce's work through a deliberately postcolonial lens that seeks to place Joyce in a literary canon of decolonization rather than European Modernism, ultimately regarding Joyce as a precursor to other exilic writers from the former British Empire such as Salman Rushdie (born 1947). In a prefiguration of much contemporary postcolonial writing, Kiberd views Joyce as a writer who condemned not only the forces of imperialism but also the postcolonial elites that supplanted the former in *A Portrait* and its references to entrance exams for the colonial civil service.[49] Furthermore, Kiberd proposes a postcolonial reading of *Ulysses* that specifically illustrates its oral characteristics – in spite of its own bookishness or textual density – the importance of which is framed by an anti-colonial resistance to the fixed textual and cartographic strictures of the imperial centre. Kiberd argues that Joyce's

■ texts increasingly substituted a sentient ear for an imperial eye, and, like his disciple Beckett, he trained himself to process the voices which came, as if unbidden, from his unconscious. *Ulysses*, judged in retrospect, is a prolonged farewell to written literature and a rejection of its attempts to colonize speech and thought.[50] □

As in Kiberd's work, Fredric Jameson's Field Day pamphlet, *Modernism and Imperialism* (1988), tries to unfold the apparently contrary canonical claims on Joyce by postcolonial and Modernist paradigms. Jameson seeks to consider Irish culture as between both First and Third

Worlds, as a European colony at the time of Joyce's writing, as part of a wider argument that the formal experimentations and dislocations of Modernism and Modernist style are brought about by imperialism. Jameson is therefore resisting the conventional reading of Modernism which is seen to be brought into being by social change in Europe, the new technologies, the radically new organization of people through urbanization and industrialization, mechanized warfare and mass slaughter on a scale never witnessed before – all of which, it is usually accepted, cause a profound disruption of traditional community, identity, subjectivity and so on. Jameson does not want to dismiss these determinants of the fragmentation of both society and literary Modernism but rather strives to add to them what he deems the ultimate cause of a new style borne out of the dislocation of the new imperial world system.

Jameson posits that, with the worldwide development in the late nineteenth century of the European empires and their economic systems, a profound change occurs in both society and consciousness. For a given European society – say, Britain – can no longer be understood by itself, within its own geographic or political borders, in its own terms, for its history is also happening elsewhere due to the development of the imperial economic system – in South Asia, or Africa or the Caribbean etc. In other words, where a nineteenth-century realist novel would seek to give a whole picture of British society by drawing together in its form upper, middle and working classes, this kind of attempted total picture of Britain is no longer possible when that society is part of a global economic system of relationships, where social classes, wealth and poverty, economic change are to be understood by what is happening not only in Manchester, London or Glasgow, but also in Calcutta, Kingston Jamaica or Nairobi. So British society no longer has the social co-ordinates internally to understand itself since any attempt to map Britain would have to take account of the external economic and political basis of its continued functioning and power.

For Jameson, then, Modernism happens directly when this spatial dislocation occurs, when traditional forms and co-ordinates are no longer able to map one's society because that society is now haunted by elsewhere, by new realities beyond the immediate perceptual or experiential grasp and understanding of people living solely within it, by the economic system that produces its wealth and the oppression of its colonized others. According to Jameson, two incommensurable realities emerge: the prosperity and development of the First World and the poverty and oppression of the Third World, and each in its own terms is unable to grasp immediately or directly the other – rather the overall system is structurally absent in its totality to each area when taken or experienced individually. Jameson insists that this Western, imperialist version of Modernism brought about by the new world system cannot be tested against the radically different experience of the Third World at the time since the fact of imperialism there is certainly brute force and open exploitation but equally the colonial subject cannot register the transformations of the First World as these are once more structurally inaccessible.

Ireland and Joyce become important to Jameson's thesis because he looks for a situation where the two incommensurable realities – of metropolitan status and colonial oppression – coincide. That is, Jameson regards Irish society at the beginning of the twentieth century as offering a unique means of understanding the new global dispensation as a systemic totality because it is both metropolis and colony at once and as such proffers a means to bring together the otherwise differential and incommensurate experiences that designate, respectively, First World development and Third World depredation. Jameson is then able to contrast Joyce's practice with that of British, metropolitan Modernists such as E. M. Forster (1879–1970) or Virginia Woolf (1882–1970). Jameson asserts that the spatial collision of First and Third Worlds in Ireland produces

■ a form which on the one hand unites Forster's sense of the providential yet seemingly accidental encounters of characters with Woolf's aesthetic closure, but which on the other hand projects those onto a radically different kind of space, a space no longer central, as in English life, but marked as marginal and ec-centric after the fashion of the colonized areas of the imperial system [...] a concept of the urban is present in *Ulysses* which contains and motivates those very encounters and intersections crucial to the modern, but lends them a different resonance.[51] □

Jameson's reading of both Joyce and Irish culture as between the designated polarities of the global imperial system also helps explain Luke Gibbons's argument that 'Ireland is a First World country, but with a Third World memory'.[52] Gibbons enables us to consider the formal experimentation of a writer like Joyce as irreducible purely to the development of European High Modernism:

■ Irish society did not have to await the twentieth century to undergo the shock of modernity: disintegration and fragmentation were already part of its history so that, in a crucial but not always welcome sense, Irish culture experienced modernity before its time. This is not unique to Ireland, but is the common inheritance of cultures subjected to the depredations of colonialism [...] In a culture traumatized by a profound sense of catastrophe, such as Ireland experienced as late as the Great Famine, is there really any need to await the importation of modernism to blast open the continuum of history?[53] □

By way of distinguishing Joyce from his High Modernist contemporaries, in the terms suggested by Gibbons's analysis, we could therefore argue that the famous review of *Ulysses* by T. S. Eliot (1888–1965) is actually a misreading. Eliot praised what he termed Joyce's 'mythical method', his use of Homer and classical literary models as 'a way of controlling, of ordering, of giving a shape and a significance to the immense panorama of futility and anarchy which is contemporary history'.[54] This interpretation is perhaps a good key to understanding Eliot's own work, especially a poem like *The Waste Land* (1922), which sought to indict the supposedly corrupt present with the fragments of the cultural glory of the past. In *The Waste Land*, amidst all the ruin and fragmentation, the dramatic tension of that epic moves towards the issues of commands by the thunder, the reconstitution of authority and order. As indicated in the critical discussion above, Joyce's work is designed to fragment and to flout authority.

Similarly, where Modernists such as Eliot or Ezra Pound (1885–1972) used the classical past to condemn the present, Joyce's *Ulysses*, which appears to make a comparable harking back to Homer, can be read as doing exactly the opposite and using the ordinary, everyday present to indict myth and the violence of the past. Joyce significantly criticized the 'epic savagery' of classical literature which he adjudged to glorify and aestheticize violence.[55] Additionally, he insisted: 'I am sure that the whole structure of heroism is, and always was, a damned lie'.[56] So in spite of the mythic framework, at another level – that of the everyday – Joyce does not have to go all the way back to classical culture (as did Eliot or Pound) to find alternatives to the slaughter and chaos of the 1910s in Europe and Ireland. Given that Joyce began writing *Ulysses* in 1914, he only goes back ten years in the quotidian structure of the novel, to 16 June 1904, to find in Bloom and others a more humane set of possibilities and alternatives to war, violence and power.

However, we can also add Emer Nolan's *James Joyce and Nationalism* (1995) to our account of key texts which intervene in these issues since she argues that liberal critics had tended to read Joyce in terms of a benign, universal cosmopolitanism. Nolan insists that Modernism and nationalism are not incompatible and her research into Joyce's letters and personal writings prove that much of the abuse which the Citizen directs towards the British in *Ulysses* is in fact taken from Joyce's own thoughts.[57] So Joyce effectively has his cake and eats it; he sends up the Irish Nationalism of the Citizen yet also uses that character to vent some of his own (Nationalist) spleen. Finally, with reference to the complication of Joyce's writing between Modernist and Postcolonial critical paradigms, Derek Attridge and Marjorie Howes's edited collection, *Semicolonial Joyce* (2000), takes its lead from a line in *Finnegans Wake* in which Shaun assumes the guise of Professor Jones who, in delivering a lecture on space and time and introducing his fable of the Mookse and The Gripes, addresses his audience in the following terms: 'Gentes and laitymen, full stoppers and semicolonials, hybreds and lubberds'.[58] Attridge and Howes glean their own sense of Joyce's work being 'semi-colonial' from this complex sentence in that its puns both invoke and collapse a variety of binary oppositions that structure identity: gender ('Gentlemen and ladies'), race and class ('high-breds and low-breds'), religion ('Gentiles' and 'laity'), and, through the distinction between full stops and semicolons, imperialist demarcations (the opposition between the indigenous and temporary inhabitants of a colonized country, or 'stoppers' and 'colonials', as well as the 'hybrids' who disturb that opposition). Attridge and Howes highlight Joyce's strategy of simultaneously evoking and complicating the oppositions that ground the formation of conventional identities with specific regard to a colonial opposition between Ireland and England:

> ■ The adjective 'semicolonial' signals our sense of a partial fit between this set of approaches and Joyce's writing [...] Joyce's writings emerge from, and take as their major historical subject, a country whose status *vis-à-vis* the imperial power, although it can be illuminated by the colonial model, cannot be understood straightforwardly in its terms.[59] □

Contesting Synge and Shaw

In addition to Joyce and Yeats, Synge's work – which, as we observed in Chapter One, was controversial enough in its own time to provoke rioting – has also become a means by which competing schools within recent Irish Studies have sought to contest the meaning of the Revival, and to elaborate conflicting views of contemporary culture and society in the Irish Republic and the North. Indeed, Synge, possibly the greatest Anglo-Irish dramatist of the Revival period, introduces further complications in how Irish literary paradigms are contested. Yes, *The Playboy of the Western World* was disrupted by nationalist rioting when performed in Dublin, but, so too, the Irish Ireland critic Daniel Corkery tried to contort his canon of Irishness to include Synge. To a degree, Corkery's effort to include Synge is based on the fact that the latter had learned the Irish language, and though Corkery's book on Anglo-Irish literature attacks that phenomenon it also struggles towards some sort of acceptance of Synge himself. Corkery's claiming of Synge is grounded in his assertion that Synge was from 'an old Wicklow family [who] had been therefore several hundreds of years in Ireland if not of Ireland'[60] Corkery's definition of Synge through his family is indicative of Irish

Ireland's view of the true nation itself as a kind of extended family, an organic and natural community. Ironically, therefore, Synge's *Playboy* can be read as a clear subversion of precisely this kind of organic, familial identity and a bold assertion of the self-creating individual.

George Watson comments that 'Synge presents us with the paradox, or seeming paradox, of a lonely and isolated man who is concerned constantly in his plays and his quasi-documentary writings with images of community and community life'.[61] Watson feels that this paradox is paradigmatic of the Protestant Ascendancy writer. In a similar vein to the later Yeats, Watson suggests, the tensions of Synge's attempt to identify with the rural peasantry in the West of Ireland cannot be finally reconciled. Watson avers: 'In the end, as his background made almost inevitable, Synge found it more congenial to imagine not the typical Irishman, but the unusual, isolated Irishman'.[62] Likewise, D. E. S. Maxwell posits: 'Typically in Synge's plays an intruder challenges the values of a small community. He is at best on the fringes of settled society. He represents the artist at odds with established usages, the wayward imagination with its exhilarating, dangerous liberation'.[63] So we can read the play as Christy Mahon's struggle to become the image of himself rather than the community's image of a hero.

However, we can also examine how it was Synge's treatment of the rural peasantry as much as the disruptive individual that induced the anger of nationalists when the play was performed in Dublin. As Robert Welch reports: 'The most frequent shout of outrage was: "That's not the West"'.[64] Synge's earthy depiction of peasant life in Mayo did not go down agreeably with an audience used to thinking of the Western poor as simple, spiritual and morally pure. But what should be stressed here is that the rioters were not peasants who took exception to Synge's representation of themselves but rather an urban, bourgeois Dublin audience of theatre-goers. Thus, Luke Gibbons explains: 'idealizations of rural existence, the longing for community and primitive simplicity, are the product of an *urban* sensibility, and are cultural fictions imposed on the lives of those they purport to represent'.[65] Synge's crime, for the nationalist pieties he offended, was to trespass on the idealization of the sacred terrain of the urban Irish Nationalist imagination – the West, which had become the symbolic guarantor and repository of an Irishness uncontaminated by Britishness or indeed the very urban, modern lifestyles afforded to the rioters themselves. The idealization of the West is, in part, due to its remoteness and the survival of the Irish language there – as Nicholas Grene summarizes adroitly: 'the West became the preserve of uncontaminated Gaelic purity.'[66]

Additionally, *Playboy* offends Irish Nationalism's self-mythology for its structure implies that violence is acceptable if framed by a good story but that its reality is unacknowledgeable. In other words, Irish Nationalism makes mythic and heroic a violence whose shoddy reality is less than ideal and must be repressed. For Seamus Deane, the hero-worshipping community, who will slovenly follow anyone who loosely fits the bill, is a damning indictment of Irish society: 'Synge is not writing out the failure of heroism. He is registering its failure in regard to society or, conversely, society's failure in regard to it'.[67] In broad agreement, Lionel Pilkington offers the following reading of *Playboy*'s demythologizing of the Revival's heroic codes and Irish Nationalism's legendary narratives of grand struggle:

> ■ What produces this adverse change in the community's attitude to Christy is not so much the people's realization that Christy's story is a fabrication, but that it has been exposed as a fabrication. The local people do not object to violence as long as it is part of a narrative, but they recoil altogether when it is committed directly in front of them [...] Pegeen's lament, 'there's a great gap between a gallous story and a dirty deed' encapsulates the point. This rural County Mayo community regenerates itself through narratives of violence that, absurdly, glamorize brutal local crimes within a larger narrative of 'holy Ireland'.[68] □

In other words, Synge's play undercuts the self-glorifying rhetoric of nationalist narratives, and indeed nationalist violence, by exposing the necessary fabrications through which localized manifestations of that violence are simultaneously incorporated and sanitized by a consummate, idealized iconography.

If Synge's play is interpreted by some nationalist critics as an unwelcome intrusion on Irish cultural and political debate, then George Bernard Shaw's *John Bull's Other Island* similarly tends to fare badly with recent nationalist critical paradigms. Declan Kiberd typifies the current Irish nationalist dismissal of the play and he judges Shaw's satiric purpose to have failed and to have in fact endorsed the overarching interpretative codes it meant to challenge: 'English audiences not only found their ancient prejudices confirmed by a witty Irish playwright, but could leave the theatre with unexpected and sophisticated evidence in support of their ancient bias'.[69] That is, Shaw's play does not radically subvert the standard paradigms of Irishness and Britishness but merely recapitulates them with exilic detachment. But, contrastingly, Nicholas Grene finds a more complex set of messages in the play, as demonstrated by its highly divergent receptions. For although the play was written from within an English rather than an Irish theatrical context – with the Dublin production apparently secondary in Shaw's mind to the London one – *John Bull* proved not only a popular success in England (despite a lukewarm critical reception) but also, to the surprise of many, an enduring favourite in Ireland. For Grene, the reason for this success on both sides of the Irish Sea was the ecumenical yet still caustic distribution of Shaw's satire against both Stage Irishness and Englishness: '*John Bull* made its way with the English and the Irish, nationalists and Unionists, by a strategy of even-handed provocativeness and iconoclasm'.[70]

In the next chapter we will cover the competing critical interpretations of another Anglo-Irish dramatist, Sean O'Casey, whose work and legacy once again have been the focus of competing paradigms in Irish Studies, especially with regard to the relationship between art and society, the nature and formation of the Irish state, and codes of heroism and political violence. More generally, we will examine how Irish Studies has assessed Irish literature since partition. As we discussed in Chapter Two, literature and criticism through this period often found itself at odds with the two states brought into being by partition, and we will remain aware of how contemporary Irish Studies – which is itself in critical dialogue with the Republic and Northern Ireland – interprets or appropriates post-partition writing in accordance with its relation to the two existing state formations in Ireland.

CHAPTER FOUR

Irish Studies Paradigms and Literature after Partition

Reinterpreting the Free State: Contesting O'Casey, Corkery, Kavanagh

This chapter offers an account of the major ways in which contemporary Irish Studies has interpreted Irish literature since the foundation of the Free State and Northern Ireland. As with our discussion of the opposing ways in which key figures in the Revival are enlisted to support current critical schools, we will evaluate how writing after partition is also deployed to endorse or refute attitudes to culture, the state and society. Obviously, in contrast to the still fluid, literally stateless energies of the Revival, the post-partition period instigated concrete state formations in both the Free State and the North so that literature, culture, ideology and both Nationalist and Unionist rhetoric had more palpable terms of reference. So the writing of this period readily lends itself to contemporary Irish Studies paradigms as a further means of negotiating with the nature of both the Republic and Northern Ireland in the present.

First we will turn to the contested legacy of Sean O'Casey. If the literature of the mainstream Revival sought to produce a heroic Ireland, or to imply that the revival of heroism was a necessary inspirational step to national rebirth, then, like Synge's, O'Casey's drama contests both the artistic hero and the nation as heroic, and it continually confronts heroic ideals with real consequences. However, as a Protestant writer who was born John Casey and who exaggerated his family's poverty in his *Autobiographies* (1939–54), O'Casey again arouses suspicion in subsequent nationalist critics – despite his time as a volunteer in the Irish Citizen Army – for his plays appear to retract his former commitment. Indeed, Seamus Deane's reaction to O'Casey neatly condenses a sense of how Irish Studies more broadly sought to resist the prevailing, international interpretation of canonical writers. For example, David Krause's study *Sean O'Casey: The Man and His Work* (1960) had celebrated O'Casey's humanism as part of a broader endorsement of his work.[1] By contrast, it is precisely O'Casey's Christian humanism (in a highly pejorative sense) that Deane disputes: 'crudely, the recipe is that we should take politics away and supplant it by humanism [...] All of O'Casey's gunmen are shadows, and consequently his aggression towards politics is a form of shadow-boxing.'[2] Declan Kiberd considers O'Casey an intrusive urban Celticist outsider: 'By depicting his inner-city Dubliners as jabbering leprechauns, he appealed to the new middle-class elites which dominated the Free State and which cast the Dublin proletarian in the role once reserved by the Anglo-Irish establishment for the stage-Irish peasant'.[3] (With regard to setting, a more nuanced insight into space in O'Casey's work is offered by Fintan O'Toole who argues that O'Casey's repeated use of the tenement was simply a means of reactivating rural notions of enclosed place and identity in an urban setting and thus avoiding the streets and the true complexity of city space.)[4]

More positively, Lionel Pilkington understands *The Shadow of a Gunman* (1923) in the context of an Ireland wracked by a Civil War engendered by competing idealisms that increasingly lost sight of real events:

■ The problem with Ireland, O'Casey's play suggests, is that nationalist anti-Treaty militancy is inspired simply by self-aggrandisement: self-indulgent role playing with no attention to consequences. The sheer irresponsibility of such militancy is the point that Davoren and the audience learn at the end when Davoren's admirer, the guileless Minnie, is shot dead by the British military.[5] □

Pilkington points to the scene where Davoren, emboldened by the community's misguided belief that he is an IRA man, takes his heroic pretence still further by agreeing to officiate in a republican court – these republican courts had been a successful means of establishing the legitimacy of the counter-state in the 1920–1 period and were replaced by government courts with the outbreak of Civil War in 1922. The farcical nature of the scene therefore suggests that pre-Treaty Republicanism was less about radical political commitment and more about egotism and posturing.[6]

However, in seeking to justify Seamus Deane's dismissal of O'Casey's simplistic humanism it can be argued that all that is offered by way of alternative to political ideologies in both *Shadow* and *Juno and the Paycock* (1924) is an idealized domestic realm and an ideal femininity. The final play in what became O'Casey's Dublin Trilogy – though admittedly he never conceived the plays as a trilogy – *The Plough and the Stars* was highly controversial as its look back to the Easter Rising coincided with the tenth anniversary of the event. The play was chaotically disrupted on the fourth night of its performance by Republican protestors. Yeats, himself looking back to the *Playboy* riots, shouted at the protestors: 'You have disgraced yourselves again'.[7] In part, some of the audience's vitriol stemmed from Republicans hostile to the signing of the Anglo-Irish Treaty and the formation of the Free State. Hanna Sheehy-Skeffington, for example, shouted 'The Free State Government is subsidising the Abbey to malign Pearse and Connolly'. But so too the audience included many bereaved family relatives of the 1916 martyrs such as Pearse's mother and the sister of Kevin Barry (1902–20) – the 18-year old whose hanging entered popular Republican mythology. Hanna Sheehy-Skeffington was herself the widow of the pacifist Francis Sheehy-Skeffington (1878–1916) who was arrested and then shot during the Rising.[8] For these family members and many more, the play was quite simply highly disrespectful to the memory of those who died in 1916. Especially controversial was Act II, in which the Tricolour and the prostitute Rosie Redmond were introduced in a pub setting. The close proximity of the national flag and a prostitute in this mundane environment seemed to symbolize a desecration of the national memory and integrity to the protestors. Grene observes in the scene that while Clitheroe proclaims 'Ireland is greater than a wife' and resolves to leave his familial obligations behind to fight for Ireland, this grandiose statement is undercut by the actions of Fluther and Rosie which suggest that a drunken night with a prostitute is preferable to the cause of Ireland:

■ It was not just prudishness or national paranoia that made the 1926 Irish audience react as they did to Act II of *The Plough* [*and the Stars*]: the very iconography of the nationalist imagination, sacralised in the Rising, was literally desecrated in the secular and mundane setting it is given.[9] □

We will return to this deep interrelation between national integrity and gender – especially the symbolic function of women – in our next chapter. But for present purposes, we can summarize that contemporary Irish Studies critics have taken O'Casey as either a proto-Revisionist whose undermining of the official state narrative of Irish Nationalism endorses Revisionism's ongoing efforts to that end, or as a writer who refuses political engagement and seeks to replace the hard-headed realities of power and the modern state with a vague, individualized perspective – the charge laid in turn by postcolonial and Field Day critics at their Revisionist adversaries.

In terms of the Free State and its official narratives, we have already considered in relation to the Revival how David Lloyd insists that mainstream Irish nationalism failed to question the idealism of identarian thinking. To Lloyd, it therefore became as such an instrument of bourgeois hegemony for the Irish Free State and latterly the Republic, so that it engages, in the terms which Lloyd takes from Deleuze and Guattari, in a reterritorialization rather than a deterritorialization of identity. A really interesting appraisal of exactly these kinds of tensions is offered by Paul Delaney's article 'Becoming National: Daniel Corkery and the Reterritorialized Subject' (2003). Delaney also uses Deleuze and Guattari as a means of shedding new light on Daniel Corkery and his effort to make a normal and national literature for Ireland. But Delaney seeks to challenge the version of Corkery as a familiar figure whose critical triumvirate of Nationalism, Religion and the Land makes him the cultural commissar for the Irish Free State. Instead, Delaney views Corkery's work as an opportunity to examine the process whereby the minor becomes major.

Specifically, Delaney uses Corkery's position between languages – as an Irish language advocate who was, nonetheless, a Professor of English – to draw a distinction between Corkery and his Irish Ireland predecessor D. P. Moran. Corkery's *Synge and Anglo-Irish Literature* had attacked 'the desire to be assessed and spoken well of by another people'.[10] But here Delaney establishes a contrast between Corkery and Moran since the latter criticizes precisely this facet of *A Treasury of Irish Poetry in the English Tongue* (1900) by Stopford A. Brooke (1832–1916) and T. W. Rolleston (1857–1920). However, Corkery actually takes up their terms in establishing his own triumvirate of Nationalism, Religion and the Land. Brooke was an Anglo-Irish rector and Rolleston a former scholar at Trinity College, Dublin. Brooke's introduction to his work with Rolleston claims that the distinctive elements of Irish literature are nationality, religion and 'what England calls rebellion'.[11] Corkery's embroilment in what for Moran would be Anglo-Irish intrusion is explained by Delaney through minor literature theory. Delaney notes how Corkery first takes up the terms of the Brooke–Rolleston model without much dispute in *The Hidden Ireland*, which was largely written before the War of Independence, but then refines the critical triumvirate in *Synge and Anglo-Irish Literature*. Notably, there is then a slippage from 'Nationality' to 'Nationalism' in Corkery's model which Delaney interprets an indicative of a move from a pre-given sense of national identity to a newly prescriptive set of nationalist indices for collective belonging.

In addition, Delaney reads the semantic shift from 'Rebellion' to 'Land' as signalling a historical change whereby the anti-colonial dynamic and rhetoric of Corkery's earlier writing is replaced by a more grounded and now dominant nationalism after the foundation of the Free State. Hence, in Deleuze and Guattari's terminology, Delaney is alert to processes not only of deterritorialization but also reterritorialization, of the reconstitution of identity, power and the law. According to Delaney, this reterritorialization is

■ predicated upon the belief in an intrinsic national essence which must be realized in some tangible territorial form – something which has the potential to be both potentially progressive (in so far as it counters imperialist myths of cultural and intellectual inferiority), and readily reactionary (as it re-articulates many of the generic groupings of imperialist discourse).[12] □

Delaney thereby understands Corkery as simultaneously subverting and reproducing imperialist forms, and, in doing so, giving insight into how Irish nationalism conceived of itself as liberating resistance to British law and power but yet, when afforded its own state and political institutions, served to reterritorialize identity, to move from being minor to being dominant or major in its own (repressive) state.

Patrick Kavanagh's writing has also lent itself to debates about the relationship between literature and the self-image of the state. Although Chapter Two has already covered Kavanagh's work in terms of its dissent from official doctrine, Antoinette Quinn's fine study *Patrick Kavanagh: Born again Romantic* (1991) insists that his writing fulfils Corkery's criteria for the native writer. In spite of acknowledging the influence of O'Connor and O'Faoláin on Kavanagh during the writing of *The Great Hunger*, Quinn asserts that this poem achieves its aim of embedding itself in the locality (in contrast to the peasant landscapes by Anglo-Irish writers so disparaged by both Kavanagh and Corkery). Quinn reads *The Great Hunger* as 'organized as a montage, as extraordinarily flexible, continually altering angle and direction [...] Maguire's life is framed with rapid changes of focus and from a deliberately diverting play of angles'.[13] Quinn argues that the juxtaposition of images inflected by shifting tones corresponds to an objective reflection of reality that encapsulates its contingency, creating the poem's aura of documentary realism. Through this form, Quinn claims: 'Kavanagh is inventing [...] an Irish social history in the guise of a social critique'.[14] Thus, for all the negative critique and the apocalyptic intensity – in fact, perhaps precisely because of the concentrated engagement and precision of his critique – Kavanagh succeeds in establishing a territory finally uncontaminated by Revivalist idealizations. Nevertheless, Quinn interprets the scream of Maguire's unborn children at the end of the hunger as the cry of those denied a history. This despair redraws the difference between Kavanagh's parish and Corkery's more officially endorsed nativism. Indeed, as Kavanagh becomes increasingly at odds with the direction of the new State and the prevailing cultural trends, Quinn finds a hastening note of despair in his later writing, journalism and criticism which left him forlornly 'flailing between two faded worlds, the county he had left and the literary Dublin he never found'.[15]

Alan Gillis's *Irish Poetry of the 1930s* (2005) grants a stimulating reading of Kavanagh that also revises the 1930s more broadly. Gillis analyzes Kavanagh's work to resist David Lloyd's argument in *Anomalous States* that the state hegemony of the time had been shored up and a pervasive ideology of essentialist identity had co-opted art and the aesthetic for these dominant and all-encompassing purposes. Gillis regards this interpretation of the post-independence state as too totalized. His counter-argument makes use of Thomas MacDonagh's 'Irish Mode' – which we discussed in Chapter One – in order to propose that far from being an imaginative nadir in which Irish poets constructed compensatory fantasies of an essentialized, pastoral nation, the 1930s proffer a divergent range of poetic dissidence: 'the "Irish Mode" could be turned against the State, in the Thirties, using the commonplaces of nationalist idealism to criticize its mundane realities'.[16] In terms of the poetry of the period and the conflicting uses of Irish modes, Gillis contrasts what he regards as Kavanagh's explosion of the 'lyrical fields' in *The Great Hunger* with the intent of Austin Clarke's social critique. To Gillis, Clarke's ruralism strives to assemble an attenuated organic poetic tradition for itself that regresses backwards in the vain hope that the Civil War might be re-fought and an Ireland uncontaminated by the new State's petty materialism be symbolically reclaimed. Conversely, Kavanagh's exasperated apocalypticism moves intensively forwards to demand insatiably the resolution of the contradictions between official ideology and the wastes of rural Monaghan:

■ Clarke's organicist desire is therefore as unquenchable as Kavanagh's, but its trajectory feeds into another world entirely. As Clarke lambasted the State for its materialistic pollution of the Republican ideal, its celebration of prosperity, Kavanagh would no doubt have welcomed a little bit of this in Monaghan.[17] □

However, a more favourable reading of Clarke's poetic is afforded by Denis Donoghue's *We Irish* (1986), which concentrates on the homonyms in Clarke's work – that is, words with the same spelling or pronunciation which but which have different meanings. Donoghue discovers a much wider import in Clarke's punning and wordplay which ensure that words do not have one meaning and one meaning alone:

■ Homonyms are crucial in Clarke's poetry because he loves to find one sound releasing two words; all the better if one word stays at home and obeys the rules while the other one runs wild and makes love upon whim and desire. This points to the dominant motif in Clarke's work, the life of freedom and impulse set against the law of institutions.[18] □

Hence, for Donoghue, this semantic play counters the monotony of State doctrine and monolithic accounts of Irishness at the time. Comparably, Terence Brown identifies in Clarke the seeds of what would become the mainstays of Revisionist criticism:

■ the fact that many of the things about which he berated his society are now part of conventional liberal opinion or on the reformer's agenda tends to make us take for granted the poet who kept resolutely on as a social critic when he was almost a lone voice, or when others had wearied at their posts.[19] □

In addition to stressing the radical terms of engagement of Kavanagh's rural Monaghan, Gillis's *Irish Poetry* is also distinctive in that it provides a key reading of Samuel Beckett's poetry – which is often starved of the critical focus granted to Beckett's plays and prose. In Beckett, Gillis discerns a different, though equally enabling and radical, trajectory to that of Kavanagh. Gillis interprets Beckett as furthering the attitude to identity that we have already established in Joyce's writing: namely, that the founding principle of both writers is a notion of Irish history as constituted by a hybridity that does not allow for demarcations. So rather than simply replace one Irish narrative with a revised version, Beckett offers a non-narrative which subsumes all narratives. Hence, to be Irish is to be anyone and everyone. But within this conception, existence is continually dissipated in a chaos of simultaneous becoming and dissolution. Resultantly, fixed constructions of identity, nation or history become impossible within Beckett's continuum. Gillis teases out the formative similarities of Beckett's and Joyce's attitudes to identity but he underlines the divergent outcomes of their work too:

■ Beckett's aesthetic [...] constitutes an attempt to deny static notions of identity, but the jocose equanimity with which Joyce dissolves history and being into processual circles is antipathetic to Beckett's existentialist intensity, ensuring rather that the world remains a virtual coliseum of pain.[20] □

The Republics of Irish Studies: Re-reading Beckett, Bowen, O'Brien and Behan

Beckett's difficult, exilic work, which sparsely and intensively journeys across languages and literary forms, also attracts the attention of David Lloyd and his effort to undermine the attenuations of identity and the aesthetic in official nationalism discourse. Though written in a very different context, Lloyd's reading of Beckett in *Anomalous States*, nonetheless, shares something of Adorno's search for the non-identical, for something other than what is, that we considered in Chapter Two. Lloyd pursues how Beckett's work sunders conventional constructions of identity, habitual doctrines of history as progress. Primarily, Lloyd seeks to problematize Beckett's supposed 'apolitical' or disengaged standpoint by examining the excremental vision of history and identity in *First Love* (written 1946; published in French, 1970; in English, 1973). For Lloyd, this work disrupts the capacity of the aesthetic to mediate subject and object. Lloyd judges such aesthetic mediation as serving a broader function reconciling individual and totality in the bourgeois state during the expansion of colonialism. In turn, Lloyd maintains that it is not only the Western imperial project and but also the cultural nationalism of the Irish state that undertakes this aesthetic coding of the individual.

Lloyd takes as one of his examples Corkery's sense of a mutual relationship between the national and normalizing functions of literature which we discussed earlier in the Guide. For this model of cultural identification, in which literature is used to develop a feeling of nationality in the Irish citizen, nationalism actually reproduces in its very opposition to the British Empire a narrative of universal development that is fundamental to the maintenance and legitimation of imperialism in the first place. Lloyd specifies two notions in the realm of aesthetics that are crucial to this process. Firstly, that the artwork serves to arouse a contemplative desire that reconciles subject and object – in other words, that the person doing the representing and that which is represented by he or she supposedly become one. And secondly, that a construction of human beings in general is extrapolated from the individual act of aesthetic appreciation – that is, there is then a generalization of the identity formed by the reconciliation of subject and object in Lloyd's first proposal. So official cultural nationalism such as Corkery's – but also, of course, the British imperialism upon which Lloyd maintains it is structurally based – instigates a regime of representation whereby difference is reconciled into sameness, and each formation of an individual is representative of a more generalized identity. Lloyd comments: 'a normal literature is a national literature, and the function of a national literature is normalizing'.[21]

So one of the main endeavours of the new Irish State's cultural nationalism is to produce a nation that is consonant with the aesthetic and historical development of other 'normal' European states. Its central task in becoming a nation is to become normal, to be the same as an apparently generalized human norm. According to Lloyd, Corkery's work strives to produce such national normality by espousing a literature which will develop from its primitive, native incoherence to the status of a representative national institution. In this regime of representation and representativeness, the individual and the nation become one and share the same ethical identity. Thus, for Lloyd, the aesthetic is a domain that seeks to reconcile the contradictions that subsist both within the subject and in the relationship between each individual subject and the state. Beckett's work is important to Lloyd because it exposes the trace of contradiction in this supposed reconciliation, its remainder. Lloyd asserts that it is the logic of Beckett's writing that the pursuit of identity produces its negation. Beckett refutes authenticity where nationalism seeks to restore it. Gender is also central to Lloyd's argument and, in *First Love*, he sees the irruptions of Ann/Lulu in the text as a challenge to a specifically paternal authority over identity. Most of all,

Lloyd wishes to reclaim Beckett's technique from High Modernist experimentation to a more marginal site of postcolonial articulation. It is this
condition that impels Beckett to dismantle the logic of identity and to
unravel the breakdown of the object and the subject in order to imagine
the threshold of another possible language and postcolonial subjectivity: 'it is whatever lies in the gapped, disjointed songs of Anna/Lulu, in
the unrepresentable of the narratives of identity which Beckett's work so
thoroughly excoriates, that the project of decolonization finds its unpredictable resources'.[22]

Lloyd develops his interpretation of Beckett in the essay 'Republics of
Difference: Yeats, MacGreevy, Beckett' (2005). Of most interest to Lloyd
is Beckett's reading of the paintings of Jack Butler Yeats (1871–1957),
brother of W. B. Yeats. Beckett picks up on Yeats's foregrounding of
his work's own material conditions of representation, its antithesis to
the simple, mimetic reflection of the world. There is a difficult relation
in both Yeats's painting and Beckett's writing between representation
and represented, medium and figure, language and its objects.[23] Lloyd
quotes Beckett's comment that

■ more and more my own language appears to me like a veil that must be
torn apart to get at the things (or the Nothingness) behind it [...] As we cannot
eliminate language all at once, we should at least leave nothing undone that
might contribute to its falling in disrepute. To bore one hole after another in
it, until what lurks behind it – be it something or nothing – begins to seep
through.[24] □

In terms of representational modes, Beckett believes that literature
has fallen behind other art forms such as music and painting in this
regard. It is therefore the primary goal of the writer, Beckett intones,
to address literature's lagging behind the other arts in self-reflexively
meditating upon its own representational confinements. In turn, Lloyd
relates these issues of the limits of representation to the dominant
ideology of the Irish Republic, which he designates a republic of homogeneity rather than of difference and which cannot represent anything
but the monotonous perpetuation of itself. Lloyd interprets a state formation's conventional aesthetics of containment – such as, for example, the call after the French Revolution by the German philosopher
Immanuel Kant (1724–1804) for a republic of the learned, not of the
people – as an effort to refute the radical claims of what Lloyd terms a
republicanism of differences.

In conventional representation, there is the subordination of the
singular, potentially eruptive manifestation of difference to a narrative
of representation that establishes a trajectory where intractable elements
are contained and assimilated by identity and sameness (realism and

symbolism being Lloyd's examples of this). In Beckett's disruption of the conventional aesthetic mediation and representation of the individual, Lloyd locates the possibility of a different, liberating kind of republicanism (and one that is, therefore, directly opposed to the state ideology of the Irish Republic as it is constituted) through its undermining of the dominant model of representation that seeks to deny difference. To explain the failure of the Irish Republic's official discourse, Lloyd professes that, under British rule, insurgent cultural nationalism sought to find alternative cultural institutions to those that the colonizer occupied politically. To do so, cultural nationalism attempts to enter a people into representation who have never been represented before, and to regulate the forms of representation in such as a way that the unity and homogenous identity of a people can be affirmed. Lloyd regards the Irish Republic as symptomatic of the inherent contradictions of this drive to representation since the nationalism which proclaims the unity of the Irish people in difference from Britain cannot accommodate or express the proliferation of difference within its own apparent unity. For Lloyd, there is a certain compulsion born of necessity that draws together the painter Yeats and the writer Beckett on the ruins of representation that follow in the wake of the national project:

■ where an aesthetic of representation that had become tied to a mode of political thinking becomes, along with the political state, a means to domination, only in the ruins of that aesthetic can an alternative be excavated. The excavation that follows is at once positive and negative: positive in its making space once more for the recalcitrant, for figures of those who had been denied representation: the tramps, rogues and derelicts that populate both artists' works; negative in the relentless interrogation of the *means* of representation that both engage formally and technically [...] The space of their work is the place made over and again for the unfit in representation, for those that dwell only among the ruins. In the ruins of representation alone, where the nation meets its end, the anticipatory trace of a republic emerges as that thing that yet eludes representation.[25] □

In broad affinity, Declan Kiberd's version of Beckett also seeks to shift the critical trajectory away from Modernism or cosmopolitanism to the postcolonial framework established in *Inventing Ireland*. Kiberd's focus is on the politics of language and he declares that Beckett's decision to write in French after his novel *Murphy* (1938) does still bespeak a series of Irish problematics about medium and form. To Kiberd, Beckett's change of language is less to do with the inherent properties of French itself and more related to a desire to resist a tendency of Irish writing in English to exaggerate wit, blarney and stock national traits. The shift to French re-educates Beckett with the literal-mindedness of a learner of a second language and his critical estrangement from or distance to all languages permits him to write in his own flat, inimitable and para-doxical style without a style. Kiberd deems French to be performing the same function for which the Irish language served Brendan Behan (1923–64): 'both men were thus enabled to express rather than exploit their Irish materials, and to transcend the confinements of revivalist eloquence'.[26]

Kiberd maintains that Beckett's work exists in the interstices between speech and writing – a terrain in which speech becomes writerly and writing retains the qualities of a speaking voice that often issues from unconscious depths – so no sooner does the form of Beckett's texts and worlds seem to take shape than they dissolve. Kiberd places him in a ruptured bardic or oral tradition to help explain this fragmentation. Moreover, Kiberd is keen to contrast the disparateness of Beckett with the Modernist fragmentation of Eliot's *The Waste Land*, which urges the reader to take each fragment and infer from it the whole of which it was an integral part before the implosion of tradition. Conversely, Kiberd continues, Beckett had no stable tradition or subject to lament since these were impossible in Ireland's gapped, discontinuous culture: 'For Beckett, the Gaelic tradition seemed posited on a void, every poem an utterance in the face of imminent annihilation, every list an inventory of shreds from a culture verging on extinction'.[27] So Kiberd's account of Beckett places him in an Irish historical continuum that has been denied its past, a culture denied its history. Yet Kiberd's analysis is also noteworthy in its effort to locate – or possibly dislocate – Beckett in an Anglo-Irish tradition with Synge and Yeats that had become displaced and rootless in the Republic. Hence, perhaps, Beckett's tramps become déclassé reworkings of that dislocation. Indeed, in providing an alter-native interpretative path to David Lloyd's reading of the negation of identity in Beckett, we could equally encounter his work in the context of a dissolution of Southern Protestant identity in the spirit of W. J. McCormack's insight that 'when the social world of the Anglo-Irish was finally eclipsed it was as if the hyphen, which had always been a signally diminished equation mark, became a minus sign, a cancellation'.[28]

It is precisely this interpretative trajectory in which Neil Corcoran evaluates the work of another Anglo-Irish writer, the novelist Elizabeth Bowen. If Beckett's tramps relate to his own exilic status, it is worth considering how many of the characters in his later plays are mired in stasis or suspended in limbo, in a manner that resonates in post-Treaty Ascendancy writing. Bowen's novel *The Last September* (1929) finds its characters wedded to the symbol of their own destruction – the Big House. The novel is set in just such an Irish Big House immediately prior to its destruction in the War of Independence. Corcoran's anal-ysis is highly instructive because it draws attention to the sometimes unacknowledged form and style of Bowen's writing, whose uneasy experimentation should make Bowen a key contributor to the development of an Irish Modernism. Corcoran recognizes *The Last September* as a narrative that is full of holes, while its dialogue is riven by lacunae and ellipses. The tone and form of Bowen's novel are highly ambivalent and they modify, and in doing so, blur generic boundaries between a comedy of manners, a resigned social commentary, the allegorical and the gothic. As Corcoran discerns, the literal often shades into the figurative, and an apparent realism becomes unsettlingly underscored by suggestive, symbolic deep-structures beneath the textual surface. To Corcoran, the novel's 'retreat towards silence is that of the Anglo-Irish class as a whole in the autumnal decline of their "last September"'.[29] Where the problematic of identity is more dispersed in Beckett's exilic art, it is certainly possible to read his work alongside Bowen's immediate detailing of the collapse of the Ascendancy and its identity. And, in *The Last September*, Corcoran reads the scene in which a crack is made in a basin by Lois as part of a broader fracture that resonates too if we consider Beckett's work. To Corcoran, it is symbolically the crack that runs between what might once have been the identity of the Anglo-Irish Ascendancy class and what it might be, or might fail to be, in an indeterminate future: 'this is an identity in transition only to abeyance. And it is that "crack", the fissure opening between a politically and historically exhausted past and a potentially non-existent future'.[30]

So far, in the work of Kavanagh, Clarke, Beckett and Bowen, we have observed how such writing is extremely, self-reflexively aware of its own modes and styles. Such artistic practice occurs for a number of competing and divergent reasons. But it, nonetheless, shares a concerted effort to find a medium able to articulate experience outwith the Irish Ireland homogeneity of official doctrine in the Free State and Republic: whether that experience emanates from a marginalized, disenfranchised peasant constituency, the cultural translations of exile or the collapse of a residually ascendant location in the culture. In turn, such writing has, as we have considered, spurred the interest of key critics in today's Irish Studies as a means of shaping their own debates about the State, society and culture. And perhaps the writer whose formal experimentations most directly impugn the institutions of the Free State and Irish Republic is Brian O'Nolan, who published in English as Flann O'Brien. O'Brien's life, like his fiction, transgresses boundaries: he was born into an Irish-speaking family in Strabane in Northern Ireland but went on to work in the state bureaucracy in the South. While always playfully parodic, his indictments of society in the Republic are no less damning for that.

Seamus Deane's *Strange Country* considers the form of O'Brien's novel *At Swim-Two-Birds* (1939) as a democratic unleashing of voices which undermines the authoritarian, residually colonialist nature of a supposedly 'free' state. Deane perceives a deeply political analogy in the novelistic form of *At Swim-Two-Birds*. He equates the omniscient, all-controlling narrator which represents all characters and events to the reader in realist fiction with the single transferable vote system in representative democracies that produces a one-party strong government nominally representing all of the people. Contrariwise, Deane associates the technique of O'Brien's novel with proportional representation and a system whereby interlocking discourses remain in uneasy alliance with one another, and no one subject or mode of representation is permitted to possess overarching control. Indeed, there is no singular discourse which could encompass the whole *mélange* of history, language, community and narratives in O'Brien's work. For O'Brien's fiction repeatedly composes and discomposes itself into so many discourses and dialects, especially and most satirically, the mock dialect of the translation of the Irish language into the stultified English of official, bureaucratic parlance.

Moreover, Deane understands O'Brien within the ongoing, often blurred set of Irish writing paradigms of realism and fantasy. These apparently oppositional paradigms appear within both the work of individual writers and the criticism that interprets such work. Within these models, Deane asserts, there is a distinction between linguistic penury and harshness on the one hand and linguistic extravagance and eloquence on the other: for example, the movement from George Moore's *Esther Waters* (1894) to *Evelyn Innes* (1898); Joyce's *Dubliners* to *Finnegans Wake*; *The Charwoman's Daughter* (1911) by James Stephens to his *The Crock of Gold* (1912); Austin Clarke's *The Vengeance of Fionn* (1917) to *Later Poems* (1961); O'Casey's *Shadow of a Gunman* to *The Silver Tassie* (1929) and beyond; and even in Synge and Yeats within individual plays. For Deane, O'Brien's conscious intervention in and across these modes enabled him, by turns, to critique the dominant representational means by which official nationalisms co-opt and order identity, to disrupt the self-exoticizing means by which Irishness was constructed, to deconstruct (as in Joyce or Beckett) the relationships between language and power, to expose the rhetoric of the state to its repressive reality, and conversely to indict a deadening reality with imaginative potential. Deane considers the conflictive, yet mutually sustaining, modes of O'Brien's critique as spanning both his fiction and his journalism. In the former, O'Brien parodies the extravagant solipsism of the Modernist author–hero in the experimental novel. In the latter, he excoriates the pre-packaged banality of newspapers and the mass media. To Deane, the only discourse which is permitted any freedom from the extremes of, on the one hand, the elitist search from uniqueness in experimental fiction, and, on the other, the deadening thirst for cliché and consensus in newspapers, is the Irish language. At least, that is, before the Irish language was corrupted in a grotesque stereotype of itself in its current use as the official language of the new State bureaucracy.

To that end, O'Brien's mock autobiography *An Béal Bocht* (1941) – which appeared in English in 1964 as *The Poor Mouth* – savagely parodies the fact that a degrading caricature of the Irish language has now become the standard, official means of Irish self-representation. So the standardized Irish of the Free State and Republic becomes a fatal deformation of the actual speech and writing of the past. But equivalently, the English language too has been rendered unrecognizable by the esoteric experimentation of High Modernism or all too recognizable by the mediocrity of contemporary journalism. Deane's thesis is that O'Brien's variations on realism and fantasy as representational modes ultimately aim to undermine both and to sunder the system of illusion by which the one relies upon the other for its definition. Increasingly, all systems of representation in O'Brien's work are interrogated. But these systems are not only to be interpreted, they are acts of interpretation themselves. As Deane puts it: 'All discourse is interpretation; all interpretation is discourse'.[31] But, he maintains, O'Brien stops short of giving himself over to an epistemological relativism where language is sufficiently autonomous to replace the world altogether. Instead, he seeks some ground from which to launch his assault on systems of representation:

■ It is in seeking such a ground that O'Brien (like Kavanagh) is an author of the Free State, the little world that succeeded to the extravagant rhetoric of the Revival and the Rising and the War of Independence and the Civil War [...] The fake nation, with its inflated rhetoric of origin and authenticity, had given way to the fake state, with its deflated rhetoric of bureaucratic dinginess. In the passage from the fantasy of one to the realism of the other, the entity called Ireland had somehow failed to appear.[32] □

In a similar vein, Sarah McKibben's article, '*The Poor Mouth*: A Parody of (Post)Colonial Manhood' (2003), deploys O'Brien to indict the appropriation of the Irish language and Irish-speaking communities by the official discourse of the State. The fact that Irish was spoken by of a minority of the population but became the first official language of the new state ensured, for McKibben, that it acquired a symbolic significance inversely proportional to its linguistic currency. Resultantly, rather than empowering existing Irish-speaking communities, this prized symbolic status actually undermined them as since it demarcated the tokenistic appropriated their language for the self-image of official nationalism.

■ If certain marginalized groups within the postcolonial state tend to keep on paying the price for liberation instead of sharing in it, (minoritized) indigenous languages also find themselves in a neo-colonial netherworld where their right to linguistic and literary self-determination is under constant threat. For these languages, decolonizing the mind – and the tongue – can hardly be a one-time event, but requires ever-renewed creativity and impudence in the face of fatal and fatalistic official demands to conform.[33] □

As we observed in Kiberd's reading of the multilingual Beckett, Brendan Behan is another writer, like O'Brien, who moves across both Irish and English languages and supplies an insight into the mechanics and failures of the institutions of the state – especially its explicitly coercive apparatuses. Due to his involvement in an IRA operation in Liverpool Behan was arrested and sent to Borstal, and on his release and return to Ireland he was again apprehended and imprisoned, this time for attempted murder. Released after World War Two under a general amnesty, he would again serve time in England and indeed he was deported to France in 1952 in a much more forced exile than that of Joyce or Beckett. It was during his time in prison that Behan began to write, and the dislocations and dissents of his life and writing are again at odds with a state seeking to establish itself in idealized homogeneity. Born into the slums of Dublin, but educated in part by his highly political family, Behan's work is a rigorous critique of state power. Notably though, his uncle, Peadar Kearney (1883–1942), wrote the lyrics to 'Amhrán na bhFiann' or 'The Soldier's Song' (1907), the national anthem of the Republic. Kiberd sees Behan as following on from O'Casey's critique of idealism, though in Behan's case tending towards nihilism ultimately or the absurdist theatre of Eugène Ionesco (1909–94), Jean Genet (1910–86) or, indeed, Beckett. For Kiberd, Behan is very much the rebel's rebel and he reads *The Quare Fellow* (1954) in terms of a post-independence social critique that will elsewhere resonate in other postcolonial settings such as India. The fact that, 30 years after the foundation of the state, Behan's play indicts the prison system but ultimately suggests life is much harder outside in society chimes, in Kiberd's mind, with the Salman Rushdie's critique of India just over three decades after independence in *Midnight's Children* (1981). Kiberd focuses on the clandestine conversations in Irish in the play between Prisoner C and the warder Crimmin, who are both from the Gaeltacht or Irish-Speaking area of Kerry, and whose use of Irish as a covert, outlaw language in one of the Free State's official institutions mordantly and symbolically devastates the state's claims to cultural authenticity and republicanism.

According to Kiberd, *The Quare Fellow* also crystallizes key themes in both Behan's writing and more widely in Irish literary paradigms. He places it, together with Behan's autobiographical *Borstal Boy* (1958), in a tradition of prison literature, which includes the *Jail Journal* (1905) of John Mitchell (1815–75), 'Ballad of Reading Gaol' (1898) and *De Profundis* (1905) by Oscar Wilde (1854–1900) and *The Gates Flew Open* (1932) by Peadar O'Donnell (1893–1987). But in addition to writing about actual incarceration, Kiberd contends that a carceral or cellular entrapment as a metaphor for an experience of the modern world also characterizes much Irish literature, such as Beckett's *Malone Dies* (1951). As Behan translated his plays like *An Giall* into *The Hostage* (1958) for the London stage, Kiberd seeks to retain the Irish dimension to his work as vitally important and in keeping with the spirit of Salman Rushdie's 'The Empire Writes Back' in which writers take possession of the imperial languages and move to confront the metropolitan centres with their work.[34] Thus, Kiberd strives to distinguish Behan radically from a more general trend in British drama in the late 1950s dealing with social change. Although Behan is sometimes lumped in with the ranks of the Angry Young Men – such as John Osborne (1929–94) – who brashly emerged in British literature in this decade and were at odds with the post-war consensus, Kiberd argues that the anger of these writers appears radical but is actually a lament for the end of empire and British influence in the world. By contrast, Kiberd insists: 'Behan felt the urge to dismantle the remains of the imperial agenda, not just in Ireland but in the imperial capital itself [...] Behan was [...] one of the first post-colonial writers to impinge on the consciousness of post-war Britain.'[35]

Reinterpreting Northern Ireland: Versions of John Hewitt

Where contemporary Irish Studies has deployed post-partition literature in the Free State and Republic to refine its own terms of engagement with the state, society and culture, the Unionist hegemony in the North has correspondingly stirred a recent critical effort to redraw an understanding of literature's support for, or dissent from, the Northern Irish state. Francis Mulhern's *The Present Lasts A Long Time* (1998) comments upon 'the stilted style of Unionist discourse, which, at its most pained, could seem to mark a radical alienation from speech itself – a kind of symbolic death'.[36] As Mulhern suggests, Unionist ideology tended to rely not on an elaborate discursive legitimation of itself, or even a cursory explanation of itself, but rather on its already attained power whose institutionalized and constitutional existence required no symbolic yearnings towards full realization. But it would be misleading to regard that Unionist ideology as all-pervasive or fully-cohered in reality. For Terence Brown, Unionist ideology has always served to repress the actual complexity and diversity of Protestant culture by reducing it instead to 'a vision of the Northern Protestant as having always belonged to a homogeneous, ideologically monolithic social group which stands for authority, law, order, loyalty, conformity, social cohesion and reason'.[37]

As we discussed in Chapter Two, there is an uneasy slippage of names for the area comprising the Northern Irish State: Northern Ireland, the North, Ulster and the Six Counties. Joe Cleary's *Literature, Partition and the Nation State: Culture and Conflict in Ireland, Israel and Palestine* (2002) argues that this semantic slippage betrays the historical anxieties and tensions faced by Unionism as it strove to legitimize Northern Ireland and lend it a narrative continuity and democratic justification:

> ■ Unionists were trapped in a bind of conflicting imperatives: they could assert Northern Ireland's Protestantism and Britishness to accentuate its separateness to the rest of Ireland, but this excluded the Catholic and Irish nationalist minority, and thus deprived the state of the consent it needed to translate political dominance into a more secure cultural hegemony.[38] □

Where we considered in Chapter Two how literature and culture offered a space of dissent from the official Unionist ideology of the North, Cleary counters that it is also necessary to consider how certain key writers have actually served to bolster a fragile Unionist hegemony. For Cleary, the North is a space where the two competing, dominant ideologies of Ireland collide. But he is notably suspicious of the regionalism of John Hewitt which Cleary reads as a cultural means of securing consent for the continued existence of a partitioned Northern Ireland:

> ■ Northern Ireland, in short, has always found it difficult to territorialise its history and historicise its geography [...] Ulster literary 'regionalism' probably represents the most sustained cultural attempt to 'solve' this dilemma [...] the project nonetheless aimed to secure cultural and emotional and ultimately political legitimacy for a more civic version of the Northern state.[39] □

According to Cleary, then, when Hewitt and other left-leaning or dissenting Protestant writers, such as Sam Hanna Bell or W. R. Rodgers (1909–69), advocate regionalism as a means of bypassing the collision of Irish Nationalism and Unionism in the North and instead offering a shared regional identification, they are in fact, despite their liberal intentions, ultimately furthering and refining a Unionist claim to the territory. Richard Kirkland's *Literature and Culture in Northern Ireland since 1965: Moments of Danger* (1996) also offers a thought-provoking and sustained critique of Hewitt's regionalist programme. Kirkland dissects Hewitt's 'Regionalism: The Last Chance' by, firstly, accusing Hewitt of a vague unsustainable individualism and a pre-lapsarian communal wholeness in his regionalism that seek to reduce actual historical complexity. Worse still, for Kirkland, Hewitt's regionalism panders to the competing tribal or sectarian dominant ideologies whose failure the Northern Irish State itself embodies. It seeks no meaningful change to the constitutional position of Northern Ireland within the United Kingdom since Hewitt's belief is that regionalism can only benefit Ulster if it remains part of a federated British Isles. Kirkland also reads Hewitt in line with David Lloyd's work, that we have discussed earlier, wherein Lloyd strives to illuminate the solving uses to which the aesthetic is put by cultural nationalism for political and social ends. Kirkland adjudges regionalism to be undertaking a comparable task of seeking to construct an aesthetic identification between individual and place that will override historical contradictions:

> ■ Hewitt's regionalism becomes interesting not through the political initiative it spectacularly failed to deliver, but through the way it allowed him to imagine a community based not on history but along aesthetic and geographical guidelines. It was a myth which idealistically claimed individual loyalty through the tropes of rootedness to the primary soil of Ulster as a 'natural', organic allegiance, and by doing so placed centrally the artist as crucial arbiter of communal judgement.[40] □

So for both Cleary and Kirkland, Hewitt's work promises dissent but registers, finally, a cultural, civic Unionist programme that would legitimize the Northern Irish State in a language of non-coercion and assent.

A much more affirmative account of Hewitt is provided by John Wilson Foster, whose work as a whole endeavours to reclaim and retrace the dissenting aspects of Protestant culture in Ireland. Foster finds in the poetry of both Hewitt and W. R. Rodgers a dissenting, nonconformist experience at odds with Unionist orthodoxy that he relates to Hewitt's lapsed Methodism and Rodgers's resignation of his Presbyterian ministry in 1946 and his separation from his wife before his departure from the North for a life dedicated to writing in London. Foster interprets Hewitt's recuperation of the vernacular poetry of the rhyming weavers, which is set in opposition to 'Colonial' and 'Provincial' poetry from Ulster written in Standard English, as an effort to construct a self-enabling tradition that reconciles Hewitt's sense of his own regionalized, dualistic identity: 'it is precisely *because* his Irishness is problematical that Hewitt's worrying of the matter for decades has enabled him to forge the conscience of the Scots-Irish in Ireland, and this may be his chief significance'.[41]

Thus Foster proposes that Hewitt's regionalism is driven by his antipathy to official Unionist ideology and his sense of exclusion, as a

Protestant, from essentialist notions of Irishness. Hewitt's response to the dilemma of his belonging, therefore, is to transmute planter uncertainty into the democratically spirited regionalist tradition which, for all its apparent radicalism and dissent, Foster nonetheless reads as actually rational and conservative: 'beneath the nonconformist independence, conscious vigilance and egalitarianism, one senses, though this need not be an ideological contradiction – Protestant reason and steady progress'.[42] For Foster, Rodgers's poetry offers a different set of nonconformist liberties that are more unmoorings than landed claims, dissenting not only from authority but also internally within the poetic self:

■ Rodgers was a blithe spirit in claiming without reservation his Irishness and it is in sober contrast that we read Hewitt's careful exploration of his cultural traditions, his self-questioning and the slow march of doubts; it is a contrast between Rodgers's cavalier assurance and Hewitt's roundheaded conscience.[43] □

So, while positioning Rodgers as more radical than Hewitt's narratives of historical continuity, Foster, nevertheless, grasps both writers as offering imaginative possibilities and alternatives that undercut the idea of a monolithic Unionist culture and State.

Questioning Northern identities: MacNeice and dissent

From a different perspective, Peter McDonald's *Mistaken Identities: Poetry and Northern Ireland* (1997), sets out to assert how the aesthetic and imaginative reordering of experience in poetry is not or should not be commandeered by the sectarian logic of identity which conventional accounts of the North tend to accept as given. In part, McDonald's arguments are driven by a hostility to postcolonial approaches to Irish literature though he has a much broader set of points to make as well. While poets such as Hewitt, Rodgers or, indeed, Louis MacNeice do emerge from complex but specific social and cultural situations, their poetry, according to McDonald, does not simply reflect circumstances but rather redraws, regalvanizes and renews the raw materials which prompt their work. Their respective aesthetics should not be solely co-opted with the identarian logic of Protestant, Scots-Irish, Ulster-Scots or variations thereon. For McDonald, Hewitt is not just a rooted regionalist or, at least, he is rooted in something more than just place alone and Hewitt's own selection and ordering of his work in his *Collected Poems* (1968) displays complicated processes of engagement and disengagement, placement and displacement. Similarly, McDonald argues, Rodgers opens identity to the challenges of artistic revision and doubt so that often in both Hewitt and Rodgers, even at times in spite of their conscious intent, the aesthetic distancing and recoding of experience cannot be reduced to one agenda. Furthermore, McDonald reads MacNeice's figure of the prism through which to look upon a multifarious world as associated dual processes of clarification and diffusion which bring about both concentration and separation. That is, McDonald avers, MacNeice's poetic is ultimately incompatible with the very concept of identity which forces thought in predetermined directions. For McDonald, a Northern Irish Protestant identity is simply the mirror image of the fundamental determinism he perceives in Irish Nationalism. Even a pluralistic conception of identity is not flexible enough to encompass the prismatic perspectives and perpetual modifications of thought in MacNeice's poetry:

> ■ Solidarity, community, place: all of these values, which strengthened and helped to mark out a generation of both sides of the Irish Sea, proved in the end less flexible and liberating than some of the creative writing they helped to bring to birth. As a part of the same complex of ideas, 'identity', whatever plurality it might claim, cannot accommodate the fluidity into which 'character' in all good writing necessarily dissolves.[44] □

Edna Longley's *The Living Stream* also provides detailed accounts of how literature and culture can resist any simplistic narrative of monolithic, identarian stagnation in the North. With regard to Hewitt and his socialism, Longley writes: 'If Yeats owed his soul to William Morris, Hewitt owed to Morris the soul of his politics'.[45] Longley concedes that there was always a dangerous thin line in radical Protestant culture between atheism or secularism and anti-Catholicism. But she finds a viable radical tradition of Protestant writing, such as that of Hewitt or Sam Hanna Bell, which finds a space for itself in Irish history through socialism or left-leaning political activity even if a mistrust of the Catholic, bourgeois Republic meant it had to go back to the Protestant involvement in the 1798 rebellion rather than the insurrections of the twentieth century. Furthermore, Longley's *Poetry in the Wars* (1986) is highly illustrative in terms of MacNeice's complex of poetic engagements. Longley highlights how section XVI of *Autumn Journal* castigates the North's mainstream culture, its pursuit of profit and stifling of dissent as part of a wider set of meditations on the pressures placed on art in the 1930s across Europe due to the rise of Fascism and Stalinism and the eventual onset of World War II. Longley reads MacNeice's polemic against Irish political insularity and British political limitation as constitutive of his humane imaginative art, its continual attention to social forces and simultaneous

refusal to become the mere mouthpiece of those forces: 'It is as if section XVI surfaces from the subconscious of *Autumn Journal* to interpret
its whole political and moral stance. By embodying the deadly alternative to liberal or tragic "doubt", MacNeice rescues it from charges of
weakness'.[46]

In Longley's interpretation, *Autumn Journal* is pitched against the
fixities and certainties of the political entrenchment of the period and
the poem's own shifting though assured formal modes shape themselves to, and thereby espouse, the movement and changes of life even
amidst dark turmoil. Just as the poem's metre is strong, yet flexible, the
poet too is responsive and active, being shaped and shaping. If, Longley
asserts, MacNeice is a poet of both flux and formal virtuosity, his rebuttal of ideological fixity should not be read as simply inviting a detached,
relativistic viewpoint or vacuous, ethically moribund pluralism (that we
could designate today as the postmodern condition):

■ Marxist critics who complain that post-modernism leaves no basis for critique should look into the thirties MacNeice [...] MacNeice's aesthetic as well
as his politics (although they cannot finally be separated) was shaped by a
recoil from Irish absoluteness. Yet he stops short of relativising the imagination into the closed circuit of infinitely deconstructible texts.[47] □

Longley also reads MacNeice's famous poem, 'Snow', and its worldly
immediacy in these terms, as suggestive of not only the richness but
also the risk of pluralities, of modern dislocations. So MacNeice's generous imaginative aesthetic is deeply concerned with social pressures
yet equally insistent that it will not be reduced solely to their terms of
engagement.

From a similar critical trajectory to Longley, Alan Gillis argues that
Irish issues figure in MacNeice's consummate aesthetic in the following
way:

■ his poetry insists that local problematics are bound up with larger historical
forces, that class inequality is part of Ireland's problem, and that Irish history
must therefore be reconfigured not in isolated terms [...] MacNeice's poetic range
indicates that the poet (and by extension every individual) is a complex array of
conflictive elements. And, just as the world is uncontainable (as is, by implication, Ireland), the modes of apprehending it are potentially illimitable.[48] □

Moreover, while the expatriate MacNeice, in contrast to Hewitt's
ongoing work in the North, appears to become disengaged from the
North in his poetry of the mid-1950s, Longley's *Living Stream* offers a
crucial recovery of the real cultural history of MacNeice's legacy and this
period more widely. MacNeice was involved in the three-year struggle

to get on to the stage the play *Over the Bridge* (1960) by Sam Thompson (1916–65). The Unionist establishment had attempted to suppress this play by Thompson, a working-class socialist and shipyard worker, who was encouraged to write for the BBC by Sam Hanna Bell and was also taught in a WEA class by John Hewitt. It was MacNeice who had recruited Bell for the BBC in the first place, and he had consistently used his influence in the London Features Department to protect the position of both Bell and John Boyd in their efforts to undermine the Unionist grip on BBC Northern Ireland.[49]

Indeed, in terms of Northern Irish culture and the State, the banning and eventual performance of Thompson's *Over the Bridge* is indicative of key tensions. Thompson attacks sectarianism in the Belfast ship-yard in his play wherein the Catholic Peter O'Boyle is victimized by a Loyalist mob, who attack O'Boyle and kill Davy Mitchell, a Protestant trade unionist who stood up for him. However, it is also worth noting that Lionel Pilkington maintains that the play's dissenting credentials are overplayed. Pilkington's archival research points out that the origi-nal rehearsal version of *Over the Bridge* concluded with the rejection by Mitchell's daughter Marian of Baxter, to whom she was engaged and who fails to back her father and instead accepts a promotion from the foreman. By contrast, the final version has Baxter criticize the foreman and support Marian's outrage and the main characters then bow their heads and pray with a Protestant clergyman. Pilkington interprets the rehearsal version as, however gingerly, admitting the Unionist working class's complicity in state power and its sectarian apparatus while the final version makes sectarianism instead the fault of O'Boyle's disruptive presence, a disruption which the play's closure seeks to repair. Pilking-ton reads the symbolism of the revised final scene in which an on-stage audience bow in reverence before a Protestant clergyman as a sign of assent to Unionist political domination. Moreover, the play's popularity, for Pilkington, should not be regarded as signalling a transition from a climate of censorship to one of artistic freedom and shifting attitudes. It is instead a sign that pressing social issues and political campaigns were being annexed and reconfigured in Unionist terms which suited the play's audiences:

■ Rather than denote a new mood of anti-sectarianism in Northern Ireland, Thompson's achievement lies in the appropriation by *Over the Bridge* of some of the principal issues of nationalist protest in Northern Ireland (in particular, anti-Catholic violence and religious discrimination in employment) – and the play's disarticulation of these from their main political expression in republi-can and nationalist protest. This is a *coup de théâtre* for the state in the sense that the theatre might be said to include nationalist minority interests while simultaneously reaffirming the terms of that minority's exclusion.[50] □

But as Longley points out the play and its reception did shake the Unionist state which Pilkington regards as endorsed by *Over the Bridge*. Furthermore, it is notable in the play's climactic scenes that the key dialogue between or across the sectarian divide and the consequent voicing of class solidarity take place in the closed room where the main protagonists are holed up while outside a baying Loyalist mob has gathered. So what should be a public space, the yard outside, the workplace, is actually a Unionist tribal possession, while the room in which the main characters converse actually becomes a public space in which meaningful debate occurs and this stands as an allegory of the stage more broadly, the ability of drama such as *Over the Bridge* to offer a public forum and political space denied by Unionist hegemony.

Thompson's play, together with the cultural climate of MacNeice, Hanna Bell and others which fostered him, do offer confirmation of art's capacity for dissent and for its formal retention of imaginative perspectives that will remain for future insight and influence even if they are stifled in their immediate context by regimes of ideological closure. The achievements of these writers, at times clawed from the darkest reaches of historical rupture, delimitation and defeat, pursue with willed purpose insights that have remained live in their influence on contemporary writing. So recent criticism – both within the Revisionist and postcolonial camps and without – has sought to comprehend literature as a means of re-conceiving the nature of culture and society North and South, as an active method of distinguishing official rhetoric from highly charged cultural conditions. But of all the inequities or problems of both states in Ireland, it is perhaps issues surrounding gender that most insistently declare their unresolved and problematic displacement. The next chapter focuses specifically on such matters of gender and nation, constructions of masculinity and femininity, sexuality, the forms of women's writing and the emergence of a feminist criticism in Ireland.

CHAPTER FIVE

Gender, Sexuality and Feminism in Irish Literature

Gender and nation

As we evaluate issues of gender and sexuality through the twentieth century, one fundamental problem faced by Irish feminism was its difficult relationship to nationalism. There were many women participants in the Irish Nationalist and Republican agitations of the Revival period, most famously Maud Gonne, Countess Markievicz and Hanna Sheehy-Skeffington. There were highly divergent views as to whether nationalism and feminism shared the same emancipatory agenda, whether feminism was an equalizing pre-requisite to nationalism, or whether national liberation must come first and then facilitate the emancipation of women once the national question had been resolved. Sheehy-Skeffington was clear that feminism had both the priority and the means to transform society more broadly in advance of national freedom. Her sense of the disempowerment of women did not just include British rule in Ireland – hence, she asks of female subjection:

■ The result of Anglicization? This is partly true; much of the evil is, however, inherent in latter-day Irish life. Nor will the evil disappear, as we are assured, when Ireland comes to her own again, whenever that may be. For until the women of Ireland are free, the men will not achieve emancipation.[1] □

In other words, it is the emancipation of women which will transform society as a whole and produce new freedoms and energies in Ireland. In stark contrast, Countess Markievicz puts the nation firmly first:

■ I would ask every nationalist woman to pause before she joined a Suffrage Society or Franchise League that did not include in their programme the Freedom of their Nation. A Free Ireland with No Sex Disabilities in her constitution should be the motto of all nationalist Women.[2] □

Which is to say, the women's movement would have to wait until the national question is resolved before pursuing its own cause fully. Prior to independence, the cause of Ireland must be the primary cause of women.

In retrospect, the repressive tenor of the Irish Free State brought about by independence obviously permits us the easy scorn of hindsight. But the purpose of the opening section of this chapter will be to understand why the usurpation of the women's movement – which was actively involved in the nationalist struggle of the early twentieth century – occurred. It is highly significant that the involvement of Gonne, Markievicz, Sheehy-Skeffington and other women was quickly forgotten, so that they became, in Margaret Ward's wonderfully insightful term, 'unmanageable revolutionaries'.[3] Ward's phrase indicates that where the other (male) heroes and martyrs of the nationalist movement were readily commemorated within the official narratives of the new State, the agency and involvement of women have in fact been highly disruptive and unsettling for patriarchal norms. This chapter will address issues of female agency and activity in the context of how such assertions of women's subjectivity challenge the conventional, purely symbolic centrality of women as figurative tropes of the nation – Mother Ireland, Cathleen Ni Houlihan and The Poor Old Woman.

In addition, the cultural and racial feminization of Ireland by Arnold's Celticism and the disempowerment of Ireland by British subordination induce core debates within feminism about whether Irish society is, therefore, particularly disposed to the liberation of women and sympathy with the dispossessed, or whether it is instead resistant to such concerns. The position of women writers will also then be addressed and we will focus specifically on the dilemma that they face in a national culture so saturated in images of women constructed by men – images designed to embody the nation itself – and so deficient in images of women representing themselves in their own terms and for their own purposes. As Clair Wills discerns: 'the motherland trope poses a very specific problem for the Irish woman writer. For the writer who rejects the association of woman and land thereby questions the relationship between poet and community, and the type of community it posits – one which excludes women'.[4]

Terry Eagleton's Field Day pamphlet, *Nationalism: Irony and Commitment* (1988), stands as one of the most influential efforts to reconcile nationalism and feminism and to suggest an affinity between oppressed groups. For Eagleton, both Irish Nationalism and feminism share a similar ontological problem: as responses to disempowerment, and indeed as efforts to overcome that disempowerment, they emerge from categories and social positions necessarily constructed for them by power in the first place. That is, Irish Nationalism strives to surmount an 'Irish' problem of being disempowered by Britain, and feminism seeks to assert the experiences of oppressed women through a womanhood that is oppressed by patriarchy. As Eagleton puts it: 'Sexual politics, like class or nationalist struggle, will thus necessarily be caught up in the very metaphysical categories it hopes finally to abolish'.[5] But the ongoing gender inequality in Ireland – North and South – requires that we consider whether nationalism and feminism undertake such a mission on an equal footing, and whether the former is able to subsume or repress the latter. Moreover, any attempt to propose a mutual disempowerment between Irish nationalism and feminism presupposes that nationality is a gender-neutral construction, and the debates we will relay below often wish to challenge that assumption. In unravelling the uneasy relationships between nationalism and feminism, we will address the pervasive use of women as symbols of the nation and the divergent contestations over the meanings of such representations.

We will commence with a consideration of the gender politics of the Revival. As already discussed, the furore surrounding both Synge's and O'Casey's plays pertained directly to the representation of women – especially the issue of female sexuality – which was central to the apparent insult to the nation's purity. In Chapter One we reported Lady Gregory's telegram to Yeats informing him that the increasingly uneasy audience had finally begun to riot upon hearing the word 'shift'. Nicholas Grene offers a rich account of why the word *shift* was so controversial by tracing, if you like, the shifts which the word undergoes in history. Grene notes how the term 'shift' had begun to displace 'smock' as a putatively more genteel word for underclothing by the seventeenth century but 'shift' itself then became supplanted by 'chemise' in the nineteenth century as a more delicate expression. These shifts in words for undergarments tell us something profound about how the contact of such clothing with the female body requires ever more refined and discreet terminologies which disclose the ongoing repression of the reality of women's bodies and physicality. As Grene comments: 'the image of woman, so central to nationalist iconography, was an insistently desexualised one, and in such a context Synge's drift of females in their shifts were scandalously erotic'.[6]

So, for the sexual proprieties of the well-to-do nationalist audiences of Dublin and Irish-America, the use of this vulgar term for 'chemise' was scandalous because it disrupted the sacrosanct gentility of Irish women. Therefore, *Playboy* was controversial not only because of its intrusion on Irish Nationalism's sacred terrain of the West of Ireland but also because it transgressed the boundaries of yet another sacred symbolic site for nationalism: the intersection of nation with gender. Most specifically, nationalism deploys the purity of its women – and its own regulation thereof – as guarantors of the nation's integrity. Under these representational conditions, women are never themselves but rather the figurative means by which men secure the symbolic coherence of their own yearning for national purity and unity. Synge's play uses a word that is not only deemed improper in itself but which also denotes an item of clothing in contact with the female body, and, in turn, it highlights the repression of female physicality and sexuality within the highly gendered symbolic codes of nationalism. *Playboy* and the reaction to it help identify how nationalism's pious defence of women is at the same time the erasure of women's actual experiences and voices, and the transmutation of real women into figurative ciphers in someone else's national imagination.

Likewise, Yeats's *Cathleen Ni Houlihan* deploys the well-established trope of personifying Ireland as female (Cathleen herself, Hibernia, the Sean Bhean Bhocht or Poor Old Woman, the Aisling or dream-vision) but it is telling that Mother Ireland's function in the play is to call *men* to action, to words and deeds. Hence, the apparent agency that Cathleen has in the play – her power to call Michael would seem to empower women and give them voice – is actually a misleading or effaced subjectivity: rather, she operates as a symbolic object whose task is to secure the subjectivity and agency of men. Furthermore, one of the key components of that male agency is the continued construction and possession of exactly such images of women. This kind of representational reversal whereby the plethora of images of Ireland as female actually attests to the exclusion of women from the imagining of the nation offers a specific example of Peter Stallybrass and Allon White's tenet that 'what is *socially* peripheral is so often *symbolically* central'.[7] In short, the continual personification of Ireland as female signifies not the empowerment of women but, rather, merely that it is men who predominantly do the representing and that their anxieties and desires find symbolic form in woman as figurative cipher.

Given the influence of Yeats's *Cathleen* on Pearse, these standard gender paradigms are recapitulated in Pearse's own writings and thought. For example, William Irwin Thompson argues of Pearse's poem 'Renunciation':

■ Pearse's poem [...] is rooted in Irish culture. In that culture virginity is considered a higher state than marriage, and the brother who becomes a priest is a greater and stronger man than the brother who, out of carnal weakness, marries [...] This is the culture of which Pearse is an almost perfect expression: he dressed in black, he praised the purity of the peasant, and celebrated the famous chastity of Irish women; if he thought about women, it was always as mothers, most often as mothers of soldiers, but never as wives. Pearse is a perfect follower of Cathleen ni Houlihan: in 'Renunciation' he turns aside from the love of a wife to accept the sharp, transforming love of death.[8] □

We can think as well about how O'Casey's plays, which appear to provide positive images of women that are intended to undercut the delusions of male heroic ideals and political fixities, nevertheless retain a purely figural hold on their female characters whose lack of complexity discloses how they are used as stereotyped objects of femininity to be either protected or corrupted as suits the point being made. The injury to Minnie's breasts, for instance, in *Shadow* is clearly a redolently symbolic means of attacking political activism by showing how it is destructive of women's avowedly 'normal' or 'natural' function. (It could be added that the stage direction describing Minnie as 'hysterical' in her moment of political commitment activates another stereotype about women to imply the unthinking, unhinged irresponsibility of political ideologies.)

With Joyce, we earlier discussed his letter to Nora Barnacle that castigated a repressive society for the treatment of his mother and this would appear to make him more sensitive to the plight of women. In *Dubliners* the eponymous protagonist of 'Eveline' is very self-consciously framed by the window in a way that suggests Joyce is aware of his own 'framing' or artistic representation of women, and Gretta's character in 'The Dead' apparently resists her husband's efforts to reduce her to a mere object in his own subjective musings. *A Portrait* implies that Stephen's representation of women is as devoid of experience and reality as any of his other stalled attempts to engage with life. *Ulysses* finally gives voice to Molly's monologue, and her celebration of sexuality is radical in a context wherein the word 'shift' can cause rioting in the *Playboy*'s audience. In turn, Molly's voice anticipates Anna Livia Plurabelle and the 'riverrun' of discourses in *Finnegans Wake*. However, as we will discuss below, feminists are divided about Joyce's gender politics and we could use the word 'yes' which cadences Molly's monologue to crystallize the competing interpretations: is it, at last, an affirmation of women, their sexuality, agency and desire? Or is it only a passive token of assent by a female character to her male author, a sign of the acquiescence of a female object defined by her body and sexuality in a stereotyped rather than liberating way?

Feminism, nation and postcolonialism

More broadly, the nationalist figuration of Ireland as female also coincides with the feminization of the Celt by Renan and Arnold and this uneasy coalescence produces tensions in feminist readings of Irish culture. The discourse of colonialism is highly gendered and tends to assert male (colonizer) authority over female (colonized) so that the norms of patriarchy are invoked to naturalize and legitimize colonial domination. A leading postcolonial critic in this field is Ashis Nandy whose work is often utilized in an Irish context. Nandy links emasculation and defeat, suggesting that colonized societies are feminized by their colonial subjugation according to the patriarchal grammar of the discourse of colonialism. Nandy then argues that one of the results of this symbolic emasculation is the construction of an over-compensatory 'hyper-masculinity' by colonized men as a degraded and contorted effort to reassert their power and agency, paradoxically in the terms of the very power that has disempowered and emasculated them:

■ Only the victims of a culture of hyper-masculinity, adulthood, historicism, objectivism, and hyperpersonality protect themselves by simultaneously conforming to the stereotype of the rulers, by over-stressing those aspects of the self which they share with the powerful, and by protecting in the corner of their heart a serene defiance which reduces to absurdity the victor's concept of the defeated and his unspoken belief that he is morally and culturally superior to his subjects, caught on the wrong side of history.[9] □

By way of an Irish Nationalist example, D. P. Moran notably castigates those not manly and virile enough to help realize his Irish Ireland through a sense of feminized impotence:

■ On all sides one sees only too much evidence that the people are secretly content to be a conquered race, though they may not have the honesty to admit it. Even the pride that frequently dignifies failure is not there. There is nothing *masculine* in the character, and when the men do fall into line with the green banners overhead, and shout themselves hoarse, is it not rather a feminine screech, a delirious burst of defiance on a background of sluggishness and despair.[10] □

Nandy's terms are picked up very effectively in Gerardine Meaney's work. Meaney follows Nandy's account of colonization as feminization to claim that colonized peoples impose and observe strictly differentiated gender roles: 'Women in these conditions become guarantors of their men's status, bearers of national honour and the scapegoats of national identity. They are not merely transformed into symbols of the nation, they become the territory over which power is exercised'.[11] Thus, for Meaney, the apparent disposition to femininity in Irish cultural, religious and political iconography actually disavows the obliteration of the reality of women's lives and experiences: 'The attractions of the traditional feminine role, particularly as the Catholic Church defines it, are grounded in a deep loathing of femininity'.[12] So Meaney uses Nandy's model to insist that the perceived feminization of Ireland by its subjugation results not in a natural sympathy between Irish nationalism and the demands of feminism as comparably disempowered and shared constituencies but rather the antithesis of this – the production of a culture and society even more ill-disposed to feminist concerns because of its hyper-masculine insecurities and compensations: 'Feminism must interrogate nationalism, must maintain its own interests and women's interests against any monolithic national identity which perpetuates patriarchy'.[13]

In this context women become the other of the other, and we can add the work of Marilyn Reizbaum to Meaney in positing the double exclusion suffered by women writing in marginalized cultures. Reizbaum does concede that nationalism and feminism would appear to share a need to overcome disempowerment and to reassert identities that have been repressed: 'Nationalism and feminism encounter many of the same vexing questions: that is, does an assertion of positive identity necessarily move toward unanimity, homogeneity, essentialism, fixity, to an ironic betrayal of the principles by which the movement is guided?'.[14] However, she maintains that any readymade commonality is disrupted by the patriarchal structure and needs of nationalism overwriting the requirements of feminism:

■ When a culture has been marginalized, its impulses toward national legitimization tend to dominate in all spheres and forms of cultural realization. What women writers in Scotland and Ireland are now addressing within their struggle to emerge is the relationship between their national and sexual identities, and in doing so they are redressing the terms by which the mainstream in their countries establishes itself – the very terms of literary production [...] The need to define nationalism in patriarchal terms in countries that have struggled against a colonizing 'father' is perhaps a response to the historical figuration of cultural 'inferiority' in stereotypes of the feminine; where the disempowerment of a culture becomes an emasculation, subjugation is gender-inflected.[15] □

The Nandian thesis of colonization as feminization also facilitates an opposing feminist trajectory, however. Anne Owens Weekes, for example, implies a shared national experience that serves to unite a people: 'colonization [...] makes female both country and people'.[16]

Additionally, Carol Coulter's work traces an existent, though sometimes forgotten, history of women's involvement in Irish Nationalist struggle – as with the involvement of Maud Gonne and Countess Markiewicz in the Easter Rising and the surrounding agitation – to claim that

■ those politically active women of the early twentieth century came out of a pre-existing tradition of women's involvement in nationalist struggle, that this offered them scope for a wider range of activities in public life than that experienced by their sisters in imperialist countries, and that all this was closed off to them by the newly-formed patriarchal state, modelled essentially on its colonial predecessor.[17] □

So despite being critical of the Irish state brought into being by nationalist struggle, Coulter is keen to preserve a still insurgent nationalism unco-opted and uncontaminated by the actions of the Free State and then the Republic (in this regard her work is similar to David Lloyd's attack on the official cultural nationalism of the state and his interest in marginalized nationalism against the state). Again, the colonization as feminization model is deployed, in contrast to Meaney and Reizbaum, as a facilitator of a feminist space in Irish society and culture:

■ Given the oppressively masculine nature of the colonial state which ruled Ireland (as well as Britain itself and the other colonies in the British Empire), it was perhaps inevitable that women would play a major role in the struggle to overthrow it, and that the battle for women for the vote and other rights gave strength to the nationalist enterprise.[18] □

Coulter's sense that a nationalist-feminist project was betrayed by the formation of an Irish State seeks to resist the interpretation that nationalism was structurally patriarchal and that the Irish Free State institutionally enacts that structure.

Ailbhe Smyth's 'The Floozie in the Jacuzzi' (1989) is an important essay in Irish feminism as it uses insights from French feminist theory and its deconstructive aspects to highlight precisely issues of underlying patriarchal structures and determinants on culture and society. Deconstructive feminisms contend that the emancipation of women does not just entail the involvement of more women in public life – in politics, employment, culture and so on. Rather, there is no neutral public space in which such emancipation can take place for patriarchy structures everything in its society including language itself. Therefore, language and all patriarchal forms require deconstruction, a radical structural sundering to open up a new, properly emancipating space. Smyth's article emerges from the building of a statue of Joyce's Anna Livia Plurabelle in Dublin in 1987 by the Smurfit Corporation and Dublin City Corporation. As to Joyce and feminism, the transformation of one of his central characters in *Finnegans Wake*, who supposedly offers a pluralistic and liberating unfolding of identity, into a statue is not a contradiction for Smyth but instead final proof of Joyce's and Irish society's repression of women:

■ *A L P* Monumental assertion of the power of patriarchy; massive appropriation of Woman, sign and symbol; pompous denial of women's right to self-definition; emphatic affirmation of the negation of women excluded from the generation of meaning [...] The name in ironic counterpoint to its own forever-fixed materiality; 'Woman' symbol of plurality, cruel insane mocking contradiction of the circumscribed realities of Irish women's lives [...] Progeny of the miscegenation of Culture and City, without legitimate autonomous existence within their walls. Produced by the brokers of male power, imaginative, economic and political, she exists to reproduce their ideas, their economy, their values, their desires. Her function is 'purely' iconic. Pure, unpolluted, uncontaminated by the actuality of actual women. Having no historical veracity/validity, she cannot represent her own plurability any more than she can represent the historically and materially rooted diversity of all/Irish/Dublin women. Her very unreality (conventional stylised allegorical figure) functioning to erase the untidy realities of fleshy women [...] A L P exists not in and for herself but in and for something *other* than herself. Essentially vacuous, receptacle without individual identity, mute spectacle, silent cipher, the symbolic female figure is incapable of *conferring* meaning.[19] □

Smyth regards woman as other of the other, and the Irish state as a structural and institutional encasement of the patriarchal codes of a nationalism whose self-empowerment is achieved through a specifically male perspective:

■ In post-colonial patriarchal culture, naming strategies have an overdetermined role, invested with an irresistible double force and double meaning. The long-denied power to name, to confer meaning, and thus (illusion?) to control material reality, is all the more powerfully experienced and pleasurably exercised when finally acquired. It is a treacherous ambivalent power if the paradigm for this exercise remains unchanged. The liberation of state implies male role-shift from that of Slave to Master, Margin to Centre, Other to Self. Women, powerless under patriarchy, are maintained as Other of the ex-Other, colonised of the post-colonised.[20] □

One thing we can draw attention to in the feminization-as-colonization model is that there is a danger that its terms of reference – masculinity and femininity – are taken as already agreed concepts or given designations. While it is vital to acknowledge the hegemony and effects of patriarchy, it does not then follow that we should accept its norms on their own terms. In other words, Nandy's model tends to assume there was or is a normal model of masculinity that is then disrupted by colonization and feminization and which may be restored or redeemed in a process of liberation. And here there is a commingling of a 'proper' national self-determination and a masculine self-reclamation. Of course, the thesis of colonial occupation as emasculation necessarily involves a male experience of that process. So Nandy reads colonization as a disruption of – and thereby a simultaneous confirmation of – patriarchal norms and the nature of both masculinity and femininity.

By contrast, a number of critics have sought to analyze the Revival period as a much more fluid and unsettling arena for standard gender paradigms. Adrian Frazier's work finds in the writing of George Moore, Edward Martyn and Yeats 'the creation of alternative male identities'.[21] Frazier concedes the dominance of the patriarchal norm of masculinity but argues that its hegemony should not be allowed to fulfil its task of masking the contradictions, disunity and alternatives which that norm strives to deny. For Frazier, Moore, Martyn and Yeats were able to refuse normative categories and negotiate 'richness in the possibilities of masculinity in the period ... before the emergent model of sexual identities (as hetero-, homo- or bi-sexual) came into force in the early twentieth century'.[22] Indeed, the fact that gendered identities are historically contingent is reinforced by Éibhear Walshe's excellent 'The First Gay Irish Man? Ireland and the Wilde Trials' (2005), which examines the relative absence of immediate interest in the trial of Wilde in Irish culture but a subsequent reclamation thereafter – even if, at times, this is undertaken by an appropriative nationalist agenda seeking to disturb perceived English norms:

■ In the hundred years since the trials of Oscar Wilde, his homosexuality has been subsumed into broader debates and discourses concerning Irish nationalism. As the unmentionable Wilde became Oscar the Irish rebel, even such a homophobic society as twentieth-century Ireland managed to locate strategies rendering homosexuality comprehensible – and even marginally acceptable.[23] □

Earlier we discussed Yeats's *Cathleen* in terms of its objectification of woman as Mother Ireland, but Elizabeth Butler Cullingford also locates in his work important ambiguities with regard to masculinity:

■ Yeats may appear vulnerable to feminist criticism on two grounds: as a love poet in a tradition that has stereotyped and silenced its female object, and as a modernist [...] Yeats's earliest work [...] is interesting precisely because of those qualities that have led male critics to denigrate it as insufficiently modern: its adoption of a feminine subject position and its 'effeminate' style and form. Yeats's tenuous and intermittent identification with traditional models of masculinity resulted in an oblique relationship to the canonical genre of the love lyric [...] one is not born a man, one becomes one; and Yeats had considerable trouble becoming a man [...] Yeats's relationship to the discourse of patriarchy was always fissured by contradictions. As a white, male, middle-class, Protestant citizen of the British Empire, with an acknowledged debt to canonical English writers [...] he belonged to the dominant literary tradition. As a colonized Irishman, however, he was acutely conscious of repression and exclusion.[24] □

In *James Joyce and Sexuality* (1988), Richard Brown's examination of Joyce comparably foregrounds the ambivalence of his work and his rebuttal of settled gender identities:

■ Critics tended to represent Joyce either as uninterested in such issues or else were led to admit, if reluctantly, that his fictional representation of women seems to fall into many of the faults against which modern feminists complain [...] Molly Bloom surely does represent a new kind of fictional woman: massive, potent and self-possessed [...] Bloom too has feminine characteristics. He is able to be sympathetic to women, in his visit to Mina Purefoy, and in smaller details such as in 'Hades' where he thinks of John O'Connell, the joking graveyard caretaker: 'Fancy being a wife'. Bloom has a 'firm full masculine feminine passive active hand' in 'Ithaca'. On Howth Head [...] he is on the receiving end of a sexually inverted kind of insemination: 'Softly she gave me in my mouth the seedcake warm and chewed'. In 'Circe' he is diagnosed by Mulligan as 'bisexually abnormal' and by Dr Dixon as 'the new womanly man' and 'about to have a baby'.[25] □

However, Kate Soper's reading of Joyce is broadly indicative of the feminist critics who ultimately dispute Joyce's feminist credentials and remain suspicious about the final positioning of his gender identities for all their apparent flux:

■ Sensitive though he is to his 'Irish' exclusion from 'English' and to the asymmetry between the two (one cannot be opposed to the other as an equally valid and cosmopolitan tongue) he nowhere in *Ulysses* shows himself sensitive to the schismatic position of women within this gaze or to the asymmetry which must dog every attempt to escape or transcend it [...] Molly Bloom is no exception to the absence of the consciousness of the 'feminine erotic' in *Ulysses* but rather the culminating confirmation of a presiding masculinity [...] the Molly chapter exemplifies to the full the 'asymmetry' of an erotic perspective in which men experience (look at, desire, etc.) women, and women experience women as being experienced by men. Molly is not simply the object of Bloom's, Boylan's, Ben Dollard's etc. 'look'. She is very much a subject too. But her subjectivity is engrossed in looking at the look, and this takes up a far larger share of her experience of the world than is the case with Bloom, Boylan, Dollard, etc.[26] □

In anticipating the following chapter of this Guide, which addresses the contemporary literatures of the Irish Republic and Northern Ireland, Edna Longley's 'From Cathleen to Anorexia', which is collected in *The Living Stream*, uses gender as a means of a wider condemnation of the dominant ideologies of both states, their limitations and their breakdown. Her title moves us from Yeats's Mother Ireland icon to the poetry of Paul Muldoon:

■ In his poem 'Aisling', written near the time of the hunger strikes, Paul Muldoon asks whether Ireland should be symbolised, not by a radiant and abundant goddess, but by the disease anorexia [...] In blaming the hunger-strikers' emaciation on their idealised cause, the poem equates that cause with a form of physical and psychic breakdown. 'Anorexia' is thus Cathleen Ni Houlihan in a terminal condition. Anorexic patients pursue an unreal self-image – in practice, a death-wish. Similarly, the Irish Nationalist dream may have declined into a destructive neurosis [...] Feminists question any exploitation of the female body for symbolic or abstract purposes. So perhaps Anorexia should, rather, personify Irish women themselves: starved and repressed by patriarchies like Unionism, Catholicism, Protestantism, Nationalism.[27] □

Longley thus targets both Irish Nationalism and Unionism in her critique, though in regard to the trope established in this section of deploying images of women to suture and resolve national anxieties and problematics, her analysis comments specifically on Irish Nationalism's female iconography and its rewriting the reality of women into a symbolic cipher. Longley maintains that the structural dynamics of Irish Nationalism privilege male experience and the symbolic use of femininity as a repository of its longings and concerns so that feminism will always be overridden by its patriarchal codes and terms.

Colin Graham's work also considers gender an important means of disrupting mainstream ideologies as part of his general undertaking and skill in engaging postcolonial theory in a very different way to its conventional use in Irish Studies. Graham undermines the use of postcolonial theory in much Irish Studies criticism in which the *post*, the *telos* or end point projected by the analysis, is the restoration of the nation in some homogeneous and uncomplicated unity. Graham acknowledges that postcolonialism is an ethical criticism in that it seeks to diagnose and morally evaluate the fundamental inequalities of the relationship between colonizer and colonized. However, Graham also argues that 'to allow the nation to monopolise the postcolonial field is to withhold [...] a more radical interrogation by the difficult ethics of the colonial encounter'.[28]

Graham specifically invokes the Subaltern Studies aspect of postcolonial criticism, which emanated primarily through the Subaltern Studies Group in India under Ranajit Guha and which derives its name from the designation of oppressed groups of people as subalterns by the Italian Marxist Antonio Gramsci (1891–1937). The term subaltern incorporates class analysis but also expands upon it to investigate how class intersects with other disempowerments related to gender, sexuality, race, colonialism and so on. Subaltern Studies professedly 'aligns itself with social groups which it sees as excluded, dominated, elided and oppressed by the state ... and as something of a necessary by-product of this mission, Subaltern Studies allows for an understanding of the post-colonial nation in a new way – no longer need the nation be regarded as the glorious achievement and fruition of the labours of an oppressed people'.[29] Hence, the nation does not have to be the ethical *telos* or ulti-mate aim of decolonization, nor should an analysis of colonialism as process be necessarily conducted in national terms.

It is notable that revisionist detractors of Ireland's postcolonial status, such as Liam Kennedy and Stephen Howe, also frame their arguments in terms of how Ireland as a *nation* benefited from British imperialism without considering disadvantages such as class and gender.[30] Graham not only astutely deems Ireland a 'liminal space', a fractured or impacted entity as a European colony both metropolitan and peripheral, but he is also alert to the further antagonisms of class, gender, religion, region and so on which complicate any neat colonizer/colonizer division with regard to colonialism itself and, moreover, any naïve celebration of unitary national liberation thereafter.[31] In his essay 'Subalternity and Gender: Problems of Postcolonial Irishness', Graham returns to the orig-inal use of the category subaltern in Antonio Gramsci's *Prison Notebooks* (1947) where Gramsci defines not only the subaltern's subordinate relationship to dominant social groups but also the subalterns' resolve to unite their diffuse concerns and form a state, and, furthermore, the subalterns' intermittent affiliation with dominant political formations. Consequently, Graham challenges David Lloyd's and Carol Coulter's reading of the subaltern, anti-colonial nature of nationalism and its solidarity with oppressed groups, such as women, through which they construct a coalition of groups in an insurgent nationalism untainted by the power and institutions of the Irish state.[32]

For Graham, nationalism still provides the ideological gel which unites Lloyd's and Coulter's diffuse subaltern groupings and it does so while attempting to suppress an acknowledgement of the state formation that Irish Nationalism has already brought into being in the Twenty-Six Counties. Graham therefore tries to trouble an easy coalition between nationalism and feminism by taking issue with what he considers the basic assumptions of Lloyd's and Coulter's ethical, oppositional mar-ginal groups. Firstly, Graham posits that both Lloyd and Coulter assume that nationalism can be viewed as orientated only towards subversion whereas in Gramsci's original model the subaltern can aim at becoming the State, and indeed subaltern groups can often affiliate themselves to dominant classes. The second problem, for Graham, in regarding nationalism and the subaltern as always insurgent is that nationalism is, therefore, only subaltern when it is unsuccessful rather than in the process of forming the State. Consequently, Graham argues, there is a considerable danger of academic revelling in the marginality of oppressed groups who must remain powerless in order for this kind of subaltern model to function. Thirdly, and with specific regard to feminism, Graham adjudges that Lloyd's and Coulter's work ultimately demotes gender issues to aspects of a more general nationalist subversion in that the model of woman-as-subaltern condemns women to exist only under the rubric of the overarching and prioritized concerns of nationalism. Contrastingly, Graham insists on the heterogeneity of the subaltern subject in order to question the false commonality of experience that usurps gender under the rubric of nationalism, and this allows Graham to resist what he sees as 'a complex, contorted intellectual nativism, rehearsing the idioms and rejuvenating the discourses of an essentialist Irishness which is always oppressed, and yet is itself oppressive of the heterogeneity with which it is confronted'.[33]

Feminism, Irish women's writing and literary form

In terms of subalternity and the position of women, a highly illustrative literary means by which we can observe how female experience is still displaced within what is apparently dissent is found in Frank O'Connor's response to the fiction of his contemporary Mary Lavin. We discussed in Chapter Three how O'Connor conceptualized the short story form as the apposite mode for 'submerged population groups', for the marginalized and disenfranchised groups in society, or subalterns in terms of the theory we have just addressed. O'Connor states that 'an Irishman, reading the stories of Mary Lavin is actually more at a loss than a foreigner would be. His not-so-distant political revolution, seen through her eyes, practically disappears from view'.[34] So in spite of his own dissident credentials, it is highly significant here that gender structures O'Connor's identification with a normal, national Irish male experience which finds odd, unfathomable and foreign the experience of women. Where O'Connor elsewhere set himself the task of criticizing aspects of the apparent normality of the Irish Republic, in this instance, he actually identifies himself (as male) with that normality and in opposition to a strange and alien femaleness. For her own part, Lavin explained the premise of her short stories in the following way: 'My interest is in recording and preserving the real life of living Irishmen and women whom I have known and seen with my own eyes. I want to note the way they acted and the things they believed, whether right or wrong'.[35] Hence, the basis of her writing and her use of the short story form are similar to O'Connor's motivations in tracing the mundane and lost realities beneath the rhetoric of the new State, but her focus on women's experience – even though she is employing the same literary form and representational modes as O'Connor – causes him to baulk at her writing and to dismiss it from his 'normal' understanding.

Therefore, O'Connor's confusion over Lavin raises key questions about literary form and representational modes as they pertain to gender politics. His reaction foregrounds key debates, which we briefly exposited in relation to Ailbhe Smyth's 'Floozie in the Jacuzzi', about whether language and form are neutral and may be deployed by women on equal terms with men, or whether they are in fact highly politicized and contain inbuilt assumptions and worldviews. Despite Lavin's avowed intention to use the short story as a form of social documentation, it is notable that she accredits Virginia Woolf with being a formative literary influence. Woolf's work, Lavin explains, 'had a great impact on me' and 'was like a painting, seen at one glance, tremendously new'.[36] So we could connect the concern in a text such a Woolf's *A Room of One's Own* (1929) with uncovering the repressed experiences of women to Lavin's effort, as Bonnie Kime Scott puts it, to express 'the life of the female mind'.[37] Woolf's work, and *A Room of One's Own* in particular, also helped to inspire one of the most formative and accomplished figures in Irish literary feminism, B. G. MacCarthy. Although her focus is not specifically on Irish literature but the development of Anglophone women's fiction more generally, MacCarthy is a hugely important figure in terms of the instigation of concerted and formalized efforts to examine writing by women. Decades before the institutional development of feminism, MacCarthy published *Women Writers: Their Contribution to the English Novel 1621–1744* (1944) and *The Female Pen: Women Writers and Novelists 1744–1818* (1947), which were reclaimed and republished in one volume after her death as *The Female Pen: Women Writers and Novelists 1621–1818* (1994). MacCarthy produced these landmarks in Irish feminist scholarship having studied as an undergraduate at University College Cork, undertaken a PhD at Cambridge, and then returned to lecture in Cork where she was a colleague of Daniel Corkery. In part, MacCarthy accepted the strictures of Corkery's view of Anglo-Irish writing, or, at least, she had to tailor carefully her feminism so as not to make women's writing appear anti-nationalist in Corkery's prevailing terms. So there is possibly a tension in MacCarthy's impressively comprehensive recovery of women's writing when it deals with Anglo-Irish novelists who are, under Corkery's rubric, not Irish enough, and Irish nationalist writing which is not feminist enough to meet her own criteria. Similarly, MacCarthy had to defer an awareness of an Irish feminism that would undermine its own national status. As Gerardine Meaney writes:

> ■ Her work remains one of the most significant achievements of feminist scholarship by an Irish woman. It also offers an explanation of the delay in the development of feminist criticism within Irish academic institutions, for the gender question and the national question became mutually exclusive questions.[38] □

Nonetheless, MacCarthy retains a sharp sense of the patriarchal power relations of society and, following on from her engagement with Woolf's *A Room of One's Own*, she is attuned to how those power relations impinge on issues of cultural and literary production:

> ■ Women's contribution to literature is no arbitrary or artificial distinction. However much the reformer may welcome or the conservative lament the growth of a harmonious sharing of ideals between men and women, that growth has been a hard-fought struggle. It has been an escape from a prison which, when it did not entirely shut out the greater world, at least enclosed a little world of education meant for women, a literature adapted to the supposed limitations of their intellect, and a course of action prescribed by their sex.[39] □

MacCarthy thus anticipates what would be cornerstones of more recent feminism: the acknowledgement that there are 'limitations' or circumscriptions placed on women, on their access to society, to education, to culture; and a resistance to biological determinism whereby women are reduced to a grossly stereotyped and naturalized idea of their sex. With regard to whether language and form are neutral or embedded in patriarchy, MacCarthy cogently displays an awareness that women are continually judged by and through masculine norms. She pitches her own historical recovery of women's writing in terms of a movement towards a more utopian moment when

> ■ having discarded the male standards by which at first they were governed, the women would choose their own canvas, their own point of view and their own technique. They can claim to have attempted almost every genre of fiction, to have enriched many and to have initiated some of the most important.[40] □

In terms of literary form, MacCarthy advances realism as the best and most prevailing means by which women have articulated and should articulate their experience. She contrasts her association of women with realism against what she deems the more male forms of the heroic epic, saga and modes such as pastoral – in all of which, it is suggested, women and the world more broadly are represented in figurative, symbolic ways rather than how they really are. Hence, MacCarthy opines of women writers that 'they can boast that the nearer fiction came towards their characteristic outlook and subject-matter the nearer it came to reality'.[41] In other words, realism offers women the means to depict the partial prison of their allocated room and, ultimately, to escape it by representing to the world its inequalities and repressed perspectives.

Nuala O'Faolain's essay 'Irish Women and Writing in Modern Ireland' (1985) offers a more recent endorsement of MacCarthy's argument from a specifically Irish literary perspective. O'Faolain argues:

■ Modern Irish literature is dominated by men so brilliant in their misanthropy – the great and elegant senses of chauvinists from Shaw and Wilde to Yeats, Joyce and Beckett – that if literature is a meaningful force, if it does arise from and reflect back upon the culture of its maker, if one knows the truth is valid on a timescale far beyond the individual life, then the self-respect of Irish women is radically and paradoxically checkmated by respect for an Irish national achievement.[42] □

O'Faolain proposes realism as a means of articulating the truth of women's experience as a counteraction against the unreal, figural tropes by which women are depicted in fantasy, myth and Modernism. She states plainly that 'It is the absence of realism from our great literary tradition which obliterates women. Because realism is the only mode available to women writers who want to write to and of women'.[43] While clearly wishing to acknowledge the achievements of a specifically Irish literary tradition, O'Faolain intimates that the development of feminism actually serves to undermine the nation or, at the very least, to uncover its inequalities: 'to women newly conscious of themselves, being Irish is neither here nor there, except to know that a vicarious share in male triumphs is no share at all'.[44] Realism, therefore, is to O'Faolain the means by which previous patriarchal untruths may be overturned and the newly feminist consciousness of women and their experience of the world may be testified.

In contrast, Eve Patten's 'Women and Fiction 1985–1990' (1990) is deeply suspicious of realism as a form of objective social truth. Patten implies that realism can actually be quite limiting with regard to the supposed social truth or reality which it allows to be represented. In particular, realism can merely endorse and reinforce a set of stereotypes about women and their experiences: 'the resort to confessional realism and the "biographical" structure are troubling in that they establish and confirm a norm – the struggling woman – contextualised by the particular social and political conditions by which she is determined, and exclusive of anything else'.[45] Which is to say, realism constructs codes of what is normal and permissible under the terms of its version of reality. Consequently, such delimitations are readily co-opted by existing patriarchal efforts to restrict the full range of female subjectivity and experience. As indicated by its title, Clair Wills's *Improprieties: Politics and Sexuality in Northern Irish Poetry* (1993) focuses on Northern Ireland and poetic form, and we will return to this book in the next chapter as a means of understanding the poetry of Medbh McGuckian. But more widely, Wills's work also provides a richly sustained and critical analysis of the politics of literary form and modes of representation that is highly germane to the discussion here. The ultimate implication of Wills's argument is that there is no neutral or objective representational form. Given that literary form is deeply imbedded in – and helps support – ongoing social, political and cultural practices, Wills avers that the task of a properly radical writing is to undermine dominant modes of representation rather than seek inclusion within them.

In this respect, Wills's work helps to distil core issues within feminism about language and form. The divisions between the private and public, the personal and the political, have always been key concerns of feminism given that patriarchy seeks to limit women to a domestic sphere and to exclude them from wider society. For feminists who espouse realism, it offers a means by which the excluded, private realm of female subjectivity may be made public. Thus a more rounded, more complete picture of society which includes women may be produced. In so doing, realism also helps to redress patriarchal imbalances by giving voice to women since, in the act of telling things as they really are, women writers thereby surmount their exclusion by making public their dissenting experience of it. However, Wills maintains that feminism does not merely need to produce or celebrate more women writers, the dissemination of whose work would therefore counteract the normal privileging of men's experiences. Rather, it is the modes of representation which produce the divisions of separate spheres, of public and private, and of gender demarcations, that need to be subverted. For Wills, a properly radical writing

■ is not the investigation and protection of interior space, it is not even the *addition* of that interior or private story to the public narrative. Instead this kind of aesthetic representation has an interventionist function. While engaging with the construction of political discourse in Ireland, it is saying to an iniquitous system of political representation, to, if you like, an unrepresentative bureaucracy – the normal processes of political negotiation have failed, and I will take no part in them.[46] □

So in terms of literary form, it is not simply the case of adding on the experiences of women to what is already established. Instead a more thorough undermining of existing literary forms is necessary so that liberated modes of subjectivity and experience can be disclosed. For Wills, a subversive literature would engage with exclusion, with the intimate or personal, but it would sunder the conventional patriarchal terms by which that personal space is usually conceived in opposition to a public sphere, and at the same time it would thereby undermine the basis of the public–private dichotomy by entirely re-conceiving the public in its own terms as well. Rather than seceding from the public realm, the intimate, the private or the enigmatic modes of women's writing can, therefore, also be directed outwards in a way that collapses the public–private division that would try to contain women's writing in the first place. But this subversion is only possible, in Wills's terms, if conventional languages and modes of representation are displaced and re-envisioned by more emancipating forms.

Comparably, Kathryn Kirkpatrick argues that the experience of Irish women does not only necessitate inclusion in the social spheres from which women were excluded, but it may also enable the renegotiation of the basis of those social spheres and their established forms: 'Irish women writers, with experiences as outsiders in both colonial and post-colonial contexts, can provide valuable alternative visions of community, identity, nation'.[47] So it is not just that the personal is political; rather the personal can transfigure the political and in so doing collapse the public–private opposition entirely. We noted in our discussion of Lavin and MacCarthy that both advanced a realist or social documentary mode of representing women's experiences but also that each wrote under the influence of Woolf, a writer is more closely associated with Modernist experimentation. Both Lavin, in her fiction, and MacCarthy, in her criticism, did share Woolf's aim of depicting repressed female subjectivities, even if their respective use and advocacy of form differed from straightforward Modernism. But Elizabeth Bowen's work perhaps takes us more towards a formal as well as a thematic affinity with Woolf. Indeed, Woolf did stay in Ireland at Bowen's ancestral home, Bowen's Court. We have already discussed Bowen in relation to a Modernist technique and through the lens of a declining Anglo-Irish Ascendancy in our previous chapter. Certainly, these determinants on Bowen's work should be properly accented. As Phyllis Lassner asserts: 'Bowen is a marginalized figure in several ways that are transformed imaginatively into a distinctive style and persona. Neither English nor Irish, she was born Anglo-Irish, an uneasy identity in both cultures'.[48] However, without forcing the issue, we could also suggest gender, however obliquely, as another determining factor on the form and technique of her fiction, in addition to her status as a marginal figure. In describing herself as one of Woolf's 'most zealous readers' and 'most jealous guardians', Bowen states that 'her aesthetic became a faith; we were believers'.[49] Undoubtedly Bowen's social class – especially as a member of the Anglo-Irish Ascendancy in the Free State – plays a significant part in shaping her work. But the gapped, deceptive fabric of her narratives, filled with suggestive aporia rather than social certainty, can perhaps also be understood in relation to the creative distance from established literary form that we have in this chapter related directly to gender politics.

In 'Why Do I Write?' (1948), Bowen registered an antipathy towards any effort to place her work in a definitive social context:

> ■ I feel irked and uneasy when asked about the nature of my (as a writer) relation to society. This is because I am being asked about the nature of something that does not, as far as I know, exist. My writing, I am prepared to think, may be a substitute for something I have been born without – a so-called normal relation to society.[50] □

It is telling that Bowen sees literature as a compensation for a 'normal' position in relation to society. In a sense, we can interpret Bowen's work as an effort to redefine the relations between the personal and the political, between the private and the social in a manner that does dovetail with the key feminist debates outlined in this chapter. The ambiguous, ambivalent tone and the lacunae-strewn narratives of Bowen's fiction do continually interrogate the social as an established, already-agreed concept, and subjective dissonance and figurative obliquity allow for no certain, singular conception of reality and truth. Indeed, part of Bowen's own artistic creed was to displace consensual stability with imaginative doubt and complexity, as she explains in 'Disloyalties' (1950):

> ■ Each time the writer disengages himself, convulsively, from a faith or theory, he spreads – and knows that he spreads – disarray in his readers' ranks: he has gainsaid the demand for stability. Does he now, then, it is asked, know his own mind? It is his own mind – and perhaps that only – with its demands and exactions and refusals to compromise, that he knows. He has once more imperilled good faith out of the need for truth – which for ever shifts and changes its form in front of him. It is when he seems most to be trusted that he mistrusts himself – may not his apparent arrival at any standpoint mean no more than a slackening-down of his faculties?[51] □

So in the context of our discussion of feminism, it is possible to find, in Bowen's self-consciously creative, enabling distance from social dogma and orthodoxy, a profound renegotiation of the relations between public and private, between a woman writer and society, that we could term proto-feminist at least.

Contemporary feminists have also reinterpreted in a similar way the work of Kate O'Brien. Eavan Boland, whose own work we will consider in detail in the next chapter, warns that it would be anachronistic to foist a contemporary feminist agenda onto O'Brien but she is equally eager to stress the capacity of O'Brien's fiction to disturbed established categories:

> ■ We live in a time when women writers of the past – they have no choice in the matter – are politicized by the present discourse about literature and gender. This is not the same as saying they are political writers. Therefore it seems especially important to me that they are not obliquely silenced by that politicization: that the complex refusals and ethical withdrawals which made up their world are not swept away by our own [...] Kate O'Brien was neither an Irish writer nor a woman writer in the accepted sense of those terms [...] new terms were therefore needed.[52] □

As to O'Brien's challenge to established categories, she does espouse – with a degree of affinity to Bowen's sense of the writer and society – a creative individualism that opposes itself resolutely to the modern world. This facet of her aesthetic is most clear in the autobiographical *Farewell Spain* (1937), which laments an individual freedom lost to both the rise of Fascism in Europe and modern, liberal democracy, even though she still hoped the latter would vanquish the tyranny of the former. Indeed, *Farewell Spain* resulted in her expulsion from Spain by the Fascist dictator General Francisco Franco (1892–1975, head of state 1939–75). In this book she wrote:

> ■ we children of the long shadows of individualism still hear a murmur in the shell for which we ask no explanation from without. It has a dying fall, perhaps, but we persist in straining for it. We seek the quickened sense of life, the accidents that jab imagination, for each of us believes the life of his breast to be his own and not a unit in another man's admirable sociological plan. We are in fact hopeless cases, who insist every now and then on getting away from it all.[53] □

However, as Gerardine Meaney summarizes: 'O'Brien outlines neither an aesthetics of indifference nor a cult of personality, but instead an aesthetics of dissidence'.[54] The effectiveness of this dissidence can be demonstrated by the fact that O'Brien's novel *Mary Lavelle* (1936) had been banned by the Irish Censorship Board due to the presence of a lesbian character and a sex scene, while *The Land of Spices* (1941) was also suppressed by the censors because of its homosexual references.

Indeed, *The Land of Spices* provides a highly dissident, yet subtle, means by which we can trace a subversion of state ideology – in this case, by taking what would apparently be one of its core institutional building-blocks, the Catholic Church, and inserting an individual re-appropriation of its central tenets and frameworks. The novel is set in the 1904–14 period in the context of the historical backdrop of the Revival and the Easter Rising. *The Land of Spices* attempts to use convent life at *Sainte Famille* not as a microcosm of the greater national religious unity and deference to authority but as a space whose cloistered position enables some degree of separation from the national life that it is actually intended to endorse. As the novel itself states: 'our nuns *are not* a nation and our business is not with national matters'.[55] To this end, Catriona Clear has argued in her study of nuns that, for all its limitations, religious vocation did supply women with some degree of autonomy and agency that was more completely denied in the society outside:

■ The convent was, indeed, offering women, especially middle-class women, an alternative to privatised domestic labour of whatever sort, from scrubbing to childbearing [...] The spread of active religious communities of women in Ireland came about at a time when the secular emphasis on women's primary domestic vocation was very strong. Most of the contemporary critics of convent life based their objections to religious women on what they saw as the flight of women from the protection – and, indeed, authority – of their father and brothers [...] the nun and the married woman [was each] called upon to serve, which was the function which women performed best [...] The Heavenly spouse did not, however, make his presence felt in the same way as the earthly spouse or male relative.[56] □

Correspondingly, Joan Hoff and Maureen Coulter contend that 'If voices of Irish women's history and solidarity begin anywhere, it is within religious sisterhoods'.[57]

However, Mary Breen offers a counter-argument which senses that the cloistered nature of the community in O'Brien's novel allows only for an attenuated freedom that does not resist but rather finally accedes to the marginalization of women from public life and culture. With reference to the French feminist Julia Kristeva (born 1941), Breen implies that seemingly willed separatism is actually forced exclusion:

■ a reading of the Sainte Famille as a counter-society would align O'Brien with [...] cultural feminists [...] who, in an attempt to reverse binarism, would like to see women embrace difference to the full in order to build a separatist female culture. It is from such a marginal and oppositional position that Julia Kristeva advocates that women should attack patriarchy. But [...] if women are to occupy a marginal position, then they are excluded from culture, and the polarisation of men and women and of male and female literature is further intensified.[58] □

Nonetheless, in taking recourse to Continental Europe to try to find some degree of individual freedom within a communal life, the novel does refract back sharply on the restrictions of society in the Irish Republic. Indeed, *The Land of Spices* provides a coded but clear undermining of the religious foundations of state censorship in the Republic. The nuns are told 'that a soul should not take upon itself the impertinence of being frightened for another soul; that God is alone with each creature'.[59] Hence the state's intervention as moral guardian against blasphemous or immoral books and films is seen to contradict the very religion it is designed to uphold. Moreover, Elizabeth Butler Cullingford argues that the juxtaposition of nationalism, authoritarianism and physical bullying in the character of Mother Mary Andrew constellates all of O'Brien's concerns at the ideological and ethical attenuations of the Irish State. The sadistic abuse which occurs in the convent can thus be linked to a wider critique, as Cullingford outlines:

> ■ It is produced by the combination of a 'neurotic' individual personality with a hegemonic church that for historical reasons is increasingly identified with the political aspirations of a nation. O'Brien's carefully nuanced analysis shows how a particular alignment between psychology, religion, and the state can produce the deformity of abuse.[60] □

In terms of gender politics and censorship in the Republic, we can also turn to John McGahern's work, not least to reaffirm that it is not only women that write about gender and sexuality, or for that matter, to dismantle the notion that there is some notional, transparent and stable masculinity against which all other subjectivities are judged. McGahern lost his teaching position on account of the ban imposed on his novel *The Dark* (1965). His fiction offers a stark portrayal of rural Ireland during times of cultural and economic insularity and repressiveness – a wider repressiveness that is often enacted through the patriarchy and the family. McGahern describes his own childhood as having a formative influence that can be traced in his fiction. Growing up in a rural police barracks in Leitrim because his father was a sergeant in the Garda Síochána, McGahern became acutely aware of both the poverty of the rural population and the hegemonic power of the Catholic Church: 'It was my first experience of the world as a lost world and the actual daily world as not quite real'.[61] This sense of the actual world as not quite real is played out in his writing, wherein, for all its obsessive detailing of a mundane reality, there is something overdetermined or implosive in its precision. Jürgen Kamm argues that McGahern is straightforwardly realist: 'It is entirely misleading to earmark McGahern as an experimental writer as his fictions are realistically told and the narrative tone is clearly indebted to the tradition of Irish story-telling'.[62] By contrast, Denis Sampson accepts that *The Dark* is 'a version of mid-twentieth-century realism' (though notably not realism itself), but he maintains that work such as *The Pornographer* (1980) 'demands a reading other than that given to conventional realism'.[63] Indeed, in an allusion to Medusa, the monstrous female figure in Greek mythology whose gaze could turn onlookers to stone but who was finally defeated by the cunning of Perseus and his use of his mirrored shield to approach Medusa without looking at her directly, McGahern himself asserts art is 'Medusa's mirror, which allows us to celebrate even the totally intolerable'.[64]

The apparently stultifying mimeticism of McGahern more often pushes writing beyond the limits of realist representation. Mimetic tendencies are frequently formally complicated by symbolic or allegorical structures beneath the surface of McGahern's work. We could draw a parallel with Brian Moore (1921–99), who, although from North Belfast, offers not only in his Belfast novels like *The Lonely Passion of Judith Hearne* (1955) but also in *Cold Heaven* (1983) or *The Colour of Blood* (1987), a form that is, if you will, realism but not quite. Terence Brown was perhaps the first critic to comment upon the nature of realism in Moore's work, upon how seemingly straightforward realist texts reveal under closer scrutiny 'something unsettling' and off-kilter.[65] Brown perceives that Moore's work explores the possibility that within 'the world in which realism seems an appropriate literary tool there may be things of which it cannot take account'.[66] With reference to McGahern, *Amongst Women* (1990), which is possibly his most well-known novel, contains precisely such formal tensions between an apparently claustrophobic realism and an underlying symbolic dimension. Antoinette Quinn posits that the novel signals a move away from the environment of the Big House tradition to the small house, to the experience of a rural Catholic family. For Quinn, *Amongst Women* therefore offers an interesting and sustained mediation on home and the family, the ideological building blocks of state ideology in the Republic: 'The syntax turns Moran and his house and farm into interchangeable entities, a complex of person and place that constitutes a fatherland'.[67] In particular, Quinn notes how Moran views his family as an extension or larger version of himself and she discerns in the military imagery of the power struggle between Moran and Rose an indication of the deep and gendered connections of nationalism and violence in the collective psyche.

In addition, Quinn argues that the enclosed rural world and the wider society of which it is an integral part disclose a profound contempt for the feminine: it is a world where the power of the paternal and patriarchal authority ousts the maternal and femininity. Hence, at the novel's close, Moran's daughters in a sense gain agency by becoming honorary males. Quinn adroitly surmises: '*Amongst Women* offers a penetrating critique of patriarchy as the refuge of the socially ill-adjusted and emotionally immature man and asks probing questions about the cult of the family'.[68] McGahern himself comments:

■ *Amongst Women* glorifies nothing but life itself, and fairly humble life. All its violence is internalised within a family, is not public or political; but it is not, therefore, a lesser evil. If the novel suggests anything, it is how difficult it is for people, especially women who until recently had no real power at all in our society, to try and create space to love and love in the shadow of violence. How they manage to do that in the novel becomes their uncertain triumph.[69] □

Thus, at one level, the novel grants a realistic indictment of an arch, controlling patriarch and a condemnation of the society he represents whose repressiveness includes a loathing of the feminine. Yet at another symbolically coded level, the identity of the apparent bastion of assured, authoritative masculinity, Moran, is sundered. For the novel's title, *Amongst Women*, not only details prosaically his day-to-day negotiations with his daughters at home but much more importantly it invokes directly the Virgin Mary through the words of the Annunciation and in turn the Rosary: 'Blessed Art Thou Amongst Women'. So the title of the novel actually serves to feminize and complicate Moran's identity and it places him in a continuum of male writing such as George Moore's trilogy of recollections *Hail and Farewell* (1911–14), whose Marian allusions make highly ambiguous his womanizing – in two senses – narrative identity.

So despite the realist detail, what is not said straightforwardly or mimetically is just as important as what is. It is in this spirit that Eamonn Hughes reads *Amongst Women*.[70] In terms of what is said and what is not said, Hughes observes that 'masculinity is an invisible but defining, defining because invisible, presence' in that it seeks both to make itself normal and set itself beyond definition. Hence, Hughes asserts, in the Irish constitution women are constantly defined, leaving men as the undefined norm.[71] It is notable in *Amongst Women* that when Moran writes to his daughter he does so in 'a clean bare style', in a manner that seeks to slip his own personality or at least achieve a kind of transparency.[72] Thus, power seeks to make itself normal, standard and transparent in the sense that otherness is defined in its difference or supposed deviance. In terms of gender, the non-realist elements of *Amongst Women* function symbolically to problematize and challenge the established assumptions of masculinity and identity. Hughes draws on the Revival and the fluid, troubled and unstable nature of masculinity that we discussed in relation to Yeats, Moore and Joyce, in order to insist that to accept masculinity as singular and coherent is to fall victim to what the dominant ideology intends. Particularly, Hughes contests the 'Fathers and Sons' section of Kiberd's *Inventing Ireland* which typifies critical readings of the father–son trope as a colonial-Oedipal masculinity by reference to the personification of Ireland as female and England as imperially male.[73] Hughes posits that this model tends to imply that the difficulties with masculinity in the Revival period and beyond are simply to be laid at the door of colonialism: that becoming a man is troublesome because the displacement or deferred imitation of the father will result in the potential male subject becoming a colonial mimic man. For Hughes, masculinity is much more ambiguous and this ambiguity arises not from a singular imposed colonial paternity but from the possibilities of masculinity, the range of forms beyond the dominant, approved versions.[74]

The unsettling of dominant modes of being, identity and belonging prepares us for our sixth chapter on contemporary literature in the Republic and the North. However, David Lloyd warns that any straightforward account of social change as progress should be problematized by acknowledging 'the displacement of indigenous forms of religion, labour, patriarchy and rule by those of colonial modernity'.[75] In other words, a new global set of power relations is taking the place of more traditional forms. While this chapter has indicated that no-one should bemoan the loss of 'indigenous' forms of patriarchy, Lloyd's point still pertains by alerting us in the following consideration of contemporary literature that ongoing concerns such as gender, class, power and marginality still prevail, in however modified a form amidst the economic change of the Celtic Tiger in the Republic and the Troubles and Peace Process in the North.

CHAPTER SIX

Contemporary Literature in the Irish Republic and Northern Ireland

Revisioning the Republic: McCabe, Tóibín, Banville

As the previous chapter suggested, John McGahern's *Amongst Women* helps illustrate a prevailing ideology of the Republic losing its normative status and, resultantly, its habituated silences become a problem rather than a sign that power needs no justification – where once the very fact of power was all the articulation it required. McGahern is therefore very much in keeping with a new dispensation in contemporary Republic culture and society. Amidst the celebratory tenor of the Celtic Tiger, a whole range of much more subterranean voices emerged restively at odds not only with the supposed economic successes of a new globalizing Ireland but also anxious to undercut the mythic past and the sacrosanct narrative of the nation. Indeed, Fintan O'Toole (born 1958) felt that by the 1990s the official narrative of Irish Nationalism had broken down and left a void which it could not itself fill: 'The grand narrative of Irish nationalist history has been destroyed, leaving a gap for the pop images to fill, not merely for the tourist but for the native as well'.[1] O'Toole's *A Mass for Jesse James: A Journey through 1980s Ireland* (1990) is perhaps the most sustained social commentary on a Republic which, in O'Toole's analysis, had lost the co-ordinates by which it had understood itself (in no small measure because those traditional codes were delusory to begin with) resulting in a deep malaise for people who had been happy to live in a dream Ireland until it became a nightmare. O'Toole viewed the 1980s as a 'petty apocalypse': the national debt was over 20 billion punts, there were a quarter of a million unemployed, while a quarter of a million emigrated, and one third of the population were living in poverty: 'A new Hidden Ireland came into being, an Ireland of undocumented aliens in their own country, invisible, unheard, with no official culture, no place in the sun'.[2]

With regard to culture, O'Toole's critique is important as it equates the social malaise with a profound imaginative dislocation and confusion that blurs reality and unreality, dream and nightmare. Making reference to a spate of reports of religious icons moving or shedding tears, the IRA Dirty Protests and Hunger Strikes in the North, political scandals and official discourse surrounding the abortion referendum of 1982, O'Toole comments:

> ■ Real life becomes as surreal as avant-garde art. How, for example, can a sculptor compete with moving statues? [...] The problem is not the problem of the way in which reality is to be aesthetically represented. It is the problem of dealing with a reality that is itself deeply aesthetic, inextricably bound up with the symbolic, the imaginary, the metaphorical.[3] □

In following O'Toole's diagnosis of a crisis in the official narrative of the Republic by the 1980s, we could argue that the dissenting visions in the literature we have examined so far had been present from the state's inception but that the decisive shift consists in the fact that such oppositional voices or divergent social experiences had become much more part of mainstream political debate and public consciousness. O'Toole regards the decade as the protracted process whereby a mainstream society set in dreamily innocent delusion by its own foundation finally had to confront the return of its repressed realities. O'Toole quotes the statement of then Taoiseach Charles Haughey (1925–2006; Taoiseach 1979–81, 1982, 1987–92) – 'When I talk about my Ireland I am talking about something which is not yet a complete reality. It is a dream that has not yet been fulfilled'[4] – in order to argue:

> ■ In the public language of Ireland in the eighties, the country was a dream, reality was incomplete, events were unbelievable even though they had happened, anything could mean everything, and everything was unprecedented [...] Traditional values needed to be publicly re-enforced precisely because they had ceased to have private meaning. The need for supposedly permanent values, for sets of words enshrined forever in a constitution, is at its greatest when nothing is really permanent.[5] □

So where Haughey, like de Valera back in St Patrick's Day 1943, continued to dream, the referenda on divorce and abortion signalled a clear insecurity about the material and constitutional realities of Ireland. If ever a writer fully actuated O'Toole's sense of there being so much body in the Irish body politic, of repressed but newly released energies rampantly transgressing the borders of official discourse, then it is the fiction of Patrick McCabe, whose grotesque, disrupted and disruptive bodies form part of a wider narrative insurgency against the officially sanctioned idealizations of both past and present. Tom Herron's essay 'ContamiNation: Patrick McCabe and Colm Tóibín's Pathologies of the Republic' (2000) provides an engaging examination of both McCabe and

Colm Tóibín as pursuing the darkest pathologies of the contemporary Republic. Herron argues that there is a continual tension in the work of both writers between the encroachment of a new Irish culture (driven by modernization, economic change, global telecommunications) and the vestiges of a 'traditional' Ireland (the family, the rural community, the official nationalist narrative and religious character of the state). Herron asserts that the fiction of McCabe and Tóibín should not be read as heralding the birth of a New Ireland or mourning the loss of an old one but rather as an uneasy and sometimes monstrous commingling of past and present: 'the interface between modernity and tradition is imagined by both writers as seriously pathological. This interface is a zone in which past and present contaminate each other; neither is settled or secure.'[6]

In McCabe, Herron identifies a continual revision and contamination of the official past, and so too, in Tóibín, a pervasive morbidity lurking underneath the impossibly heroic rhetoric of the State and emerging from its silences, in the petrifaction of state ideology. In the first sentence of McCabe's *The Butcher Boy* (1992), whose retroactive narration offers itself as a kind of national return of the repressed, there is a significant temporal slippage whereby the events could have happened 20, 30 or 40 years ago. Most specifically, the childlike narrative of the novel, which is, nonetheless, the actual voice of a middle-aged psychopath, Francie, is an apt medium for a return of the repressed. For just as Freud saw childhood as the causal site of both traumas and later repressions, so McCabe's novel sets about divesting the 1950s of its supposed innocence. *The Butcher Boy* locates in that decade child abuse, paedophile priests, social dysfunction and abject poverty amidst prosperity for a few, in a way that speaks directly to its own immediate context of official scandals and disclosures in the contemporary Republic. Herron notes that McCabe's novel is able to excavate the underside of official narratives of both tradition and modernization. *The Butcher Boy* addresses issues of family, community and religion at a key period (1957–62) in the history of the Republic when de Valeran socio-economic conservatism was finally supplanted by the modernizing vision of Seán Lemass (1899–1971, Taoiseach 1959–66). Although this period can be viewed as a time of liberalizing potential, Herron's analysis discerns how *The Butcher Boy* also links Francie's descent into madness with international events such as the Cuban Missile Crisis (1962) and the Cold War's nuclear threat of Mutually Assured Destruction. So while the novel does uncover the horrors beneath the innocent façade of a traditional Ireland, it also harbours a deep ambivalence about modernization.

In *The Butcher Boy*, the Nugent family represent and possess everything that is unavailable to Francie – a car, television, piano, boarding school for Philip – whereas Francie is a terminally damaged Borstal boy like his father. Indeed, McCabe's naming of the Nugents is deeply resonant since they represent a newly emergent middle class: they are 'new gents' – suggesting both a new bourgeois modernity and a con-comitant recasting of colonial forms of authority, an aping of the British gentry. The nicknaming of the Bradys as filthy 'pigs' is also telling since Francie ends up working in an abattoir helping to kill pigs in a sym-bolic act of self-annihilation. Francie inhabits a border zone between identities and ends up with none. In keeping with O'Toole's proposal of a cultural void, Francie notably does not know who he is nor how to behave, and though he tries to mimic a whole array of possible models of behaviour – his father, figures of authority, popular culture, comic books and film – none of these, tragically, enable him to construct a coherent identity of belonging. As Herron affirms, it is not so much that Francie disrupts a settled society and its mythical pastoral vision but instead he exposes its concealed, repressed and constitutive violence. Equally, though, Francie's character allows us to retain a circumspection about the dislocations of modernization and the disjuncture between the winners and losers or liberalization and economic change. For just as Francie represents the untold underside of de Valera's cosy vision of official nationalism, so too Francie is not included in the mainstream version of a new modern Republic.

Herron also discusses Tóibín's *The Heather Blazing* (1992) and relates how the name of its central figure, the judge Eamon Redmond, combines de Valera's first name with the surname of John Redmond (1856–1918), the leader of the Irish Parliamentary Party at Westminster from 1900 to 1918. Redmond supported the British war effort in 1914, a stance which led directly to a split in the Irish Volunteers and indirectly to the 1916 Rising, which in turn precipitated the eclipse of the Irish Parliamentary Party (IPP) by Sinn Féin in the 1918 General Election. So Redmond's name harnesses antagonistic histories and narratives, antagonisms that the official national narrative seeks both to repress and reconcile. Herron interprets the novel's continual metaphors of erosion, paralysis, aphasia, restriction and repetition as a critique of the republican nation-state, of what can be said and what cannot. As a judge, Redmond has the power to speak in court and to silence others, yet he is haunted by silences and absences; these are compounded by the strokes and physical and speech dysfunction suffered initially by his father and then his second wife Carmel. Herron notes that for all Redmond's imposition of silence on others in the public sphere, he is privately inexpressive to his wife, and unable to discuss his unmarried daughter's pregnancy. The Constitution is the script for his carefully prepared judgements or the political election rally speech he gives which he memorizes by heart. Yet he remains incapable of expressing himself privately. As Herron adroitly observes:

■ Under the thrall of the hieratic power of the Constitution, Eamon is a man who must be listened to in the public sphere, the one who hands down judgement from on high. In the private domain, however, he is the silent one, the one who cannot communicate, who will not speak, who cannot listen.[7] □

The conclusion of the novel is highly ambiguous – when playing on the beach with his grandson, Michael, Redmond goes to the sea to swim but realizes that the water is too cold for the youngster and returns to the shore. Throughout the novel, water functions as a space of non-meaning into which Redmond plunges to escape from the pressures of work, family and language. It is unclear whether, at last, communication or understanding happens but in that realm beyond language, or simply that another evasion and deferral has occurred. Herron recognizes the ambiguity of the novel's close but argues that it can be interpreted as gesturing, however uncertainly, to 'the promises of changed circumstances, to different ways of living, and to new discursive and emotional possibilities'.[8]

If *The Heather Blazing* does open up imaginative possibilities we can read Tóibín's writing more generally as a kind of Revisionism put into in literary practice. In his review of the *Field Day Anthology* he had pointedly opposed the possibilities of art to the circumscriptions of political fixity:

■ Each artist in the great Irish tradition has invented an Ireland. Each has done so in order to survive. Yeats's Protestant Ascendancy, Brian Friel's history lessons, Seamus Heaney's Catholic Derry childhood [...] In the Field Day enterprise itself, however, such manoeuvrings for the sake of art, such distortions, such single-mindedness have been stripped of their origin in artistic necessity and presented to us as a political manifesto, the political truth. A number of men have come to believe in their own dreams.[9] □

Another writer who can be thought of as a kind of oblique revisionist in his fiction is John Banville, who is keen to resist any overarching national aim or structure to literature by Irish authors: 'there is no such thing as an Irish national literature, only Irish writers engaged in the practice of writing'.[10] So although Banville is antipathetic to a national Irish literary canon, we can discern in his writing key techniques and tropes that he shares with a number of writers discussed in this guide – in addition to finding that his resistance to fixated, homogeneous renderings of truth is embedded in contemporary Irish literary debate. Banville's comment, that 'life is complicated, history does not run to symmetry',[11] is intended to challenge the ordering of life's contingencies by official narrative modes. Banville states polemically: 'Most of Irish writing is within a nineteenth-century tradition where the world is regarded as given. Everybody knows what the reality is and people sit down to write stories which occur in the known world with known values'.[12] In his own terms, Banville views his writing as self-referentially destabilizing the construction of truth and habituated knowledge: 'I wished to challenge the reader to go on suspending his disbelief in my fiction in the face of an emphatic admission on my part that what I was presenting *was* fiction and nothing more – and everything more'.[13]

Banville's sense of art's resistance to fixed ideologies of the self and identity also helps explain his recurrent use of twins and doubles in his fiction, as in *Birchwood* (1973) or even *The Untouchable* (1997) which is loosely based on the spy Anthony Blunt (1907–83) and the multiplicity of roles he performed. Banville asserts that the twin or double is 'a powerful metaphor for the act of fiction: in telling a story the writer too becomes someone else. But it goes much deeper than that [...] it's the divided self that everyone feels'.[14] However, in terms of doubleness there is an awareness, which is actually a recurrent one in Irish writing, of being immersed in someone else's communicative medium. Banville sees in the Irish use of English a consequent mistrustfulness of words:

> ■ What I am talking about is something subversive, destructive, and in a way profoundly despairing. Listen to any group of Irish people conversing, from whatever class, in whatever circumstances, and behind the humour and the rhetoric and the slyness you will detect a dark note of hopelessness before the phenomena of a world that is always *out there*.[15] □

Whether there are specific Irish determinants on the form and technique of Banville's work, or whether the reader wishes to place him more in a wider Western European intellectual milieu of a postmodern circumspection about representation and truth, Banville's fiction is undoubtedly self-consciously aware of its own medium and form and it refuses to accept language and representation as neutral or objective modes of figuring reality. Banville calls for 'an art which knows that truth is arbitrary, that reality is multifarious, that language is not a clear lens'.[16] Hence, in *Doctor Copernicus* (1976) there is a profound unease about the limits of science and truth, and representation itself. Copernicus's dialogue with Rheticus signals a loss of faith in the adequacy of his own means of expression and representation, and a collapse of the relationship between word and thing, discourse and experience. *Birchwood* sees Gabriel concede the arbitrariness of his own fictions and in *Kepler* (1981) and *Mefisto* (1986) it is the local and provisional that define 'truth'. Throughout his oeuvre Banville disrupts the totalizing role language plays in the functioning of knowledge and power. Hence, as Seán Lysaght confirms, 'there is no scope in this world for innocent mimesis'.[17] Joseph McMinn discerns that in Banville's writing: 'Language creates fictions, and should not be confused with a reality that invites perception but defies analysis'.[18] Additionally, Richard Kearney regards Banville as parodying and demythologizing the pieties of official national culture. In *The Newton Letter* (1982), for example, the narrator is entrapped in a labyrinth of indecisions and revisions, fictional interpretations which turn out to be mistaken, so that, Kearney argues, even the narrator's one 'real' experience – his affair – is 'conducted through the intermediary of a story, a memory. History keeps revising itself in the mind of the creator'.[19]

In the field of drama, there is perhaps no better an example of a play which engages with issues of historical revision than *Bailegangaire* (1984) by Tom Murphy. The play uncovers a lost history at odds with the conventional narrative of colonial subjugation and national liberation. Although the play was written in 1984 and Murphy was conscious of George Orwell's nightmare vision of totalitarian social control *Nineteen Eighty-Four* (1949), the play's account of the senile grandmother Mommo and her middle-aged granddaughters Mary and Dolly actually deals with lives who are definitely not the object of official scrutiny but are instead lost and vanquished. However, the play's historical revisions should also not simply be read as a bland endorsement of progress. As Nicholas Grene observes, *Bailegangaire* insists on poverty and social disadvantage as constitutive factors in Murphy's version of Irish history: 'His history is not that of Irish against English, Protestant versus Catholic, landlord and peasant; it is above all a history of poverty and its consequences'.[20]

The Western Ireland setting in the play is a direct re-working of the topography of Revival drama by the likes of Synge and Yeats, though notably outside Mommo's cottage there is a trade union meeting about the future of a Japanese-owned computer factory and *Bailegangaire* accesses the lives of those marginalized by the new Republic of economic boom and global technology. The fragmentary, jumbled histories which Mommo grotesquely narrates disclose a profound degree of historical rupture and exclusion. Grene argues that the plight of the play's three main female characters, in addition to foregrounding poverty and the deprivations of social class, also offers a stringent feminist critique that confronts

> ■ the problems of latter-day Irish women with an inheritance of repressive patriarchy. Murphy's Ireland involves a reconception of the country cottage of Synge, Yeats and Gregory to create an Irish drama which tells a different story from the theatre of national politics.[21] □

To that end, the next section will begin with an appraisal of the poetry of Eavan Boland which also offers a feminist redress to culture in the Irish Republic.

Gender, class, pluralism and the Republic

In an *Irish Times* review, Boland questions Heaney's objections to being
included in *The Penguin Book of Contemporary British Poetry* (1982) in
terms that disclose her own sense of her own writing and the claims
laid upon it: 'Poetry is defined by its energies and its eloquence, not
by the passport of the poet or the editor; or the name of the nationality. That way lie all the categories, the separations, the censorships
that poetry exists to dispel'.[22] Boland pitches her writing as a feminist
intervention in the context we have established wherein a nationalist
iconography deploys women merely as symbols or ciphers. Her work,
Boland asserts, induces 'the strange scenario of what happens to a tradition when previously mute images within it come to awkward and vivid
life: when the icons returns to haunt the icon-makers'.[23] Indeed, Boland
regards the very fact of the assertion of her poetic voice – whatever its
subject – as a politically and socially resonant act: 'merely by the fact
of going upstairs in a winter dusk, merely by starting to write a poem
at a window that looked out on the Dublin hills, I was entering a place
of force. Just by trying to record the life I lived in the poem I wrote, I
had become a political poet'.[24] So even the most personal experience
is political, in feminist terms, where the experiences of women have
been denied access to the public spaces of society. Boland writes that
the poem is where she can 'follow my body with my mind and take
myself to a place where they could heal in language: in new poems, in
radical explorations'.[25] So her work offers a feminist space in which the
repressed agency of both women's bodies or corporeal realities and
their voices may take shape and articulate their prior exclusion, sup-
pression and suffering. With regard to Boland's critical reception, however, Edna Longley accepts that Boland undertakes a feminist project
that redraws the conventional subject but argues that it fails to achieve
a similar subversion of the nation. As part of her attack on how feminism in Ireland has been hampered by nationalist paradigms, Longley
writes:

■ The Northern women's movement has been divided and retarded; while the
Southern movement, preoccupied with church-and-state, has largely avoided
'nation'. Eavan Boland's feminist poem 'Mise Eire' (I am Ireland) destabilises
Mise but not Eire – 'my nation displaced / into old dactyls'. There is some
reluctance, partly for fear of further division, to re-open the ever-problematic,
ever-central issue of 'Nationalism and feminism'.[26] □

For Longley, Boland's poetry leaves the nation unreformed and its
national narratives undisturbed by seeking to find room for women
within existing traditions and assumptions.

A slightly different though comparable challenge to Boland's work is provided by Clair Wills who does admittedly view Boland as a kind of cultural 'suffragette' engaged in making literature more representative of society through the inclusion of female perspectives. Wills observes that 'a trope of privacy appears in place of the motherland trope, the function of which is to allow women to accede to the role of poet'.[27] Yet Wills is suspicious that Boland's effort to make Irish literature more representative with regard to gender is doomed to fail because the trope of privacy leaves unchallenged the basis and foundation of the (patriarchal) national tradition to which Boland seeks access. So both Longley and Wills would maintain that it is precisely that national tradition which has excluded women in the first place. It is therefore unlikely that any attempt at inclusion within the existing terms of that tradition will amount to anything more than tokenism or indeed the depleted appropriation of women's voices by the authority of the national tradition. By contrast, Boland clearly feels that she can enrich and expand the nation rather than merely reject it out of hand: 'I wanted to relocate myself within the Irish poetic tradition. I felt the need to do so. I thought of myself as an Irish poet, although I was fairly sure it was not a category that readily suggested itself in connection with my work'.[28]

In addition to the issues which Longley and Wills raise about Boland's attitude to the national tradition, Gerardine Meaney is circumspect about the feminist import of Boland's writing. Meaney asserts that it is not only nation that remains in its unchecked unitary state, but also femininity which remains an already-agreed and already-defined identity, in Meaney's terms, 'a homogenous and self-contained entity'.[29] However, a much more positive evaluation is proffered by Andrew J. Auge, who wishes to resist to these critiques of Boland's work as simplistic in both national and feminist terms. For Auge both gender and nation in Boland's poetry are never fixed or secure entities but always fissured and multiple:

■ Throughout Boland's poetry, a profoundly lyric sensibility intersects with an exilic sense of displacement, generating verse in which intimacy and estrangement are frequently conjoined. Ironically, this is nowhere more evident than in Boland's poetic reflections on maternity, the supposed locus of her essentialism.[30] □

The poetry of Brendan Kennelly also intervenes in debates about the national narratives and the iconography of the nation, perhaps most directly in *Cromwell* (1977). This complex imaginative voyage works through Oliver Cromwell (1599–1658) – somewhat understandably a hate-figure for Irish Nationalism – and his alter ego *Buffún* in order to tap into key psychic touchstones and tensions in the national imagination. For Richard Kearney, it is the freedom which Kennelly's individual, artistic imagination achieves that overturns outworn, collective ideological stereotypes. According to Kearney, Kennelly's poem, by tangling its competing versions of Cromwell, refutes any notion of a pure or unitary Irish identity and history. In addition, the poem acknowledges the fracture of Irish history, yet at the same time moves beyond the ruins of the past by creating a new, imaginatively liberated mythology:

> ■ the poet imagines the possibility of another kind of home in history [...] Kennelly is liberated into a positive ignorance, free to reconnect with foreclosed dimensions of being. The dissolution of orthodox myth releases new energies for the re-creation of utopian myth.[31] □

Kearney's post-nationalist perspective is also drawn to the poetry of Paul Durcan, whom he considers 'one of the most innovative and iconoclastic of the younger generation of Irish poets'.[32] For Kearney and critics of a Revisionist or post-nationalist mind, Durcan, who is the son of a judge in the Irish Republic, offers a body of writing which seeks to find in poetry imaginative possibilities and alternatives to official nationalist doctrine. Durcan's sequence, 'Daddy, Daddy', in his collection *Daddy, Daddy* (1990) offers a kind of generational rite of passage through which the poet is able to think afresh. Edna Longley reads the sequence, in which father and mother function to symbolize, respectively, what is endorsed or legitimized by the state and that which is repressed yet still offers liberating potentialities, as an attempt to construct a kind of matriarchal utopia that dissolves the social and patriarchal authority embodied by the poet's father. Longley maintains that Durcan's poem offers 'an originary speech which the state or Nation has forgotten, but poetry, women and the father's better self remember. Durcan's future-oriented (epochal) vision undermines patriarchal foundations by imagining [...] a new symbolic order'.[33] Moreover, and by way of indicating that Revisionism is informed not just by social change in the Republic but also by the conflict in the North, Neil Corcoran finds in Durcan's poetry 'a view of the North which flies in the face of all nationalist sentiment with a critique of the IRA and its apologists'.[34] However, we can regard not only official nationalism but also the post-nationalist narrative of a new, plural Republic buoyed by the economic boom of the Celtic Tiger as an emergently dominant version of the South.

As with the lost voices of McCabe's fiction or Murphy's play *Bailegangaire*, the politics of social class, and, in particular, the plight of the Dublin working-class drives a body of writing termed, by turns, 'Northside Realism', 'Dirty Realism' or 'Dublin Realism', which once more seeks to undermine official discourse, but in this case by depicting the urban deprivation that is the flipside of the Celtic Tiger. The fiction of Dermot Bolger has spearheaded this movement, while the Booker Prize-winning Roddy Doyle perhaps offers it a more mainstream gloss. Of all the criticism of this form of Dublin writing, perhaps most notably it is Declan Kiberd who maintains that it exaggerates and oversimplifies inequality and poverty in the contemporary Republic. Kiberd attacks Bolger's *The Journey Home* (1990) and *The Woman's Daughter* (1987; revised and enlarged edition, 1991) as much less subversive than they would appear. Specifically, Kiberd finds a gross exaggeration of the social tyranny of priests, teachers and politicians in Bolger's work and a simultaneous sentimentality in the representation of young people as victims. Kiberd posits that Bolger resorts to 'the conceptual clichés of a strangely caricatured Dublin landscape of horses in high-rise flats and doomed young things in squalid bed-sits'.[35] Ironically, therefore, in Kiberd's analysis, Bolger's fiction does not instigate a new, gritty urban writing in the Republic but instead reinforces existing pastoral versions of Ireland by implying that the city is a hellish and finally impossible place to live.

Nevertheless, in 'The Right to the City: Re-Presentations of Dublin in Contemporary Irish Fiction' (2000), Gerry Smyth offers a more approving interpretation of *The Journey Home* which suggests that Bolger's work is much more nuanced than Kiberd would allow. Smyth regards the novel as appearing to want to move beyond the hellish city and deadening suburbs to a mythical home beyond Dublin but yet actually mapping out a more complex sense of the city. The flux and change – for better and for worse – of city life in *The Journey Home* provide a means, Smyth contends, of finding alternatives to both stultifying squalor and an irrecoverable rural ideal:

■ If this is where Northside Realism left itself vulnerable to accusations of counter-mythologizing, it is also where it begins to move back towards Joyce and his representations of the city as a space offering modes of experience above and beyond the limiting terms of the national imagination.[36] ☐

In Smyth's terms, Bolger's fiction not only and necessarily attests to urban poverty but also grasps the city as a space whose complications, contingencies and unrelenting movement provide a means of forging new identities which are neither fixed, stable nor homogeneous and which therefore counterpoint the ordering of the official national narrative: 'Dublin is [...] increasingly the arena in which the paradoxes, ironies and complexities of a modern Irish identity are played out. As the supremely ambivalent national space, it is, after all, eminently endowed to do so'.[37]

In his book *The Novel and the Nation* (1997), which provides a good survey of contemporary Irish fiction more generally, Smyth also makes a case for Doyle's work that pays specific attention to its narrative form and technique. Smyth regards voice in Doyle's fiction, and Doyle's effort to allow his characters to speak in their own idiom rather than being superintended and regulated by an omniscient narrative discourse, as facilitating a democratic process that blurs the conventional linguistic hierarchy of the novel wherein vernacular or demotic voices are explained and controlled by a standardized voice. In turn, Smyth continues, this formal technique also democratizes the reading process for it is the reader who actively fills in the gaps in the narrative rather than being passively directed by an authorial narration:

> ■ Doyle refuses to patronise or pander to the reader by telling everything about the characters or the action; by the same token, his novels insist that the reader does not adopt an ironic or patronising tone with regard to the characters or their concerns, but takes the world of the text on its own terms.[38] □

If the occluded realities of working-class life concerned the counter-imagining of the city in 'Dublin Realism', writing by a number of contemporary women writers highlights ongoing repressions surrounding gender and sexuality. In her article, 'Petrifying Time: Incest Narratives from Contemporary Ireland' (2000), Christine St Peter examines the work of Dorothy Nelson (born 1952) and Edna O'Brien in the context of domestic violence and abuse that is either systemically hidden or even condoned. Indeed, St Peter points to an instance in 1995 when the Court of Criminal Appeal decided to reduce the sentence of a man who raped his daughter's 14-year-old friend in 1992 (in the immediate aftermath of which the state tried to prevent the victim and her parents from travelling to England to obtain an abortion). This incident directly impinges on O'Brien's novel *Down By the River* (1987) but St Peter locates an important precursor to that work in Dorothy Nelson's *In Night's City* (1982). This novel is an unremitting, bleak and claustrophobic account of a family damaged by violence and its narrative moves between Sara, an abused girl, her mother Esther and Maggie, Sara's alter ego. Comparably, O'Brien's *Down By the River* details the story of Mary MacNamara, a 14-year-old girl who has been raped by her father and it takes the bullying father figure of O'Brien's earlier novels, such as *The Country Girls* (1960) or *A Pagan Place* (1971), to a brutal extreme. *Down By the River* is also notable in O'Brien's oeuvre in that it moves from the private realm of her earlier fiction into the public and political sphere and it seeks to make the whole of society guilty. There is a different trajectory from *In Night's City*, and O'Brien's novel concludes very ambiguously with Mary dreaming of happier times and a happier nation, as she rises to sing at a disco sometime in an indeterminate future. St Peter comments:

■ the rebirth of hope in Mary's heart may suggest more than just a romantic dream, although it is certainly that [...] Having witnessed petrifying horrors, the reader is now privy to tentative hope. But *Down By the River*, like *In Night's City*, pushes the imagination beyond the fictive text and into the world where real change has to be created.[39] □

Antoinette Quinn's 'New Noises from the Woodshed: the Novels of Emma Donoghue' (2000) gleans its title from Donoghue's survey of Irish lesbian fiction, 'Noises from the Woodshed', which itself honours Mary Dorcey's collection of lesbian short fictions, *A Noise from the Woodshed* (1989).[40] Quinn asserts that the fiction of Emma Donoghue articulates lesbian experience in the Republic in a more confident manner than before while not shying away from homophobia. Quinn regards Maria Murphy's journey in *Stir-Fry* (1994) as signalling an effort by Donoghue to tap into a broader coming into consciousness in Irish society. Subsequently, Donoghue's *Hood* (1995) focuses on single week in the life of Pen, or Penelope O'Grady, following the death of her lover Cara, and the narrative works through flashbacks back across their relationship. While Pen does come out to her mother, Quinn asserts that the novel is more complex than this stock lesbian fictive trope as it deals with the emotional depth of its lesbian relationship in a manner that is less about either stigmatizing or exotic interest and more concerned with humanizing and integrating Pen's experience:

■ In refusing to construct a monument to gay pride or to gay victimization, Donoghue brings the Irish lesbian novel out of the ghetto. Towards the end of the narrative, Pen, observing the Saturday afternoon shoppers on Grafton Street, experiences an epiphany of a human continuum of grief and suffering that transcends barriers of sexual or political identity.[41] □

So across the literature and criticism we have covered, there are clear interstices where tradition and modernity collide, where older forms of culture and identity residually blunt newer constellations. But we have sought to retain an awareness that such changes, particularly as they apply to gender, sexuality or social class, are not always uncomplicatedly affirmative and may actually be, in some cases, harbingers of new forms of disadvantage and disenfranchisement. Ray Ryan's edited collection, *Writing the Irish Republic: Literature, Culture, Politics 1949–1999* (2000), provides an array of critical voices who are all attuned to the changes which have occurred in the Republic. In Ryan's own contribution, he arraigns what he deems a detached and individualized liberal pluralism. Ryan argues:

> ■ Liberalism must offer some substantive and coherent conception of what is good, and not withdraw to hermetic and private universes in defence of the right not to be assaulted by tradition and history. In Ireland, our conception of ourselves as private citizens is not, after all, completely divorced from the public identity we establish through cultural practice.[42] □

That is, such forms of liberalism are a privileged disengagement bought by a secure social status which allows for a wishy-washy rather than a substantively meaningful assertion of individual freedom. In a sense, the new pluralism is fine for those who can afford it, a luxurious detachment in which less empowered groups in society have no stake. We will bear Ryan's forceful point in mind as we turn to contemporary Northern Irish literature, for in the critical accounts of it we again find tensions between the traditional and the new. Specifically, the political conflict and the Peace Process, which followed it, provide a forum for contemporary critics to intervene in issues of profound social and cultural change.

Contemporary literature and the North: Heaney, history and the Troubles

The violence in the current phase of the Troubles in the North, which began in the mid-1960s with a series of Loyalist murders and attacks and escalated around 1969 with the arrival of British troops and the formation of the Provisional IRA, places enormous, at times impossible, pressure on writing and culture to respond, articulate or resolve. Writers found themselves being shuffled, rightly or wrongly, into polarized sectarian camps or constituencies, and either willingly assented or resisted. As we will discuss, literature has been regarded, variously, as complicit in the conflict, irresponsibly detached from it, or as a site of restorative perspectives and alternatives. Edna Longley, for example, in *The Living Stream*, acknowledges the problems and losses of the Troubles but also views the North as offering possibility as much as entrenchment. Longley sees the Troubles as the culmination of the imperatives of the exclusive, intransigent dominant ideologies of Irish Nationalism and Unionism, yet she also proposes the North as 'a cultural corridor', a space of ambiguity and interchange where the dominant ideologies may be seen to break down and be surmounted: 'a zone where Ireland and Britain permeate one another'.[43]

Similarly, Richard Kirkland interprets the conflict in the North less as a self-contained aberration and more as an opportunity to dissect prevailing ideologies: 'Northern Ireland offers itself as an implicit critique of both the bourgeois liberal British state and the triumph of the bourgeois-nationalist project in the Republic.'[44] Furthermore, Eamonn Hughes insists that the North should not be seen as a place apart, as an anachronistic, stagnant blight cordoned off from the rest of the world where change does happen. Hughes argues that the Troubles are part of a set of wider, international processes of change from the 1960s to the present, which includes Civil Rights protests in the US and elsewhere, uprisings in Paris by students and workers, profound socio-economic transformation and a world where traditional borders and boundaries are being redrawn or transgressed. Hughes reads Northern Ireland, being both British and Irish at once, as part of a highly modern dilemma and dislocation:

■ Northern Ireland is a place in which identity does not confront difference; rather identity is difference [...] identity must always be formed on terms of intimacy with whatever one chooses to regard as the other. Far from making Northern Ireland a peculiar place, from which the modern world turns embarrassed equally by its anachronism and passion, this makes it central to the experience of the modern world.[45] □

While acknowledging the damage done by sectarian violence, Hughes maintains that possibilities also emerge from 'the always-at-least-dual nature of the Northern Irish and their cultures, which is made possible by the recognition that borders can be crossed'.[46] For Hughes, the point of sectarianism and the mainstream account and management of the Troubles according to a sectarian paradigm are attempts to thwart those processes of change. Hughes is especially keen to resist depictions of Northern Ireland as historically static because it has achieved its fate, in the sense that the conflict is interpreted as merely culminating an intractable sectarian history. With regard to culture, Hughes observes how the thriller form (in both fiction and film about the North) is most often used to shore up this kind of interpretation of Northern Ireland as an irresolvable, strange anomaly, as in *Patriot Games* (1987) by Tom Clancy (born 1947). Hence, Hughes asserts that when Irish writers employ the thriller form to deal with the conflict in the North, as with *Proxopera: A Tale of Modern Ireland* (1977) by Benedict Kiely (1919–2007), *Cal* (1983) by Bernard MacLaverty's (born 1942) or Brian Moore's *Lies of Silence* (1990), more often than not they recapitulate and reactivate this view of the North as fated, enclosed and irresolvable: 'The failure of the novel in regard to Northern Ireland is that, by accepting the image of the North as fate, it has not allowed for the interplay of characters, form and circumstances'.[47]

Seamus Heaney's work comprises one of the most sensitive but also, for some, controversial efforts to deal with the pressures of contemporary Northern society. Heaney was at times criticized by some Nationalists for not voicing their concerns directly enough yet he was also threatened by Loyalists and consequently left the North for the Republic in the 1970s due to those death threats, as poignantly meditated upon in his poem 'Exposure'. Heaney acknowledges the enormous weight placed upon him as a writer: 'The main tension is between two often contradictory commands: to be faithful to the collective historical experience and to be true to the recognition of the emerging self'.[48] Resultantly, Heaney's poetry is highly charged with both a need for artistic freedom and an obligation to find an imaginative means of responding to the conflict in the North. Heaney, as with most writers of his generation, found that trying to compete with media images, with photographs of killings and television footage of bomb blasts, was ill-conceived and instead he and others sought more oblique or considered means of trying to comprehend events. With a backward glance to our discussion of the gender politics of the Revival period, it is striking that Heaney's sense of the antagonistic core Northern conflict is structured by a highly gendered model of feminine Irish and masculine British polarities:

■ There is an indigenous territorial numen [a presiding spirit or deity], a tutelar of the whole island, call her Mother Ireland, Kathleen Ni Houlihan, the poor old woman, the Shan Van Vocht, whatever; and her sovereignty has been temporarily usurped or infringed by a new male cult whose founding fathers were Cromwell, William of Orange [1650–1702; King of England 1689–1702] and Edward Carson [1854–1935], whose Godhead is incarnate in a rex or Caesar resident in a palace in London.[49] □

Elsewhere Heaney writes of the rosary: 'all the devotions were centred towards a feminine presence [...] There's something faintly amorous about the "Hail Mary"'.[50] So it is tempting to discern a melding of Nationalist and Catholic (male) imaginations in Heaney's gendered account of the conflict, its structural causes and necessary sacrifices to this feminine presence. Most particularly, Heaney's own mission to find historical parallels or other cultural and political situations by which he could comprehend and contextualize the Troubles was sharply focused P. V. Glob's *The Bog People* (1965; trans. 1969). Glob's book detailed a series of archaeological finds in Scandinavia in which the bodies of the victims of ancient sacrificial rites were exhumed, having been preserved for centuries in peat bogs. Notably, Heaney discovers in these archaeological specimens not merely parallel deaths with which to compare contemporary violence but, more resonantly for him, confirmation of recurrent historical patterns of violence and human behaviour:

■ Taken in relation to the tradition of Irish political martyrdom for that whose cause is Kathleen Ni Houlihan, this is more than an archaic barbarous rite: it is an archetypal pattern. And the unforgettable photographs of these victims blended in my mind with photographs of atrocities, past and present, in the long rites of Irish political and religious struggles.[51] □

In part, Heaney's recourse to archetypes and archetypal patterns through which to understand the Troubles as the return of inexorable imperatives is due to his reading of the psychology of Carl Jung (1875–1961) with its masculine and feminine archetypes of *animus* and *anima*, and its assertion that there is a supra-historical collective unconscious which shapes culture and society.[52] Indeed, with regard to efforts to transpose this kind of archetypal psychology onto the social conflict in the North, it can be observed, admittedly somewhat mischievously, that there is a curious correlation between Jung's ideal self and the Field Day vision, of which Heaney was a part, of a 'fifth province'. Jung's idealized and total self contains a secret, resolving centre: 'it is as if the leadership of affairs had gone over to an invisible centre'.[53] Field Day's utopian impulse of a fifth province borrows from Mark Hederman and Richard Kearney in the journal *The Crane Bag*, where they noted that Irish word for province is *cóiced*, meaning fifth. Hence, they propose 'Uisneach, or the secret centre, was the place where all oppositions were resolved, the primeval unity'.[54] Accordingly, Field Day took up this idea of a fifth province, as described by Brian Friel: 'A province of mind through which we hope to devise another way of looking at Ireland, or another possible Ireland ... a place for dissenters, traitors to the prevailing mythologies in the other four provinces'.[55] Moreover, one of the paradigms of the *'mandala'* – a recurrent symbol of the self concentrically arranged in the dreams of the Jungian collective unconscious – is a fourfold geometric figure structured around a central point that is echoed in the Field Day conception of an Ireland in which the secret centre of Uisneach configures and totalizes the four actual provinces.[56]

To return to Heaney, in addition to trying to find a historical structure in his bog poems through which to understand the Troubles, Heaney's poetry also reworked its own existing sense of place and landscape as a means of considering the conflict in communal, territorial terms. From the first poem of his first collection, 'Digging', Heaney had clearly rooted his work in the ground of his own locale and the influence of Kavanagh's universal parish is evident in both *Death of a Naturalist* (1966) and *Door into the Dark* (1969). However, by his third collection, *Wintering Out* (1972), Heaney resolved to 'politicize the terrain and the imagery of the first two books'.[57] Hence, poems such as 'Broagh' and 'Anahorish', open up the familial belonging of the parish to a wider communal territorial claim in which language, self and place cohere in establishing an identity that excludes those deemed outsiders or others. To this end, Heaney asserts that 'I think that poetry and politics are, in different ways, an articulation, an ordering, a giving form to inchoate pieties, prejudices, worldviews, or whatever. And I think that my own poetry is a kind of slow, obstinate papish burn, emanating from the ground I was brought up on'.[58] This effort to ground both his own communal identity and a concomitant understanding of the political violence culminates in *North* (1975), which for his more severe critics, finds Heaney becoming bogged down in his own archetypal patterns. Indeed, it is noteworthy that, in contrast to the sensual immediacy and perceptive paths of his earlier poems – which owe something to the nature poetry of Ted Hughes (1930–98) – *North* was conceived according to a template: 'I'm certain that up to *North*, that that was one book; in a way it grows together and goes together ... I had a notion of *North*, the opening of *North*: those poems came piecemeal now and again, and then I began to see a shape. They were rewritten a lot'.[59] Hence, some critics argue that *North* is too preconceived and the poetry consequently becomes petrified both formally and imaginatively, losing the sense of discovery of his earlier work. Edna Longley contends that the poems in *North* polarize 'song and suffering ... as if history were only suffering and poetry were only song'.[60] Notably, Paul Muldoon, when compiling his *Faber Book of Contemporary Irish Poetry* (1986), almost completely ignored *North* and Heaney's bog poems, while we will consider the objections of Ciaran Carson to Heaney's archetypal method below in relation to Carson's own work.

However, Neil Corcoran finds all Heaney's work, including *North*, 'scrupulously self-critical, it constantly makes enquiry into its own resources and potential, its affiliations and responsibilities; into, in the end, its own exemplary status'.[61] Corcoran argues that Heaney's early poetry takes self-instruction on its own art by drawing analogies between his writing and the agricultural labour of his family and community. In this continuum of labour dedicated to the service of the community, poetry thus becomes part of the community's work, even if these analogies assuage an anxiety or guilt about Heaney's education and literary career divorcing him from the experiences of that community. Corcoran maintains that the relationship between the poetic self and the community is always a complex and reflective one that is not as reductive or straightforward as some critics assume. Corcoran focuses on the landscape poem 'Gifts of Rain', from *Wintering Out*, and its ghostly voices imploring Heaney not to forget the Famine, as a means of understanding the development of Heaney's work towards *North*. Here, for Corcoran, Heaney's poetic self is responsively alert to the voices of its communal ancestry who had been consigned to silence. The poetic and the political are collapsed together since the poetic self assumes its self-conferred responsibility for articulating communal concerns. But this responsibility is not without self-reflection. Consequently, Corcoran interprets the counsel offered by the Viking longship in the title poem of Heaney's most controversial collection, 'North', in a manner very different from critics who dismiss Heaney's inexorable historical parallels of violence. Corcoran accepts that the Viking voices do indeed insist on an atavistic imperative of violence that takes Heaney to 'kinds of recognition not normally made in civilized literary discourse', but he asserts that Heaney's poetry remains self-dividedly alert to its own potential to give offence'.[62]

In his own terms, Heaney posits that *North* and his next collection *Field Work* (1979) were 'negotiating with each other'.[63] And Corcoran's analysis allows us to comprehend how this dialogue is anticipated by 'Exposure', the closing poem of *North*, which undercuts the historical and political certainties of the rest of the collection and returns to the speculative range of his earlier work, while also adumbrating his interrogation of political and communal belonging in *Field Work* and individual poems like 'Casualty'. Corcoran reads 'Exposure' as a poem guided by the tentative, muted counsel of the rain: 'The rain is therefore a counsellor who feelingly persuades the Heaney of 'Exposure' what he is: not committed to the solidarity of an original community, but anxiously, even guiltily, pledged to the complicated freedoms and responsibilities of the poem itself.'[64]

Indeed, Heaney remarked that after *North*: 'I no longer wanted a door into the dark – I want a door into the light'.[65] There is a move away from the dark historical imperatives of *North* and the literally grounded certainties of identity and belonging are displaced by differing elements of air, light and water in subsequent collections. An instructive way by which readers can assess a shift in Heaney's aesthetic is to consider the change in attitude to Kavanagh's parish in his critical work: the more grounded home turf of the essay 'From Monaghan to the Grand Canal' is transfigured in 'The Placeless Heaven' where Heaney accredits Kavanagh's parish with a visionary lucency that transforms 'luminous spaces'.[66] In his poetry, we can follow this imaginative reconstruction and reclamation of the parish through the early poems to 'Glanmore Sonnets', 'The Harvest Bow', 'The Mud Vision' and the lambency of 'Clearances' in *The Haw Lantern* (1987).

Given the highly gendered structure of Heaney's archetypal understanding of the conflict in the North, there have been a number of important feminist critiques of his work. Patricia Coughlan offers a thorough analysis in which she compares the female figures of Heaney's poetry with those of John Montague (born 1929). As with our discussion of gender and nation in Chapter Six, Coughlan asserts that female figures appear in various guises in the work of both Heaney and Montague but they do so once more merely as ciphers facilitating the voice of male subjectivity. Coughlan observes:

> ■ A particular contradiction is discernable in Montague and Heaney between the project of speaking for a politically oppressed and therefore hitherto unspoken group, Northern Catholics [...] and their failure, in general, to perceive their own reliance upon and tacit approval of the absence of women as speaking subjects and of female disempowerment.[67] □

This process, according to Coughlan, may be traced in the hag figures of Montague poems such as 'The Sean Bhean Bhocht', 'The Music Box' or 'Procession', or the mythic maternal and goddess personae of 'The Leaping Fire', 'For the Hillmother' or 'The Hero's Portion'. So too Heaney's work, from his earlier parish landscapes to his more politicized middle-period terrain, tends to displace women even when seemingly offering a voice to the experience of women as in 'The Wife's Tale'. Indeed, Heaney's 'Punishment', which parallels ancient sacrifice with the punishment of young Catholic women in Derry who socialized with British troops, is one of the most controversial poems in *North* and it, like the communitarian imperative it shares, belies a specifically male anxiety about the control and possession of women as guarantors of tribal purity. Coughlan argues the poem's apparent effort to sympathize with the plight of the victim is undermined by both the communal identification of the poetic voice with the punishers and the masculine subjectivity of the poet's gaze: 'The compassion is equivocal not just because of the half-sympathy with the punishers, but because of the speaker's excitement at the scopic spectacle of the girl's utter disempowerment'.[68]

However, we can also note that Heaney places 'Punishment' in direct dialogue in *North* with 'Strange Fruit', which gleans its title from the Billie Holiday (1915–59) version of a blues song about racism in the United States – the strange fruit being the burned, mutilated bodies of African Americans lynched and hanged from trees by white racist mobs. 'Strange Fruit', while featuring another female victim, revises 'Punishment' for in this case the victim remains nameless and horrific, she cannot be named and made archetypal and mythically and tribally significant as the victims of 'Punishment' are. Indeed, the corpse in 'Strange Fruit' outstares and resists the gaze of the poet. But with regard to gender politics and the position of women in Heaney's work, it is also significant that in this instance where a female figure is allowed agency of her own, we are left with an anomalous agency characterized more by absence than presence since the poet is confronted by the stare of a headless corpse. In Heaney's bog and landscape poems there is a notable distinction between the female body – whether as a personified landscape that threatens and makes demands upon men ('Bog Queen' for example) or a mutilated victim in 'Punishment' and 'Strange Fruit' – and the male body which is often perfected or made whole again by the artistry of the poem and its historical memory.

To that end, Rand Brandes argues that the body in Heaney's poetry mediates a complex relationship to history and society. Brandes uses the literary trope of metonymy to explain how dismembered body parts in Heaney's poetry contain a range of meanings (metonymy being the substitution of one associated word for another in a process where the part object stands for something else in an association of contiguity rather than direct similarity as in metaphor. For example, in the popular expression, 'the pen is mightier than the sword', 'pen' actually stands for 'writing' and 'sword' for 'violence'; or, as another brief illustration, the common usage of 'The Crown' actually refers to the current monarch). Brand reads 'Digging' as a poem highly charged by tensions between inheritance and independence, memory and history, culture and labour – all of which are figured through the body, or parts of the body. Brandes asserts that the references to the speaker's finger and thumb and to his father's shoulder, rump and knee seek to pass on the skill of his father's labour. So the speaker's finger and thumb become metonymical representations of the whole man and his profession as it breaks from family tradition. Brandes comments: 'Metonymy predisposes us not to take the image literally, but to construct whatever is missing – to compensate for the partiality of meaning in regard to the absent whole, to make the absent present'.[69] If 'Digging' is a work which uses fragments of the body to attempt to reconcile Heaney's break from family tradition, to gesture to things made whole again, then this metonymic trope of gesturing to a reconciliation and a wholeness is intensified in Heaney's more political work with regard to history and society. Brandes argues that in 'Tollund Man' the bog body represents history itself, a history that must be redeemed and preserved out of its fragments with a renewed intactness and integrity, just as the bodies of 'Funeral Rites' must remain whole: 'As in "Digging", the body is always there in History and the body of History is always whole in the metonymy of memory'.[70] So the effort to restore the male body in Heaney's bog poems can be interpreted as an effort to suture a set of historical ruptures and anxieties, and to assemble a communal or wider national identity based on the perfected male subject in a mythic fashion against the contingencies and challenges of historical change.

Thomas Docherty provides a slightly different, postmodern take on these issues. Docherty argues that postmodernism problematizes the relationship between subject and object, particularly any transhistorical or mythic subject and that this in turn has implications for Heaney's sense of belonging, place and identity – especially the use to which he puts supposedly natural landscape and the bog bodies. Docherty observes: 'The reality which is supposed to ground our representations, be it the presence of History as exterior fact or the presence-to-self of the supposed transcendental Subject, has itself become an image'.[71] So for Docherty, postmodernism troubles the cartographic imperatives of Heaney's construction of landscape through which avowedly organic identities and belongings are secured. Docherty argues that the corpse in 'The Grauballe Man' is 'strangely androgynous', his testicle becomes an ovary, his body takes on a female cast and he is pregnant with the presence of a future, giving birth to himself just as the poem is giving birth to itself.[72] For Docherty, 'Grauballe Man' is 'a latent unconscious for the poet, his Imaginary; and the writing of the poem is the therapeutic act of recovering what had been repressed and facing it. In these terms, the atrocities of violence in Ireland are a return of the repressed pagan rites of sacrifice [...] Heaney here is not map-making, but history-making'.[73] While Docherty's analysis reinforces the idea that the body in Heaney's poetry is deployed to mediate and repair historical turmoil and disjunction, the postmodern androgynous poetic voice giving birth to itself would appear to challenge the interpretation of Heaney's work as establishing the ground of a secure male subjectivity. However, from a feminist perspective, we could be more circumspect and consider, from an early instance like 'Poem' in *Death of A Naturalist* through to 'The Wife's Tale' or 'Undine', that Heaney's poetry does not offer disruptively androgynous identities but rather a much more conventionally masculine and patriarchal voice which appropriates the female's creative role in giving birth for its own purposes: namely, the creation of a settled self and community that is empowered simultaneously both to incorporate and transcend the feminine.

Field Day, identity and the North

With regard to communal politics, or at least the interpretation of the North as a conflict of two traditions and communities, Heaney's work has a paradigmatic and contested legacy. A poem such as 'The Other Side' was an effort to reach out from one tradition to another, in that specific instance, by opening up a dialogue with John Hewitt's work. However, Richard Kirkland expresses a wariness of a reading whereby 'John Hewitt is perceived as the poetic voice of Protestant Ulster and Seamus Heaney as his Catholic counterpart [...] in this way they are not simply rendered as embodiments of a community but become mutually defining'.[74] We can pursue Kirkland's sense of how the 'Two Traditions' model serves to delimit a full acknowledgement of culture in the North in relation to the work of Heaney's Field Day colleague Brian Friel, whose play *Translations* (1980) was very much the flagship production by the company. Seamus Deane states of the play: 'It was originating for Field Day, the more appropriately so because it quite literally mapped a territory by writing about the remapping of a territory'.[75] *Translations* is set in Baile Beag as it is being renamed as Ballybeg during the first Royal Ordnance Survey of 1833 wherein the British administration resolved to map and rename Ireland.

Although the play is written and performed almost exclusively in English, with some phrases and quotations in ancient Greek and Latin, the audience is required to imagine that the Irish characters speak in their native tongue during the play – one of many translations in a work that traces the imposition of the English language on Ireland as part of a wider political and social hegemony. Hence, Deane comments: 'in *Translations*, there are two Irelands, two languages, two kinds of violence'.[76] W. B. Worthen argues that the imaginative leap required by the audience to believe that the native characters are speaking Irish is itself instructive of the cultural and social collision embedded in the play: '*Translations* stages an image of that past at the moment of its subjugation to the colonial order; it offers a "translation" of an absent text, an "origin" now available only in translation, a text that has been systematically obliterated'.[77] Friel's own account of the linguistic politics of *Translations* is significantly tied to a spatial (and militarized) metaphor that coalesces the play's concern with how both language and the power it represents map a territory and culture: 'The problem with the Northern situation is how you can tip-toe through the minefields of language where language has become so politicized. You see, wherever you have a war, language is the first casualty'.[78]

In keeping with Heaney's intimate tribal communities, it is telling that Irish – or at least the audience's imaginative reconstruction of it – is conceived by *Translations* as the 'language of the tribe' and the play also confers upon both Irish and English languages a 'private core'.[79] The danger here is that, although *Translations* endeavours to confront the political conflict of language, Friel's polarization of Irish and English ends up treating each language as internally homogeneous and given. So, reflecting upon Kirkland's postulation that this kind of tribal binary precludes other concerns, to take each language as homogenous tends to eschews issues such as gender, class or regions and so forth which always trouble the unitary credentials of any national language. Friel does consider the play and the Field Day enterprise in general as attempts to enter into a cultural and political dialogue but it is noteworthy that, perhaps like Heaney's 'The Other Side', the debate is couched in terms of already agreed, identifiable constituencies: 'We are talking to ourselves as we must and if we are overheard in America, or England, so much the better [...] we must continually look at ourselves, recognise and identify ourselves. We must make English identifiably our own language'.[80]

Friel's comment additionally raises the issue of how both the play and Field Day itself sought to remap Irish culture and society as part of a reclamation that redresses the displacement into the English language and British political domination that *Translations* depicts. Sarah's character in *Translations* most clearly broaches the key issues of losing one's own language and culture and being redefined by someone else's terms and power. Deane reads Sarah, about whom the stage directions inform us that she has a profound speech impediment and is considered locally to be dumb, as a highly symbolic character: 'Sarah loses her self-possession when she loses her name ... Having one's name spoken is different from speaking one's own name, especially when one *cannot* speak that name'.[81] Similarly, Heaney, in his review of the play, seizes upon Sarah's inability to say her own name before the English officer Captain Lancey: 'It is as if some symbolic figure of Ireland from an eighteenth-century vision poem, the one who once confidently called herself Cathleen Ni Houlihan, has been struck dumb by the shock of modernity'. In mitigation of this voicelessness, Heaney claims that Friel's work provides Ireland with 'a powerful therapy, a set of imaginative exercises that give her the chance to know and say herself properly to herself again'.[82] Notably, here are two male writers seeking to give voice to a feminized personification of the nation. If we recall our discussion of gender and nation, one of the issues concealed by Friel's model of a homogenous tribal language is therefore gender politics. While the play seeks to understand how Ireland might recover its voice and re-articulate its identity, the figural means by which this dilemma is framed tries to forget that Sarah was muted by her local community to begin with before the translation of that community into English. Deane asserts that 'the naming or renaming of a place, the naming or renaming of a race, a region, a person, is, like all acts of primordial nomination, an act of possession'.[83] But Sarah's character enables us to collapse the play's colonial binary and uncover its obsessive concern with the ritual of naming as the site of an internal gendered insecurity – an insecurity which manifests itself in the christening and subsequent death of Sarah's baby – about the power of a male national subject to use women as the guarantors and ciphers of its communal unity.

In terms of *Translations'* insistence on two languages and two identities, Edna Longley represents the severest of Field Day's critics.

She regards the colonial binary of this model and the whole Field Day aim of remapping and redefining Irishness with circumspection. Firstly, she argues that Northern Nationalism is out of step with the revision of nationalism in the Republic, and deliberately so, in order to sustain its colonial interpretation of the Northern conflict (to this end, she contrasts Friel's drama with Murphy's *Baliegangiare* in the Republic). Additionally, Longley dismisses the efforts of the Field Day company to reach out to Unionism or Protestantism as tokenistic gestures in what is in reality a Nationalist monologue or a reductive 'talking to ourselves', to re-employ Friel's phrase. And equally, Longley contends, the Field Day pamphlets by the international scholars Said, Jameson and Eagleton pander to notions of a unitary Irish people.[84]

From a different perspective, Shaun Richards also challenges the Field Day claim to be thinking anew and opening up new dialogues and debates. Richards draws on the play *Pentecost* (1987) by Stewart Parker, the Field Day production of which Longley concedes was a genuine attempt to reach out to different cultural perspectives. Richards views *Pentecost* as a work that, although set against the Ulster Workers' Strike of 1974, is strong on personal relationships and the domestic sphere but weak in translating that microcosmic realm into a political sphere. In fact Richards construes *Pentecost* as recapitulating the apolitical, Christian humanism that we noted Deane accused O'Casey's drama of propagating in the Revival and his critique sardonically echoes the Field Day aim of rewriting and re-reading all Irish literature: 'What *Pentecost* presents ... is a moving modernization of the plea of O'Casey's Juno to "Take away our murdherin' hate, an' give us Thine own eternal love". Not so much a re-reading as a reprise'.[85] Richards focuses on the Field Day company's troubled relationship with the work of Frank McGuinness to develop his argument that the whole project does not live up to its own stated intentions of critical, meaningful debate and dialogue. Field Day had rejected McGuinness's *Observe the Sons of Ulster Marching Towards the Somme* (1985), a play which delved deeply into Ulster Protestant identity. And McGuinness would later withdraw his play *Carthaginians* (1988), a blend of tragedy and farce which focused on a group of social misfits in a Derry graveyard 16 years after Bloody Sunday in 1972 when 13 unarmed civilians were shot dead by the British army, over apparent artistic differences with Field Day.

To return to poetry, we will now cover a range of poets whom critics have tended to read against the grain of Heaney's aesthetic. Paul Muldoon is the writer accredited most fully by Edna Longley with undermining the religious and communal identities and archetypes in Heaney's work.[86] Where Heaney's poetry develops from his parish symbolically structured by his father, Muldoon's disrupts such patriarchal and placed certainties with a series of vertiginous, visionary voyages as in 'Immram' and 'The More A Man Has the More A Man Wants' in which identities are fluid and glide in and out of one another and the quest for an originary paternal presence is always frustrated and satirized. Although Muldoon shares with Heaney a rural Catholic background, in his case the Moy in Armagh, Longley notes that though interested in Kavanagh's parish from his earliest poems, Muldoon's Moy is transfigured through the looking-glass into terrains foreign to Kavanagh's symbolic landscape. A key poem, 'Why Brownlee Left', disrupts the fixed sectarian certainties of names and locales and crystallizes many of Muldoon's central concerns. Brownlee's name suggests a brown meadow, or a ploughed field, so that his end is his name, his identity and life are to be determined by his name. But yet he escapes his fate in a collection where identity is often kaleidoscopic and uncertain. As Longley explains: 'In reaction against predestination, Muldoon's hall of metamorphic mirrors shatters fixed identities (not only Irish ones) by reflecting multiple and ambiguous human faces'.[87]

Where Heaney in a poem like 'The Other Side' does admittedly and generously seek cultural accommodation, he does so on the basis of already agreed and distinct identities. In Muldoon, however, the neat divisions between communal and indeed personal identities are continually transgressed and modified. Hence, his collection *Mules* (1977) uses the hybrid nature of the mule to consider the possibilities of being in-between, neither one nor the other, or indeed both at once and more than both. His work considers the benefits of openness, of getting the best of both worlds, yet it never loses sight of polarization and division. Tim Kendall, in his excellently informed and accessible guide to Muldoon's work, interprets *Mules* as both a conscious subversion of sectarian polarities and a concomitant refusal to be defined purely in terms of sectarian debate.[88] Kendall also reads 'The Right Arm', which recalls Muldoon's childhood home in Eglish where his father owned a shop and features a boy plunging his arm in a sweet-jar for the last piece of clove-rock, as a critique of the tribal fixity and religious identity of Heaney's place-name and landscape poems. Notably, 'The Right Arm' wedges Eglish between *ecclesia* and *église*. Kendall analyzes the poem's mediation on naming as follows (with reference to the Irish literary tradition of *dinnseanchas* or 'place-name lore' which delves into the origins of place-names and the intertwining of landscape and being):

■ The poem is about entrapment: Eglish, from the Irish for 'church', is jammed – etymologically rather than alphabetically – between two foreign words also meaning 'church', so that its character is rigidly fixed by its name [...] 'The Right Arm' is an example of the Gaelic *dinnseanchas* genre, but now the place-name's equation with its roots ensures only confinement.[89] □

Another poet whom critics tend to contrast with Heaney is Derek Mahon. Mahon's work thinks deeply not only about the conflict itself but also the status of art and the position of the poet – though with differing conclusions to Heaney's work. Indeed, Mahon's 'Lives', which is dedicated to Heaney, contains a dialogue with Heaney's bog poems and directly refutes their mythic patterns since the identities of both poet and bog bodies are in flux and subject to historical contingency. As with a Muldoon poem like '7 Middagh Street', Mahon's 'Afterlives' self-consciously meditates on the place of poetry and the poet in society and retains a self-criticism simultaneously with a defence of the poetic imagination and indictment of stagnant ideologies. Similarly, 'The Last of the Fire Kings' skilfully equilibrates, with the solving ambiguity Mahon finds in MacNeice, a romantic longing for sheer artistic freedom and social responsiveness and responsibility. Edna Longley comments: 'Mahon insists on the poet serving humanity on his own terms. He should feel, but resist, the contrary pressure that would make him in the image of the people'.[90] In one of Mahon's most famous poems, 'A Disused Shed in Co. Wexford', a sympathy with the lost voices of history's victims is expressed through the understated, yet ultimately generously encompassing, symbol of mushrooms. Longley intuits the poem as instructive of Mahon's whole poetic and as exemplifying a fundamental point about poetry made by Edward Thomas (1878–1917):

■ 'A Disused Shed in Co. Wexford' makes and proves Edward Thomas's point, fundamental to the issue of poetry and politics, as to poetry in general: 'Anything, however small, may make a poem; nothing, however great, is certain to' [...] Mahon receives a defenceless spirit into the protectorate of poetry.[91] □

Comparably, Peter McDonald posits that the poem shows that history is not constituted solely by what is politically accessible or momentous by focusing instead on those forgotten by the cruel necessities and indifferences of history:

■ Mahon does not anatomize a given community when he encounters its plight; rather, he sets that plight deep in a context of change and human isolation. The poem seems to be a vindication of Mahon's determinedly cold and detached perspectives, and his insistence of seeing straight even when it means seeing straight through what we might want to be there.[92] □

In its own thoughtful, oblique and highly particular idiom, the poetry of Medbh McGuckian also offers a disruption of the essentialist or naturalized relationship between language, land and identity, whether in Heaney's work or in wider Irish Nationalist discourse. In keeping with his post-nationalist perspective that we discussed in relation to contemporary writing in the Republic, Richard Kearney interprets McGuckian as making ironic the myths she deploys and substituting her own personal meanings for communal orthodoxies (especially those pertaining to myths of an Irish motherland). A history of women's experience is recovered through what Kearney views as a prism of private witness in which lived metaphors of body, sex and childbirth bring private life into conflict with public myths. For example, McGuckian's poem, 'Dovecoat', examines the Nationalist response to the Hunger Strike of 1981 through a parallel framework of the private attempt of a woman to restore her self-identity or body and mind after giving birth and a collective attempt by the Catholic community to recover its self-definition during the campaign in Long Kesh. Kearney reads the Dovecoat itself as a symbol of both the woman's body after childbirth and the desire of both the woman and the Catholic community to be at one, to be undivided. The doves, Kearney argues, are the strikers at the mercy of the Nationalist people who use them to consolidate their own sense of Ireland. Kearney posits that the poem reviews the public myth of martyrdom through the prism of personal experience. Ultimately, according to Kearney, the habitual nationalist use of women as symbols and ciphers is subverted:

■ In contrast to the culturally debilitating emblems of the Sean Bhean Bhocht, Mother Eire or Caitlín ní Houlihán, McGuckian re-empowers the image of Irish women as sexually complex [...] Woman finds herself in a place where she is of no use to the ideological agenda, nationalist or imperialist. Women's fertility becomes unappropriable for male mythology [...] Words and women revitalize the *idées fixes* of myth by giving birth to an unpredictable, utopian future.[93] □

Moreover, as demonstrated in Chapter Five, Clair Wills grants a sustained reading of McGuckian that accredits her poetry with a radical re-definition of the public–private dichotomy by which women and their writing are often marginalized. Wills avers:

■ despite the dangers of a reading which would merely serve to reconfirm notion's of women's concerns as primarily personal, it is important to be aware of the ways in which a seemingly personal or confessional poet (such as McGuckian) is radical precisely in her attempts to talk about public and political events through the medium of private symbolism.[94] □

For Wills it is not simply that McGuckian is an expressive female poet giving voice to her intimate sphere; rather, her formal strategies fragment the traditional lyric and its social symbolism. As with Kearney's interpretation, Wills foregrounds McGuckian's mode of reading public and political events through the changes occurring in the contours of her body, and her experience of sex and childbirth. As Wills concludes: 'This is perhaps precisely because as a woman writer she lies outside the tradition of poetry as public statement – she does not have access to the language of poetic "responsibility"'.[95]

The City, pluralism and the North

The work of Ciaran Carson offers also a very different terrain and historical perspective from Heaney, and we can trace his trajectory in his damning review of Heaney's *North*. Carson latches upon the claim in 'Exposure' to have 'escaped from the massacre' in order to assert: 'No one really escapes from the massacre, of course – the only way you can do that is by falsifying issues, by applying wrong notions of history, instead of seeing what's before your eyes'. Carson condemns Heaney as 'the laureate of violence – a mythmaker, an anthropologist of ritual killing, an apologist for "the situation", in the last resort, a mystifier'.[96] So, for Carson, Heaney's bog poems of historical archetypes mythologize, aestheticize and naturalize violence. In Carson's urban landscapes the grounded stability of Heaney's versions of identity and history is rendered untenable. Belfast, a city built on unstable 'sleech' or mud, is continually shifting in a manner that is embodied in the formal metamorphoses of Carson's writing.

Carson's resistance to fixed cartographic or historical paradigms is evident in both his poetry and prose. Perhaps the ambiguity surrounding the etymology of Belfast's very name, brilliantly traced in *Belfast Confetti* (1990), is apposite: does it derive from *Béal*, the mouth or mouth of a river, in this case the Farset or *Feirste*; or from *Fearsaid*, a sand-bar or sand-bank at the crossing point or ford of two rivers, the Farset and the Lagan? In many ways, the city can be all these things: a crossing point, a fluid place of transgression, the mouth of a river flowing with innumerable voices. The linguistic and historical shifts and contingencies of Carson's work therefore directly undermine the settled significations and identities of Heaney poems like 'Broagh' or 'Anahorish'. Nevertheless, Carson's urban aesthetic also foregrounds issues of power and socio-economic disadvantage in the city, as in 'The Ballad of HMS Belfast' where the imaginative voyage begun on April Fools' Day is sundered by the carceral realities of power and hegemony. Carson's labyrinthine geographies are not facilitated by some hybrid free-play of urban movement but are rather produced by socially conditioned and socially coded situations. Alan Gillis adeptly grasps the central tenets of Carson's labyrinthine urban vision in the following terms:

■ when Carson attempts to reconceive the cartography of Belfast, he is implicitly attempting to reconfigure certain historical paradigms [...] Maps petrify the potential for historical transformation. By rendering a cultural space static, they are inherently past-tense, because the present, for Carson, is dynamically open to the future.[97] □

The challenges and problems of urban space are also addressed in two important articles by Eamonn Hughes who analyzes the city as disrupting traditional social co-ordinates and identities in a way comparable to Gerry Smyth's account of Dublin in our discussion on the Irish Republic. Hughes's essay, '"What Itch of Contradiction?": Belfast in Poetry' (2003), gleans its title from a phrase in John Hewitt's 'Conacre' and it considers how poetry seems more inclined to pastoral and rural landscapes yet the actual topographies of Northern poetry are much more complex and interesting. Hughes discerns contradictions in how a range of poets, including Hewitt, MacNeice, Mahon, Michael Longley (born 1939) and others, represent Belfast. Belfast is often depicted, in MacNeice's 'Belfast', 'Valediction' and 'Autumn Journal' as a city full of oppositions: hot–cold, hard–soft, foundational mud, land and water. So too in Mahon's 'Day Trip to Donegal', Belfast is sleeping yet changing, and in Mahon's 'An Unborn Child' and 'Ecclesiastes' there are fixities and hard certainties yet also the imaginative possibilities by which these poems gain energies from what they attack. Hughes observes:

■ Hewitt's 'itch of contradiction' is then to be found not just in a division between Belfast and the rural, but within Belfast itself as its fixity and certainty, its very setting and geology, become fluid and indeterminate. If poets flicker in and out of Belfast, then Belfast itself flickers in and out of vision. Like the Ireland in which it may or may not be located it is caught in an endless chain of signification, self-divided and always deferred. The ultimate Belfast binary is whether it is a living city or a necropolis (and this, even more than other self-divisions, is profoundly accentuated by the Troubles).[98] □

Hughes asserts that Heaney's poetry has difficulty dealing with the city and approaches it indirectly through a range of other literary works or cultural mediations (as in 'A Northern Hoard' or the MacNeice-influenced 'Docker'). In particular, Hughes regards Heaney's sense of belonging and identity in his pastoral landscapes as impossible in the city and contrasts Heaney with Michael Longley and MacNeice, whose urban topographies foreground a sense of the commercial and economic relations of the city. Hughes argues that the city requires very different identities and co-ordinates than those demanded by the tribal certainties and rigidly bordered belongings of Irish Nationalism and Unionism: 'The city affronts the sense of the nation as homogenous'.[99]

Hughes also elaborates his argument in relation to prose in his article '"Town of Shadows": Representations of Belfast in Recent Fiction' (1996), where he contends that in contemporary writing there has been a redress of the relative absence of Belfast in fictional representation.[100] Hughes argues that in the second half of the twentieth century a change occurs due to the growth of Belfast, the consequences of more wide-spread educational opportunities, a securely city-based and educated audience for these writings about the city, and broadcasting and elec-tronic technologies that give Belfast dwellers a sense of themselves as not living in a small marginal city but partaking of the global experience of being urban. Hughes also highlights the issue of migration and avers that in the early twentieth century the city was where people went when they lost their land or were economically displaced, but that the city served as a place of transition for a further move out of Ireland – and Hughes's example here is the mixture of shame, guilt, loss and nostalgia in the Belfast novels of Michael McLaverty (1904–92). Yet, Hughes con-tinues, the Irish abroad are urban – as in Kilburn or Bermondsey in London, Manchester or Birmingham, parts of New York and Boston – and Irish culture has slowly had to catch up with the urban experiences of Irish peoples. This urban dispensation takes some getting used to – not only for Irish writers but for all people who have to undergo the shocks of modernity. In Sam Hanna Bell's 1951 novel, *December Bride*, the complexity and dazzle of Belfast defeats the old countryman Petie Ogle to the point of death, and the city is described as 'a confused blur'.[101] Hughes interprets this new, dislocating confusion of established, tradi-tional belongings in the context of Joyce's effort to come to terms with Dublin in *A Portrait*. But while the city certainly offers a challenge to the writer, once its shocks and disruptions are harnessed, then its com-plexity also facilitates a breach of the dominant ideologies of Ireland: 'where the rural produces an essentialist and organic identity, cities produce relational and constructed identities. The rural is the site of homogeneous Ireland; the urban is resisted precisely because it is the site of heterogeneous Ireland'.[102]

Hughes's analysis does not shy away from issues of social poverty and class inequality, but it maintains that the recurrent mainstream depiction of Belfast as hell has less to do with an ethical effort to depict such depredations and more to do with the distrust and fear which the city engenders in both Irish Nationalism and Unionism. The city can be a space of the transgression of accepted codes or traditional boundaries. Hughes points to how Poll in Hanna Bell's *A Man Flourishing* (1973) dresses as a woman, how Theresa in *Hidden Symptoms* (1987) by Deidre Madden (born 1960) crosses gender boundaries. There are also the homosexu-als in the fiction of Maurice Leitch (born 1933) and in Brian Moore's

The Emperor of Ice Cream (1966), and even the stereotypical 'across the barricades' love or friendship of Ripley and Deirdre Curran in *Ripley Bogle* (1989) by Robert McLiam Wilson, or Mal and Francy in *Burning Your Own* (1988) by Glenn Patterson. Additionally, Hughes invokes the study of the French poet Charles Baudelaire (born 1821–67) by the German critic Walter Benjamin (1892–1940), wherein the mystery of the city is ultimately the mystery of the self, and he accredits McLiam Wilson and Patterson with developing a meaningful and subversive urban consciousness that redefines place and identity in Northern culture.[103]

With regard to McLiam Wilson's and Patterson's fiction, Laura Pelaschiar's critical work, especially her *Writing the North: The Contemporary Novel in Northern Ireland* (1998), is indispensable in tracing the emergence of a new Northern consciousness and its contravention of existing literary paradigms.[104] As with Hughes's analysis, Pelaschiar finds McLiam Wilson's *Eureka Street* (1996) to be the apotheosis of a rewritten Belfast of possibility as well as fracture: 'Belfast is clearly Everycity, its inhabitants Everyman'.[105] Elsewhere in her criticism, Pelaschiar locates in McLiam Wilson, Patterson and the generation of which they are a part, a sustained effort to rethink and recast the North that opens up a potential for reconciliation and renewal. For Pelaschiar the city becomes 'a laboratory for opportunities, a post-modern place depicted as *the* only place where it is possible to build and articulate a (post) national conscience, the only location for any possible encyclopaedic, multivoiced and multi-ethnic development of Northern society.'[106] Elmer Kennedy-Andrews's *(De-)Constructing the North: Fiction and the Northern Ireland Troubles since 1969* (2003) offers a comparably important and consummate survey of contemporary prose through which McLiam Wilson, Patterson and their peers are contextualized as embodying a new postmodern or deconstructive turn which undermines the prevailing ideologies of Irish Nationalism and Unionism:

■ The fiction itself, we might say, exhibits a postmodern multiplicity and heterogeneity, a plurality of viewpoints, a resistance to closure and totalisation [...] issues of identity, justice, freedom, and so forth are constantly subject to imaginative interrogation and reconstruction, constantly to be debated, revised and determined.[107] □

However, Richard Kirkland's *Identity Parades* provides a counterargument to the celebration of a new postmodern Northern fiction and the multiplicity and pluralism it represents. Kirkland suspects that underpinning such postmodern plurality is a bourgeois ideology which is engaged in the reconstitution of its dominance in the North and more globally. So what appears as liberation from traditional constraint is actually a more socially coded individualism ultimately conditioned by consumerism and the economic logic of bourgeois society. Hence, Kirkland reads the apparent newly pluralistic and diverse cultures of Patterson's *Fat Lad* (1992), McLiam Wilson's *Eureka Street, Cycle of Violence* (1994) by Colin Bateman (born 1962), *Kissing the Frog* (1996) by Annie Dunlop (born 1968) and *A Wreath Upon the Dead* (1993) by Briege Duffaud as emanating not from multiplicity but from the same underlying socio-economic imperative:

■ While each novel charts a form of resistance it is possible for the individual to take when faced with the perceived constrictions of Nationalist and/or Unionist ideology, at the same time they all acknowledge (although to varying degrees) the futility of attempting to resist the onward march of postmodern capitalism.[108] □

In terms of social class, we can also turn to the novel *No Mate for the Magpie* (1985) by Frances Molloy. This book is frustratingly often out of print and Molloy's untimely death leaves only this novel and a collection of short stories, *Women Are the Scourge of the Earth* (1998), as her brilliant but sadly curtailed legacy. *No Mate* is a highly significant work in that its narrative is driven solely by working-class, County Derry vernacular. This is unusual since where a working-class voice does appear in a lot of Northern Irish fiction it does so only at the level of dialogue, whereas *No Mate* disrupts the conventional hierarchy of the novel in which a Standard English register superintends the narrative so that working-class vernacular is reduced to a behavioral trait while it is only the Standard voice which is capable of insight, thought, psychological complexity and so on. Conventionally, while the novels by writers from working-class backgrounds may use vernacular in dialogue and speech, the fact that the narrative itself is composed in a standard register discloses the ultimate (middle-class) designation and destination of the work. Molloy's novel lacerates the complicity between such formal conventions and a middle-class perspective and the absence of any comparable work in Northern Irish culture – as opposed, say, to a whole body of writing in Scotland produced by James Kelman (born 1946), Tom Leonard (born 1944) and others – indicates how the conventional sense of language as caught up in either a tribal, sectarian division or a reductive Irish-English dichotomy ultimately serves to occlude class conflict and identity. To that end, Kennedy-Andrews comments that *No Mate* grants 'a voice that works against socio-political and cultural centralisation, signalling from the beginning the importance of class, hierarchy and status – and therefore issues of power and authority'.[109] In the conclusion we will now reprise the unresolved ethical exigencies and creative ambiguities of Irish Studies as the discipline encounters the twenty-first century.

CONCLUSION

Irish Studies Today

Our examination of literature and criticism in the Irish Republic and the North concluded in each case with an acknowledgement of the globalized networks now coursing through Irish society. For some, this global dispensation promised a new open, pluralist possibility through which to vanquish the repressive fixities of the past. Other writers and critics, we observed, while certainly not harking back to unrealizable ideals, equally remained more circumspect about the economic changes and realignments of power which this new global context brings forth. An important and engaging intervention in debates about a new Ireland or new Irish cultural constellations is granted by *Multi-Culturalism: The View From the Two Irelands* (2001), which comprises parallel essays by Edna Longley and Declan Kiberd. Each assesses, respectively, the North and the Republic with regard to multiculturalism and the possibilities and limitations of social pluralism.

Longley is suspicious of the term multiculturalism in that, while it implies many cultures as opposed to one culture or monoculturalism, it does not necessitate any meaningful engagement across or between cultures but rather holds each culture as an already agreed or self-contained entity. Her own preferred term is *inter-culturalism* which does indicate much more fully a dialogue and a creative encounter. Additionally, Longley wishes to resist a relativized interpretation of multiculturalism wherein all things are equally viable and above criticism. With reference to the consociational model of the Good Friday Agreement (i.e., that the 'Two Communities' must learn to live together), Longley explains both her own terms and the dangers of allowing self-contained cultures to wallow in their own delimited identities under the rubric of multiculturalism:

> ■ Perhaps 'inter-cultural' is a better term than the somewhat ambiguous 'multi-cultural' for the project of engaging with genuine differences and making them fruitful [...] Our consociational Agreement fits how most people now effectively live in Northern Ireland. The population-shifts caused by the Troubles, whether involuntary or voluntary, mean fewer mixed areas; greater social apartheid; unreasonable demands for local self-sufficiency. (In some

people's heads Northern Ireland is a vast prairie which might be infinitely
devolved so that nobody ever has to encounter anything that might disturb
their cultural complacency).[1] □

Kiberd's essay on the Irish Republic reflects on a globalized Ireland
where immigration is now a significant factor, where once the Irish
nation had to reconcile itself to the emigration of its own citizens. This
history of emigration, and the international Irish community that it
produced – as institutionally recognized under the presidency of Mary
Robinson (born 1944; President of Ireland 1990–7) – fruitfully intersects,
Kiberd maintains, with this new era of economic migration to Ireland
to embolden a sense of the nation as open-ended and plural.[2] Therein,
no one is a stranger in that we are all strangers, we all have identities
that shift the terms of earlier conceptions of nations or identities:

■ Ireland itself was always multi-cultural, in the sense of being eclectic, open,
assimilative. The best definition of a nation was that given by Joyce's Leopold
Bloom: the same people living in the same place [...] The recognition during Mary Robinson's presidency that the overseas Irish were also part of the
national family suggested a corollary: that many immigrant peoples living on
the island of Ireland might also have their own global communities over and
above the immediate society to which they belong. In such a context, the word
'foreigner' may begin to seem a little preposterous.[3] □

However, both Longley and Kiberd also refer to the rise in racism
and racist attacks against immigrants in both the North and the Republic which would tend to suggest that, as Longley suspects, monocultural
and exclusivist ideologies persist under the cloak of multiculturalism and
that those ideologies are just as capable of venting their purist politics
against migrants as against their established indigenous 'tribal' others.
    In regard to gaps in awareness of racial issues, perhaps most notably
Roddy Doyle's *The Commitments* (1987) proclaimed: 'The Irish are the
niggers of Europe ... An' the Dubliners are the niggers of Ireland ...
An' the northside Dubliners are the niggers o' Dublin. – Say it loud,
I'm black an' I'm proud.'[4] At best, there is a profound danger here that
Doyle's version of an Irish disadvantaged group – in a seeming moment
of solidarity – actually commandeers and appropriates the suffering
of others in order to bolster its own credentials of being oppressed. In
this context, Suzanna Chan's work is highly valuable and instructive in
uncovering the varying degrees of blindness and transparency by which
race (especially the mainstream whiteness of Irish society) is either
ignored or distorted in contemporary debate. Chan's focus is on feminism and the deployment of a homogenous 'woman', which precludes
any consideration of race, but she also contextualizes her critique with

reference to the 2004 referendum in the Irish Republic that redefined citizenship in terms of bloodline:

■ by focussing solely on gender, feminist criticism can neglect its intersections with axes of differentiation such as 'race'; or result in one-dimensional analogies between 'Irish' women and 'Black' and 'Third World' women. The importance of 'race' to the construction of identity in an Irish context was underscored by the 2004 Referendum on Citizenship, which defined Irish national identity on a white-centred patriarchal basis, and renders 'nonnational' women doubly 'other'. Following the 2004 referendum, the Irish Constitution will be amended to define citizenship on a *jus sanguinis* basis, whereby it is transmitted through parental bloodline. Many migrants in Ireland thus face deportation, while the right to citizenship of the 'Irish diaspora' is affirmed.[5] □

So despite Kiberd's anticipation that the global diaspora of the Irish and the migration to Ireland by new workers would mutually affirm one another in a dialogue of openness and generous difference, Chan notes how constitutionally a much more unequal encounter takes place that confers Irishness on the diaspora and withdraws access to that same Irishness for those migrants actually living in Ireland. With regard to mainstream Irish feminism, Chan argues that Ailbhe Smyth's work contains a totalizing category of Irish feminism alongside a correspondingly undifferentiated sense of non-white, non-Western women that inevitably results in generalizations.[6] Simultaneously, Chan continues, such a dichotomy leaves little space for acknowledging the experiences of non-white women in Ireland, or indeed for becoming aware that such women may also *be* Irish. With reference to the overwhelming majority (79 per cent) of the electorate who voted in favour of amending the Republic's constitution to define Irish citizenship on a bloodline basis which simultaneously excludes 'others', Chan argues:

■ Against these racialised 'others', women and men of the Irish electorate identified themselves differentially as a 'white' majority, in a stark example of the reproduction of Irish national identity through gendered discourses of whiteness. Not only does this highlight the inadequacy of feminist approaches that remain with a dualistic model of sexual difference and miss the intersectionality of 'race' and gender [...] it also underscores Ireland's white-centredness.[7] □

Moreover, from a socialist perspective, Francis Mulhern asserts that the continual dwelling on the national question, upon the colonial trauma, as the primary identification of the Irish people generations after Independence in the Republic is redolent of a 'postcolonial melancholy'.[8] This wilful, perverse nostalgia serves to exonerate the State and ruling classes in the Republic for any culpability for the shortcomings and ills of society. However, Mulhern also stresses that his alternative to this postcolonial melancholy is not postmodern relativism but rather a renewed (socialist) uncovering of issues of power and social inequality:

■ 'Difference' and 'discontinuity', valorized without regard for their specific contents and real conditions of existence, are the alibi of conformists and chastened doctrinaires. There will be a day for a Europe (and a world) of differences, lived as a history without closure, but its precondition is a general social transformation that will not come through the free proliferation of particularities. The strong alternative to a flawed grand narrative is surely a critically revised one, not a winsome anthology of (very) short stories.[9] □

Comparably, Terry Eagleton asserts the importance of the Field Day project as a regalvanized effort to highlight concrete inequalities in Irish society in a way that defeats a bland pluralism where all things are merely cultural difference. Eagleton posits that what is at stake in Irish Studies debates is much less a conflict between tradition and modernity, than one between modernity and postmodernity. Eagleton equates modernity with political discourses of rights, justice, oppression, solidarity (and nationalism, liberalism and socialism are his constitutive parts of this worldview). The political language of postmodernity is identity, marginality, locality, difference and desire. Eagleton maintains that there are extreme tensions between the two registers, yet equally he regards each as urgently in need of the other. For Eagleton, it is the spirit of the Field Day project that encapsulates the fruitful bringing together of these two discourses:

■ Within Ireland, the best aspects of what might be called the Field Day case have tried to do exactly this – to argue that genuine identity, true difference and authentic pluralism can finally be established only on the basis of political justice and emancipation.[10] □

As this Guide has indicated, David Lloyd's work is wary of the forms of neo-colonialism. In *Ireland After History* (1999) he invokes – in order to critique – the 'end of history' thesis espoused by Francis Fukuyama (born 1952), which posits, with the collapse of the Soviet Union, that capitalism and liberal democracy have won and that there are no meaningful ideological or political conflicts left to resolve. Fukuyama regards the present as the fulfillment of history and its reformist, ameliorative promises, and he equates post-Cold War global capitalism (and indeed American imperialism) with democracy to create, in his own terms at least, a utopia of a world supposedly beyond political division, ideological conflict or historical change.[11] By contrast, Lloyd's work – and its affirmation of those either outside of, on the receiving end of, or directly resistant to, these dominant historical narratives – seeks to rebut this grandiose conclusion of historical debate. Lloyd comments of his own work:

> ■ Ireland faces its own forms of subjection to a New World Order that has long been in preparation. *Ireland After History* gestures towards other possibilities that have persisted outside the mainstream of developmental history, and suggests that they might be liberated from the regulatory force of an historical ideology that has governed political and economic decisions globally over the last two centuries.[12] □

Colin Graham's *Deconstructing Ireland* (2001) is as comfortable examining Joyce as it is with analyzing popular cultural kitsch, though Graham's take on popular culture is very different from David Lloyd's. Graham's deconstructive approach proposes that all attempts to define Ireland serve – with both positive and negative consequences – to postpone or defer its final definition in a manner that frustrates certain fixating or unitary urges yet sustains more fluid potentialities: 'Ireland's origins and futures are produced and reproduced again and again as mirages and as impossible, but tantalising, utopian presences'.[13] In terms of a globalizing Irish culture, Graham's mastery of both reading and applying deconstructive and postcolonial theory makes him excellently equipped to address the key concerns of twenty-first century Irish Studies. His grasp of kitsch popular cultural versions of Irishness latches on to kitsch's infinite reproducibility in contrast to the supposed authenticities and exclusive collectabilities of cultural antiques:

> ■ Kitsch scatters the remnants of Irish authenticity around the globe, allowing forms of ownership to visitor, emigrant and citizen alike [...] Selling itself and 'Ireland', kitsch recognises the brand name as the sign of a never-to-be-realised and thus never-to-be-broken promise.[14] □

This Guide has sought to trace in the field of literature various promises of Ireland and Irishness from the imaginings of the Revival through world war, national conflict, despair, isolation, hope, solidarity and the apparently benign futures of the present. Literature and the critical instinct retain a capacity to be of the world but not bounded by it. The aesthetic and formal distances of the literary and the critical from the world do not entail mere escapism but help produce spaces where the world may be rethought, refigured or resisted. And that capacity is ongoing in Irish literature and the multifarious, contradictory, frustrating and enabling conditions in which it is made.

Notes

INTRODUCTION

1 Terence Brown, *Ireland: A Social and Cultural History 1922–79* (Glasgow: Fontana, 1981), p. 45.
2 Thomas Kinsella, *The Dual Tradition: An Essay on Poetry and Politics in Ireland* (Manchester: Carcanet, 1995), p. 116. For an engaging range of articles on Kinsella see a special issue on his work in *Irish University Review* 31.1 (Spring 2001).
3 Kinsella (1995), p. 5
4 Seamus Deane, *Celtic Revivals: Essays in Modern Irish Literature* (London: Faber, 1985), p. 13.
5 For a good collection of essays on the Celtic Tiger see Luke Gibbons et al., eds, *Reinventing Ireland: Culture, Society and the Global Economy* (London: Pluto Press, 2002).
6 These lectures are published as Matthew Arnold, *On the Study of Celtic Literature* (1867), and collected in R. H. Super, ed. *Lectures and Essays in Criticism* (Ann Arbor: University of Michigan Press, 1962).
7 Ernest Renan, *The Poetry of the Celtic Races* (London: Walter Scott, 1897), p. 14.
8 Renan (1987), p. 7.
9 Renan (1897), p. 8.
10 Arnold (1962), p. 343.

CHAPTER ONE

1 Yeats, 'The Celtic Element in Literature', *Essays and Introductions* (London: Macmillan, 1961), pp. 175–6.
2 Yeats (1961), p. 178.
3 Yeats (1961), p. 179.
4 Yeats (1961), p. 182.
5 Yeats (1961), p. 187.
6 Yeats, 'The Theatre', *Essays and Introductions* (London: Papermac, 1989), p. 166.
7 Standish O'Grady, *History of Ireland: The Heroic Period* Vol. 1 (London: Sampson, Low, Searle, Marston and Rivington, 1878), p. vii. For an excellent guide, see Michael McAteer, *Standish O'Grady, AE and Yeats: History, Politics, Culture* (Dublin: Irish Academic Press, 2002).
8 O'Grady (1878), p. vii.
9 Douglas Hyde, 'The Necessity for De-Anglicizing Ireland', *Languages, Lore and Lyrics* (Blackrock: Irish Academic Press, 1986), p. 153.
10 Hyde (1986), pp. 169–70.
11 Thomas Davis, 'Our National Language', *Essays Literary and Historical By Thomas Davis* (Dundalk: Dungalgan Press, 1914), p. 173.
12 Yeats, 'Irish National Literature', *Uncollected Prose* (Houndmills: Macmillan, 1975), p. 373.
13 Yeats (1975), p. 362.
14 Yeats, 'Nationality and Literature' (1975), p. 273.
15 Yeats, 'The Literary Movement in Ireland' (1975), pp. 187–8.
16 Yeats (1975), p. 196.
17 Yeats (1975), p. 274.
18 Yeats, 'Poetry and Tradition' (1961), p. 251.
19 Yeats, 'Preface' to *Michael Robartes and the Dancer* (Dundrum: Cuala Press, 1921).

20 George Orwell, 'W. B. Yeats' (1943). Reprinted in W. H. Pritchard, ed. *W. B. Yeats: A Critical Anthology* (Harmondsworth: Penguin, 1972), pp. 190–1.

21 Yeats, *Collected Letters* (Oxford: Clarendon, 1986), p. 813.

22 Yeats (1986), p. 885.

23 Lady Gregory, *Our Irish Theatre: A Chapter in Autobiography* (New York: Putnam, 1913), p. 101.

24 Synge quoted in Ann Saddlemyer, ed. *J. M. Synge: Plays* (Oxford: Oxford University Press, 1977), pp. 101–2.

25 Synge quoted in George Watson, *Irish Identity and the Literary Revival: Synge, Yeats, Joyce and O'Casey* (Washington, D.C.: Catholic University of America Press, 1994), p. 39.

26 Gregory (1913), pp. 9–10.

27 Gregory (1913), p. 115.

28 G. B. Shaw, *Preface for Politicians* [1906], in *John Bull's Other Island* [1904] (London: Penguin, 1984), p. 1.

29 W. B. Yeats to George Bernard Shaw, quoted in John P. Harrington, ed. *Modern Irish Drama* (London: W.W. Norton, 1991), p. 482.

30 Shaw, *Preface* (1984), p. 10.

31 D. P. Moran, *The Philosophy of Irish Ireland* (Dublin: Duffy & Gill, 1905), p. 11.

32 Moran (1905), p. 26.

33 Moran (1905), p. 25.

34 Moran (1905), pp. 77–8.

35 James Joyce, *Critical Writings*, Ellsworth Mason and Richard Ellmann, eds, (Ithaca: Cornell U P, 1989), p. 70.

36 Joyce (1989), p. 71.

37 Joyce (1989), p. 71.

38 Joyce (1989), pp. 165–6.

39 Joyce, *A Portrait of the Artist As A Young Man* [1916] (London: Penguin, 1977), p. 203.

40 Joyce (1977), p. 253.

41 Joyce (1989), pp. 171, 173.

42 Joyce in Richard Ellmann, ed. *Selected Letters of James Joyce* (New York: Viking Press, 1975), p. 25.

43 Joyce (1989), pp. 173–4.

44 Joyce in Stuart Gilbert and Richard Ellmann, eds, *The Letters of James Joyce* (New York: Viking Press, 1957–1966), Vol.2, p. 134.

45 Joyce (1989), p. 45.

46 Joyce quoted in Willard Potts, ed. *Portraits of the Artist in Exile: Recollections of James Joyce by Europeans* (London: University of Washington Press, 1979), pp. 27–8.

47 Joyce (1977), p. 189.

48 Joyce (1989), p. 198.

49 Thomas MacDonagh, *Literature in Ireland: Studies Irish and Anglo-Irish* (Dublin: Talbot, 1916), p. 169.

50 MacDonagh (1916), p. 57.

51 MacDonagh (1916), p. vii.

52 Pádraic Pearse quoted in Pronsias Mac Aonghusa and Liam Ó Réagáin, eds, *The Best of Pearse* (Cork: Mercier Press, 1967), p. 152.

53 Lady Gregory, *Poets and Dreamers: Studies and Translations from the Irish* (Dublin 1903), p. 129.

54 Pádraic Pearse, 'About Literature', *An Claidheamh Soluis* (26 May 1906), p. 6.

CHAPTER TWO

1 Daniel Corkery, *The Hidden Ireland: A Study of Gaelic Munster in the Eighteenth Century* [1924] (Dublin: Gill and Macmillan, 1989), p. 12.

2 Corkery, *Synge And Anglo-Irish Literature* (Cork: Cork University Press, 1931), p. 14.

3 Corkery (1931), p. 2.

4 Corkery (1931), pp. 9–10.

5 Corkery (1931), pp. 7, 11.

6 Corkery (1931), pp. 7–8.

7 Corkery (1931), p. 3.

8 Corkery (1931), pp. 12–13.

9 Corkery (1931), p. 19.

10 For a good account of this legislative context see Elizabeth Butler Cullingford, *Gender and History in Yeats's Love Poetry* (Cambridge: Cambridge University Press, 1993), p. 142.

11 George Russell, 'Art and National Life' *Irish Statesman* Vol.10, no.2 (May 1928), p. 227. For an excellent account of Russell's life and work, see Nicholas Allen, *George Russell (AE) and the New Ireland, 1905–1930* (Dublin: Four Courts Press, 2002). A good collection of some of Russell's writings is offered by *Selections from the Contributions to the Irish Homestead by G.W. Russell*, edited by Henry Summerfield (Gerrards Cross: Colin Smythe, 1978).

12 George Bernard Shaw, 'The Censorship', *Irish Statesman* Col.11, no.11 (November 1928), pp. 621–2.

13 Quoted in Terence Brown, *Ireland: A Social and Cultural History 1922–79* (Glasgow: Fontana, 1981), p. 146.

14 Sean O'Faoláin, 'Silent Ireland', *The Bell* 6.5 (1943), p. 464.

15 'Seumas' is collected in *The Hounds of Banba* [1920] (New York: Books for Libraries, 1970).

16 'The Patriot' is collected in *Midsummer Madness and Other Stories* [1932] and reprinted in *The Collected Short Stories of Sean O'Faoláin* (Boston: Little Brown, 1983).

17 For an informative survey see Michael L. Storey, *Representing the Troubles in Irish Short Fiction* (Washington, D.C.: The Catholic University of America Press, 2004).

18 Frank O'Connor, 'The Future of Irish Literature', *Horizon* Vol.5 No.25 (Jan 1942), p. 56.

19 Frank O'Connor, *An Only Child* (London: Macmillan, 1965), p. 210.

20 O'Connor (1965), p. 237.

21 For an excellent anthology of writing from this journal see Sean McMahon, ed. *The Best from the Bell* (Dublin: O'Brien Press, 1978).

22 Sean O'Faoláin, 'This is Your Magazine', *The Bell* (Oct 1940), pp. 5–6.

23 Sean O'Faoláin, 'Ulster', *The Bell* Vol.2, no.4 (1941), p. 9.

24 Frank O'Connor, *The Lonely Voice: A Study of the Short Story* (London: Macmillan, 1963), p. 18.

25 O'Connor (1963), p. 45.

26 Benedict Anderson, *Imagined Communities: Reflections on the Origin and Spread of Nationalism* (London: Verso, 1991).

27 For a critical account which regards the Irish novel as specifically problematic in these terms see Terry Eagleton's *Heathcliff and the Great Hunger: Studies in Irish Culture* (London: Verso, 1995).

28 O'Connor (1963), p. 21.

29 Frank O'Connor, *The Mirror on the Roadway: A Study of the Modern Novel* (London: Harvard Summer School Lectures, 1957), p. 253.

30 O'Connor, (1957), p. 257.

31 Sean O'Faoláin, 'The Dilemma of Irish Letters', *The Month* Vol.2, No.6 (1949), pp. 375–6.

32 Patrick Kavanagh, *Collected Pruse*, (London: MacGibbon and Kee, 1967), pp. 19, 13.

33 Kavanagh (1967), pp. 282–3.

34 *Kavanagh's Weekly*, 1.1 (12 April 1952), p. 7.

35 Patrick Kavanagh, 'Paris in Aran', *Kavanagh's Weekly*, Vol.9 (7 June 1952), p. 7.

36 Austin Clarke, Letter to the Editor, *The Irish Statesman* (20 Feb 1926), p. 740.

37 Quoted in Jonathan Bardon, *A History of Ulster* (Belfast: Blackstaff Press, 1992), pp. 538–9.

38 Quoted in *Irish News*, 13 April 1948.

39 Quoted in *Belfast Telegraph*, 10 May 1969.
40 John Hewitt, 'Regionalism: The Last Chance' (1947) in Tom Clyde, ed. *Ancestral Voices: The Selected Prose of John Hewitt* (Belfast: Blackstaff Press, 1987), p. 122.
41 John Boyd, 'Introduction', *Lagan* No.1 (1943), p. 6.
42 O'Faoláin, 'An Ulster Issue', *The Bell* (July 1942), p. 230.
43 Hewitt (1987), p. 117.
44 Hewitt, 'The Bitter Gourd: Some Problems of the Ulster Writer', *Lagan* 3 (1945), p. 104.
45 Hewitt (1945), p. 108.
46 Sam Hanna Bell, *Erin's Orange Lilly: Ulster Custom and Folklore* (London: Dennis Dobson, 1956), pp. 7–8.
47 Hanna Bell, 'A Banderol: An Introduction', in Sam Hanna Bell, John Hewitt and Nesca A. Robb, eds. *The Arts in Ulster: A Symposium* (London: Harrap, 1951), p. 19.
48 Hanna Bell (1951), p. 13.
49 Louis MacNeice quoted in Edna Longley, *Poetry in the Wars* (Newcastle: Bloodaxe, 1986), p. 202.
50 Samuel Beckett in Beckett et al., *Our Exagmination Round His Factification For Incamination Of Work In Progress* [1929] (London: Faber, 1961), p. 4.
51 Beckett (1929), p. 14.
52 Eugene Jolas in Beckett et al. (1929), p. 79.
53 It should be pointed out that New Criticism focused its close attentions on the short poem and, arguably, had greater difficulty in dealing with longer (e.g., narrative) poems.
54 Denis Donoghue 'Notes Towards A Critical Method: Language As Order' *Studies*, 42 (1955), p. 181.
55 Donald Davie, 'Reflections of an English Writer in Ireland' *Studies* 44 (1955), p. 440.
56 Vivian Mercier, 'An Irish School of Criticism?' *Studies* 45 (1956), pp. 84–5.
57 Mercier (1956), p. 86.
58 Vivian Mercier and David H. Greene 'Introduction' to Mercier and Greene, eds, *1000 Years of Irish Prose: Part 1 – The Literary Revival* [1952] (New York: Devin-Adair, 1953), p. xx.
59 Vivian Mercier, *The Irish Comic Tradition* (Oxford: Oxford University Press, 1962), p. 246.
60 Vivian Mercier, *Beckett/Beckett* (Oxford: Oxford University Press, 1977), p. xii.
61 Theodor W. Adorno, 'Trying to Understand *Endgame*', in Brian O'Connor, ed. *The Adorno Reader* (Oxford: Blackwell, 2000), p. 322.
62 Adorno, *Negative Dialectics*, Trans. Brian Ashton (London: Routledge, 1973), pp. 380–1.
63 Richard Ellmann, *James Joyce* (New York: Oxford University Press, 1959), p. 1.
64 Richard Ellmann, *The Consciousness of Joyce* (London: Faber, 1977), p. 13.
65 Hugh Kenner, *Dublin's Joyce* (London: Chatto & Windus, 1955), p. 12.
66 Kenner (1955), p. 132.
67 Kenner, *Joyce's Voices* (London: Faber, 1978), p. 17.
68 Kenner, *A Reader's Guide to Samuel Beckett* (London, Thames and Hudson, 1973), p. 134.
69 Kenner, *A Colder Eye: The Modern Irish Writers* (New York: Alfred A. Kopf, 1983), p. 3.
70 Kenner (1983), p. 7.
71 Seamus Deane, *Heroic Styles: The Tradition of an Idea* (Derry: Field Day, 1984), p. 17.
72 Declan Kiberd, *Inventing Ireland* (London: Cape, 1995), p. 345.
73 See Ngũgĩ wa Thiong'o, *Decolonizing the Mind: The Politics of African Literature* (London: Heinemann, 1986).

CHAPTER THREE

1 George D. Boyce and Alan O'Day, *The Making of Irish History* (London: Routledge, 1996), pp. 5–6.
2 Francis Shaw, 'The Canon of Irish History – A Challenge', *Studies* 61 (Summer 1972), p. 119.

3 R. F. Foster quoted in Seamus Deane, ed. *The Field Day Anthology of Irish Writing* Vol.3 (Derry: Field Day, 1991), p. 586.

4 Seamus Deane quoted by Mitchell W. Harris, 'An Ersatz Ministry of Culture: The Political Cultural Function of the Field Day Theatre Company' in C. C. Barfoot and Rias van den Doel, eds, *Ritual Remembering: History, Myth and Politics in Anglo-Irish Drama* (Amsterdam: Rodopi, 1995), p. 159.

5 Quoted in Marilynn Richtarik, *Acting Between the Lines: The Field Day Theatre Company and Irish Cultural Politics 1980–1984* (Oxford: Clarendon Press, 1994), p. 135.

6 Deane, 'What Is Field Day?', Programme Notes for the Field Day Production of *Three Sisters*, 1981.

7 Seamus Deane, 'Introduction' to *Nationalism, Colonialism and Literature* (Minneapolis: University of Minnesota Press, 1990), pp. 3, 6.

8 R. F. Foster, *Paddy and Mr Punch* (London: Penguin, 1993), p. xv.

9 Deane (1990), p. 15.

10 Deane, 'General Introduction' (1991), p. xix.

11 Declan Kiberd, *Inventing Ireland* (London: Cape, 1995), p. 116.

12 Seamus Deane, *Civilians and Barbarians* (Derry: Field Day, 1983), p. 12.

13 Tom Paulin, *The Faber Book of Political Verse* (London: Faber, 1986), pp. 41–2.

14 W. J. McCormack, *Ascendancy and Tradition in Anglo-Irish Literary History* (Oxford: Clarendon, 1985), p. 12.

15 Gerry Smyth, *Decolonization and Criticism: The Construction of Irish Literature* (London: Pluto Press, 1998), p. 73.

16 Conor Cruise O'Brien, *Passion and Cunning and Other Essays* (London: Wiedenfeld & Nicolson, 1988), p. 41.

17 George Watson, *Irish Identity and the Literary Revival: Synge, Yeats, Joyce and O'Casey* (Washington, D.C.: Catholic University of America Press, 1994), p. 103.

18 Watson (1994), p. 110.

19 Watson (1994), p. 127.

20 Seamus Deane, *Celtic Revivals: Essays in Modern Irish Literature, 1880–1980* (London: Faber, 1985), p. 28.

21 Deane (1985), p. 38.

22 David Lloyd, *Anomalous States: Irish Writing and the Post-Colonial Moment* (Dublin: Lilliput Press, 1993), p. 69.

23 Seamus Deane, *Heroic Styles: The Tradition of an Idea* (Derry: Field Day, 1984), pp. 5–6.

24 Deane (1984), pp. 9–10.

25 Deane (1984), p. 18.

26 Paul Scott Stanfield, *Yeats and Politics in the 1930s* (Basingstoke: Macmillan, 1988) p. 185. Elizabeth Butler Cullingford's *Yeats, Ireland and Fascism* (London: Macmillan, 1981) also provides a good account of Yeats's politics and seeks to defend him from accusations of outright Fascism.

27 Edna Longley, *The Living Stream: Literature and Revisionism in Ireland* (Newcastle: Bloodaxe, 1994), p. 23.

28 Longley (1994), p. 26.

29 Edward W. Said, 'Yeats and Decolonization' in Deane, ed. (1990) pp. 69–70.

30 John Wilson Foster, *Colonial Consequences: Essays in Irish Literature and Culture* (Dublin: Lilliput Press, 1991), p. 208.

31 Longley (1994), p. 29.

32 Longley (1994), p. 31.

33 Yeats, 'Irish National Literature', *Uncollected Prose* (Houndmills: Macmillan, 1975), p. 360.

34 Longley (1994), pp. 135–6.

35 Longley (1994), pp. 83–4.

36 For full, rich critical bibliographies of Yeats, see Terence Brown's *The Life of W. B. Yeats: A Critical Biography* (Oxford: Blackwell, 1999); and R. F. Foster's *W. B. Yeats: A Life*

Vol.1: The Apprentice Mage 1865–1914 (Oxford: Oxford University Press, 1997); *W. B. Yeats: A Life Vol.2: The Arch Poet 1915–1939* (Oxford: Oxford University Press, 2003).

37 Marjorie Howes, *Yeats's Nations: Gender, Class, Irishness* (Cambridge: Cambridge University Press, 1996), p. 162.

38 Deane (1984), pp. 16–17.

39 Deane, *Strange Country: Modernity and Nationhood in Irish Writing since 1790* (Oxford: Clarendon Press, 1997), pp. 156–7.

40 Joep Leerssen, *Remembrance and Imagination: Patterns in the Historical and Literary Representation of Ireland in the Nineteenth Century* (Cork: Cork University Press, 1996), p. 35.

41 Leerssen (1996), p. 37.

42 Gilles Deleuze and Felix Guattari, *Franz Kafka: Towards A Minor Literature* (London: University of Minnesota Press, 1986), p. 16.

43 Deleuze and Guattari (1986), p. 17.

44 David Lloyd *Nationalism and Minor Literature: James Clarence Mangan* (London: University of California Press, 1987), p. 22.

45 Deane (1985), p. 92.

46 Lloyd (1993), p. 106.

47 Lloyd (1993), p. 109. Colin MacCabe's *James Joyce and the Revolution of the Word* (Houndmills: Palgrave Macmillan, 2003) also offers a superb account of the narrative politics of Joyce's fiction. MacCabe argues that Joyce's multiplicity of discourses undermines 'meta-language', the conventional novel's usual privileging of one, authoritative narrative register.

48 Vincent J. Cheng, *Joyce, Race and Empire* (Cambridge: Cambridge University Press, 1995), p. 291.

49 Kiberd (1995), p. 333.

50 Kiberd (1995), p. 355.

51 Fredric Jameson, *Modernism and Imperialism* [1988] in Deane, ed. (1990), pp. 61–2.

52 Luke Gibbons, *Transformations in Irish Culture* (Cork: Cork University Press, 1996), p. 3.

53 Gibbons (1996), p. 6, 167.

54 T. S. Eliot, '*Ulysses*, Order and Myth', *The Dial* 75.5 (November 1923), pp. 480–3; p. 483. (See also Frank Kermode, ed. *Selected Prose of T. S. Eliot* (London: Harvest, 1975), pp. 175–8.

55 James Joyce, *Critical Writings*, Ellsworth Mason and Richard Ellmann, eds, (Ithaca: Cornell University Press), p. 44.

56 Joyce, *The Letters of James Joyce*, Stuart Gilbert and Richard Ellmann, eds, (New York: Viking Press, 1957–1966) Vol.2, p. 81.

57 Emer Nolan, *James Joyce and Nationalism* (London: Routledge, 1995).

58 Joyce, *Finnegans Wake* [1939] (London: Penguin, 1995), p. 152.

59 Derek Attridge and Marjorie Howes, 'Introduction', *Semicolonial Joyce* (Cambridge: Cambridge University Press, 2000), pp. 3–4.

60 Daniel Corkery, *Synge and Anglo-Irish Literature* (Cork: Cork University Press, 1931), p. 28.

61 Watson (1994), p. 35.

62 Watson (1994), p. 85.

63 D. E. S. Maxwell, 'Irish Drama, 1899–1929' in Deane, ed. (1991) Vol.2, p. 566.

64 Robert Welch, *The Abbey Theatre, 1899–1999: Form and Pressure* (Oxford: Oxford University Press, 1999), p. 42.

65 Gibbons (1996), p. 85.

66 Nicholas Grene, *The Politics of Irish Drama: Plays in Context from Boucicault to Friel* (Cambridge: Cambridge University Press, 2002), p. 97.

67 Deane (1985), p. 53.

68 Lionel Pilkington, *Theatre and the State in Twentieth-Century Ireland: Cultivating the People* (London: Routledge, 2001), pp. 56–7.

69 Kiberd (1995), p. 61.

70 Grene (2002), p. 21.

CHAPTER FOUR

1 David Krause, *Sean O'Casey: The Man and His Work* (London: Macmillan, 1960).

2 Seamus Deane, *Celtic Revivals: Essays in Modern Irish Literature* (London: Faber, 1985), p. 109.

3 Declan Kiberd, 'The Elephant of Revolutionary Forgetfulness' in Maírín Ni Dhonnochadha and Theo Dorgan, eds, *Revising the Rising* (Derry: Field Day, 1991), p. 18.

4 Fintan O'Toole, 'Going West: The Country Versus the City in Irish Writing', *The Crane Bag* 9.2 (1985), p. 114.

5 Lionel Pilkington, *Theatre and the State in Twentieth-Century Ireland: Cultivating the People* (London: Routledge, 2001), p. 90.

6 Pilkington (2001), p. 92.

7 Quoted in Nicholas Grene, *The Politics of Irish Drama: Plays in Context from Boucicault to Friel* (Cambridge: Cambridge University Press, 2002), p. 139.

8 Grene (2002), pp. 140–1.

9 Grene (2002), p. 144.

10 Daniel Corkery, *Synge and Anglo-Irish Literature* (Cork: Cork University Press), p. 3.

11 Stopford A. Brooke, 'Introduction', *A Treasury of Irish Poetry in the English Tongue* (London: Smith, Elder & Co., 1900), p. xix.

12 Paul Delaney, 'Becoming National: Daniel Corkery and the Reterritorialized Subject' in Alan Gillis and Aaron Kelly, eds, *Critical Ireland: New Essays in Literature and Culture* (Dublin: Four Courts, 2001), p. 47.

13 Antoinette Quinn, *Patrick Kavanagh: Born Again Romantic* (Dublin: Gill and Macmillan, 1991), p. 130.

14 Quinn (1991), p. 153.

15 Quinn (1991), p. 283.

16 Alan Gillis, *Irish Poetry of the 1930s* (Oxford: Oxford University Press), p. 15.

17 Gillis (2005), p. 95.

18 Denis Donoghue, *We Irish* (Berkeley: University of California Press, 1986), p. 248.

19 Terence Brown, *Ireland's Literature: Selected Essays* (Gigginstown: Lilliput Press, 1988), p. 133.

20 Gillis (2005), p. 137.

21 David Lloyd, *Anomalous States: Irish Writing and the Post-Colonial Moment* (Dublin: Lilliput Press, 1993), p. 46.

22 Lloyd (1993), p. 56.

23 See Ruby Cohn, ed. *Samuel Beckett, Disjecta: Miscellaneous Writings and a Dramatic Fragment* (New York: Grove Press, 1984).

24 Cohn, ed. (1984), pp. 171–2.

25 David Lloyd, 'Republics of Difference: Yeats, MacGreevy, Beckett', *Third Text* 19.5 (2005), pp. 473–4.

26 Declan Kiberd, *Inventing Ireland* (London: Cape, 1995), p. 535.

27 Kiberd (1995), p. 538.

28 W. J. McCormack, *From Burke to Beckett: Ascendancy, Tradition and Betrayal in Literary History* (Cork: Cork University Press, 1994), pp. 52–3.

29 Neil Corcoran, 'Discovery of a Lack: History and Ellipsis in Elizabeth Bowen's *The Last September*', *Irish University Review* 31.2 (Autumn/Winter 2001), p. 315.

30 Corcoran (2001), p. 320.

31 Seamus Deane, *Strange Country: Modernity and Nationhood in Irish Writing since 1790* (Oxford: Clarendon Press, 1997), p. 161.

32 Deane (1997), p. 161.

33 Sarah McKibben, '*The Poor Mouth*: A Parody of (Post)Colonial Irish Manhood', *Research in African Literatures* 34.4 (2003), pp. 96, 112.

34 See Salman Rushdie, *Imaginary Homelands: Essays and Criticism, 1981–1991* (London: Granta, 1992).

35 Kiberd (1995), pp. 528–9.
36 Francis Mulhern, *The Present Lasts A Long Time* (Cork: Cork University Press, 1998), p. 21.
37 Terence Brown, *The Whole Protestant Community: The Making of a Historical Myth* (Derry: Field Day, 1985), p. 5.
38 Joe Cleary, *Literature, Partition and the Nation State: Culture and Conflict in Ireland, Israel and Palestine* (Cambridge: Cambridge University Press, 2002), pp. 70–1.
39 Cleary (2002), pp. 71–2.
40 Kirkland, *Literature and Culture in Northern Ireland since 1965: Moments of Danger* (London: Longman, 1996), p. 29.
41 John Wilson Foster, *Colonial Consequences: Essays in Irish Literature and Culture* (Dublin: Lilliput Press, 1991), p. 118.
42 Foster (1991), p. 120.
43 Foster (1991), p. 123.
44 Peter McDonald, *Mistaken Identities: Poetry and Northern Ireland* (Oxford: Clarendon Press, 1997), p. 40.
45 Edna Longley, *The Living Stream: Literature and Revisionism in Ireland* (Newcastle: Bloodaxe, 1994), p. 117.
46 Edna Longley, *Poetry in the Wars* (Newcastle: Bloodaxe, 1986), p. 90.
47 Longley (1994), pp. 257–8.
48 Gillis (2005), pp. 60–1.
49 Longley (1994), p. 127.
50 Lionel Pilkington, *Theatre and the State in Twentieth-Century Ireland* (London: Routledge, 2001), p. 184.

CHAPTER FIVE

1 Hanna Sheehy-Skeffington quoted in Margaret Ward, *In Their Own Voice: Women and Irish Nationalism* (Dublin: Attic Press, 1995), p. 3.
2 Countess Markiewicz quoted in Ward (1995), p. 31.
3 Margaret Ward, *Unmanageable Revolutionaries: Women and Irish Nationalism* (London: Pluto Press, 1983).
4 Clair Wills, *Improprieties: Politics and Sexuality in Northern Irish Poetry* (Oxford: Clarendon Press, 1993), p. 57.
5 Terry Eagleton, *Nationalism, Irony and Commitment* (Derry: Field Day, 1988), p. 6.
6 Nicholas Grene, *The Politics of Irish Drama: Plays in Context from Boucicault to Friel* (Cambridge: Cambridge UP, 2002), pp. 81–3.
7 Peter Stallybrass and Allon White, *The Politics and Poetics of Transgression* (London: Methuen, 1986), p. 5.
8 William Irwin Thompson, *The Imagination of an Insurrection: A Story of an Ideological Movement* (New York: Oxford University Press, 1967), p. 124.
9 Ashis Nandy, *Exiled at Home: At the Edge of Psychology, The Intimate Enemy and Creating a Nationality* (Delhi: Oxford University Press, 1998), p. 100.
10 Moran (1905), p. 6. Indeed, Moran would use the pages of *The Leader* to pillory George Russell as the 'Hairy Fairy'.
11 Gerardine Meaney, *Sex and Nation: Women in Irish Culture and Politics* (Dublin: Attic Press, 1991), p. 7.
12 Meaney (1991), p. 5.
13 Meaney (1991), p. 13.
14 Marilyn Reizbaum, 'Canonical Double Cross: Scottish and Irish Women's Writing', in Karen E. Lawrence, ed. *Decolonizing Tradition: New Views of Twentieth-Century 'British' Literary Canons* (Chicago: University of Illinois Press, 1992), p. 167. See also Marilyn Reizbaum,

'Not A Crying Game: The Feminist Appeal; Nationalism, Feminism and the Contemporary Literatures of Scotland and Ireland', *Scotlands* 2 (1994), pp. 24–31.

15 Reizbaum (1992), pp. 171–2.

16 Anne Owens Weekes, *Irish Women Writers: An Uncharted Tradition* (Lexington: University of Kentucky Press, 1990), p. 5.

17 Carol Coulter, *The Hidden Tradition: Feminism, Women and Nationalism in Ireland* (Cork: Cork University Press, 1993), p. 3.

18 Coulter (1993), p. 19.

19 Ailbhe Smyth, 'The Floozie in the Jacuzzi' *Irish Review* 6 (1989), pp. 8–9.

20 Smyth (1989), p. 10.

21 Adrian Frazier, 'Queering the Irish Renaissance: The Masculinities of Moore, Martyn and Yeats' in Anthony Bradley and Maryann Gialanella Valiulis, eds, *Gender and Sexuality in Modern Ireland* (Amherst: University of Massachusetts Press, 1997), p. 9.

22 Frazier (1997), p. 11.

23 Éibhear Walshe, 'The First Gay Irishman? Ireland and the Wilde Trials', *Éire-Ireland* 40.3–4 (2005), p. 56.

24 Elizabeth Butler Cullingford, *Gender and History in Yeats's Love Poetry* (Cambridge: Cambridge University Press, 1988), pp. 5–6.

25 Richard Brown, *James Joyce and Sexuality* (Cambridge: Cambridge University Press, 1988), pp. 89, 100, 104.

26 Kate Soper, 'Stephen Heroine' in *Troubled Pleasures: Writings on Politics, Gender and Hedonism* (London: Verso, 1990), pp. 260–2.

27 Longley, *The Living Stream: Literature and Revisionism in Ireland* (Newcastle: Bloodaxe, 1994), p. 73.

28 Colin Graham, *Deconstructing Ireland* (Edinburgh: Edinburgh University Press, 2001), p. 82.

29 Graham (2001), p. 83.

30 See Liam Kennedy, 'Modern Ireland: Postcolonial Society or Postcolonial Pretensions?', *Irish Review* 13 (Winter 1992/1993), pp. 107–121; and Stephen Howe, *Ireland and Empire: Colonial Legacies in Irish History and Culture* (Oxford: Oxford University Press, 2000).

31 See Colin Graham, '"Liminal Spaces": Post-Colonial Theories and Irish Culture', *The Irish Review* (Autumn/Winter 1994), pp. 29–43.

32 See David Lloyd's 'Nationalisms Against the State; Towards a Critique of the Anti-Nationalist Prejudice' in T. P. Toley et al., eds, *Gender and Colonialism* (Galway, 1995); *Ireland after History* (Cork: Cork University Press, 1999); *Anomalous States: Irish Writing and the Post-Colonial Moment* (Dublin: Lilliput Press, 1993); and Carol Coulter's aforementioned *The Hidden Tradition*.

33 Colin Graham, 'Subalternity and Gender: Problems of Postcolonial Irishness' in Claire Connolly, ed. *Theorizing Ireland* (Houndmills: Palgrave Macmillan, 2003), p. 158.

34 Frank O'Connor, *The Lonely Voice: A Study of the Short Story* (London: Macmillan, 1963), p. 203.

35 Robert L. Stevens and Sylvia Stevens, 'An Interview with Mary Lavin' *Studies* 86.341 (1997), p. 46.

36 Maurice Harmon, 'From Conversations with Mary Lavin', *Irish University Review* 27.2 (1997), p. 289.

37 Bonnie Kime Scott, 'Mary Lavin and the Life of the Mind', *Irish University Review* 9.2 (1979), p. 278.

38 Gerardine Meaney, 'Aesthetics and Politics' in Angela Bourke, ed. *The Field Day Anthology of Irish Writing: Irish Women's Writing and Traditions* Vol.5 (Cork: Cork University Press, 2002), p. 1072.

39 B. G. MacCarthy, *The Female Pen: Women Writers and Novelists 1621–1818* (Cork: Cork University Press, 1994), p. 1.

40 MacCarthy (1994), pp. 500–1.

41 MacCarthy (1994), p. 501.

42 Nuala O'Faolain, 'Irish Women and Writing in Modern Ireland' in Eilean Ní Chuilleanáin, ed. *Irish Women: Image and Achievement. Women in Irish Culture from Earliest Times* (Dublin: Attic Press, 1985), p. 132.

43 O'Faolain (1985), p. 132.

44 O'Faolain (1985), p. 133.

45 Eve Patten, 'Women and Fiction 1985–1990', *Krino* 8.9 (1990), p. 4.

46 Wills (1993), p. 77.

47 Kathryn Kirkpatrick, 'Introduction' in Kirkpatrick, ed. *Border Crossings: Irish Women Writers and National Identities* (Tuscaloosa: University of Alabama Press, 2000), p. 6.

48 Phyllis Lassner, *Elizabeth Bowen* (Maryland: Barnes and Noble, 1990), pp. 142–3.

49 Elizabeth Bowen, 'Preface to *Orlando*' in Hermione Lee, ed. *The Mulberry Tree: Writings of Elizabeth Bowen* (London: Virago, 1986), p. 131.

50 Elizabeth Bowen, 'Why Do I Write?' (1948). This is a transcript of a BBC radio broadcast from 10 July 1948. Quoted in Bourke, ed. (2002), p. 1096.

51 Bowen quoted in Bourke, ed. (2002), p. 1098.

52 Eavan Boland, 'Continuing the Encounter' in Eibhear Walshe, ed. *Ordinary People Dancing: Essays on Kate O'Brien* (Cork: Cork University Press, 1993), p. 16.

53 Kate O'Brien quoted in Bourke, ed. (2002), p. 1084.

54 Meaney, quoted in Bourke, ed. (2002), pp. 1072–3.

55 Kate O'Brien, *Land of Spices* [1941] (London: Virago, 1988), p. 15.

56 Catriona Clear, *Nuns in Nineteenth Century Ireland* (Dublin: Gill and Macmillan, 1987), pp. 143, 147.

57 Joan Hoff and Maureen Coulter, 'Editors' Note' in Hoff and Coulter, eds, *Irish Women's Voices: Past and Present. Special Issue: Journal of Women's History* 6.4 (1995), p. 10.

58 Mary Breen in Walshe, ed. (1993), p. 179.

59 O'Brien (1988), p. 22.

60 Elizabeth Butler Cullingford, '"Our Nuns Are Not A Nation": Politicizing the Convent in Literature and Film', *Éire-Ireland* 41.1 (2006), pp. 27–8.

61 John McGahern quoted in Eileen Kennedy, 'Q & A with John McGahern', *Irish Literary Supplement* 3 (Spring 1984), p. 40.

62 Jürgen Kamm, 'John McGahern' in Rüdiger Imhof, ed. *Contemporary Irish Novelists* (Tübingen: Narr, 1990), p. 187.

63 Denis Sampson, *Outstaring Nature's Eye: The Fiction of John McGahern* (Dublin: Lilliput Press, 1993), pp. 35, 138.

64 McGahern, 'The Image', *Canadian Journal of Irish Studies* 17.1 (July 1991), p. 12.

65 Terence Brown, *Ireland's Literature: Selected Essays* (Gigginstown: Lilliput Press, 1988), p. 175.

66 Brown (1988), pp. 183–4.

67 Antoinette Quinn, 'A Prayer for My Daughter: Patriarchy in *Amongst Women*', *Canadian Journal of Irish Studies* 17.1 (July 1991), p. 81.

68 Antoinette Quinn (1991), p. 83.

69 John McGahern, 'The Solitary Reader', *Canadian Journal of Irish Studies* 17.1 (July 1991), p. 23.

70 Eamonn Hughes, '"How I Achieved This Trick": Representations of Masculinity in Contemporary Irish Fiction' in Elmer Kennedy-Andrews, ed. *Irish Fiction since the 1960s* (Gerrards Cross: Colin Smythe, 2006), p. 123.

71 Hughes (2006), p. 130.

72 John McGahern, *Amongst Women* (London: Faber, 1990), p. 66.

73 See Kiberd, *Inventing Ireland* (London: Cape, 1995), pp. 380–94.

74 Hughes (2006), p. 125.

75 David Lloyd (1999), p. 2.

CHAPTER SIX

1 Fintan O'Toole, *Black Hole, Green Card: The Disappearance of Ireland* (Dublin: New Island Books, 1994), p. 41.

2 Fintan O'Toole, *A Mass for Jesse James: A Journey Through 1980s Ireland* (Dublin: Raven Arts Press, 1990), p. 10.

3 O'Toole (1990), pp. 8–9.

4 Quoted in O'Toole (1990), p. 12.

5 O'Toole (1990), pp. 13–14.

6 Tom Herron, 'ContamiNation: Patrick McCabe and Colm Tóibín's Pathologies of the Republic', Liam Harte and Michael Parker, eds, *Contemporary Irish Fiction: Themes, Tropes, Theories* (Houndmills: Macmillan, 2000), p. 168.

7 Herron (2000), p. 186.

8 Herron (2000), p. 189.

9 Colm Tóibín quoted in Edna Longley, *The Living Stream: Literature and Revisionism in Ireland* (Newcastle: Bloodaxe, 1994), p. 25.

10 Banville quoted in Longley (1994), p. 179.

11 John Banville, 'The Ireland of de Valera and O'Faoláin', *Irish Review* 17–18 (Winter 1995), p. 151.

12 Banville quoted in 'Novelists on the Novel', *Crane Bag* 3.1 (1979), p. 76.

13 Rüdiger Imhof, 'My Readers, That Small Band, Deserve a Rest: An Interview with John Banville', *Irish University Review* 11.1 (Spring 1981), p. 5.

14 Banville quoted in 'Out of Chaos Comes Order: John Banville Interviewed by Ciaran Carty', *Sunday Tribune* (14 September 1986), p. 18.

15 John Banville, 'A Talk', *Irish University Review* 11.1 (Spring 1981), p. 14.

16 Banville (1981), p. 17.

17 Seán Lysaght, 'Banville's Tetralogy: The Limits of Mimesis', *Irish University Review* 21.1 (1991), p. 99.

18 Joseph McMinn, 'Naming the World: Language and Experience in John Banville's Fiction', *Irish University Review* 23.2 (1993), p. 192.

19 Richard Kearney, *Transitions: Narratives in Modern Irish Culture* (Manchester: Manchester University Press, 1988), p. 97.

20 Nicholas Grene, *The Politics of Irish Drama: Plays in Context from Boucicault to Friel* (Cambridge: Cambridge University Press, 2002) p. 236.

21 Grene (2002), p. 221.

22 Eavan Boland quoted in Edna Longley, *Poetry in the Wars* (Newcastle: Bloodaxe, 1986), p. 199.

23 Eavan Boland, 'Writing the Political Poem in Ireland', *The Southern Review* 31.3 (Summer, 1995), p. 485.

24 Eavan Boland, *Object Lessons: The Life of the Woman and the Poet in Our Time* (London: Vintage, 1995), p. 183.

25 Boland (1995), p. 110.

26 Longley (1994), p. 173.

27 Clair Wills, *Improprieties: Politics and Sexuality in Northern Irish Poetry* (Oxford: Oxford University Press, 1993), p. 61.

28 Boland (1995), p. 147.

29 Gerardine Meaney, 'Myth, History, and the Politics of Subjectivity: Eavan Boland and Irish Women's Writing', *Women: A Cultural Review* 4.2 (Autumn, 1993), p. 148.

30 Andrew J. Auge, 'Fracture and Wound: Eavan Boland's Poetry of Nationality', *New Hibernia Review* 8.2 (Summer 2004), p. 121.

31 Kearney, *Postnationalist Ireland* (London: Routledge, 1996), pp. 139–40.

32 Kearney (1996), p. 132.

33 Longley (1994), pp. 65–6.

34 Neil Corcoran, *After Yeats and Joyce: Reading Modern Irish Literature* (Oxford: Oxford University Press, 1997), p. 120.

35 Kiberd, *Inventing Ireland* (London: Cape, 1995), pp. 609–10.

36 Gerry Smyth, 'The Right to the City: Re-Presentations of Dublin in Contemporary Irish Fiction', Liam Harte and Michael Parker, eds, *Contemporary Irish Fiction: Themes, Tropes, Theories* (Houndmills: Macmillan, 2000), p. 26. Gerry Smyth also offers a wide-ranging account of place in Irish culture more generally in his *Space and the Irish Cultural Imagination* (Basingstoke: Palgrave Macmillan, 2001). Another interesting analysis of the importance of spatial concerns in Irish culture is offered by Oona Frawley, *Irish Pastoral: Nostalgia in Irish Literature* (Dublin: Irish Academic Press).

37 Smyth (2000), p. 30.

38 Gerry Smyth, *The Novel and the Nation: Studies in the New Irish Fiction* (London: Pluto, 1997), p. 69.

39 Christine St Peter, 'Petrifying Time: Incest Narratives from Contemporary Ireland' in Michael Parker and Liam Harte, eds, *Contemporary Irish Fiction: Themes, Tropes, Theories* (Houndmills: Macmillan, 2000), p. 142.

40 See Emma Donoghue, 'Noises from Woodsheds: Tales of Irish Lesbians, 1886–1989' in L. O'Carroll and E. Collins, eds, *Lesbian and Gay Visions of Ireland* (London: Cassell, 1995), pp. 158–70; and Mary Dorcey, *A Noise from the Woodshed* (1989).

41 Antoinette Quinn, 'New Noises from the Woodshed: The Novels of Emma Donoghue' in Parker and Harte, eds, (2000), p. 165.

42 Ray Ryan, 'The Republic and Ireland: Pluralism, Politics, and Narrative Form' in Ryan, ed. *Writing the Irish Republic; Literature, Culture, Politics 1949–1999* (Houndmills: Macmillan, 2000), p. 98.

43 Longley (1995), pp. 194–5.

44 Kirkland, *Identity Parades: Northern Irish Culture and Dissident Subjects* (Liverpool: Liverpool University Press, 2002), p. 4.

45 Eamonn Hughes, 'Introduction: Northern Ireland – Border Country' in Eamonn Hughes, ed. *Culture and Politics in Northern Ireland* (Milton Keynes: Open University Press, 1991), pp. 3–4.

46 Hughes, 'Introduction', p. 10.

47 Hughes, 'Introduction', p. 7.

48 Seamus Heaney, 'Envies and Identifications: Dante and The Modern Poet', *Irish University Review* 15.1 (Spring 1985), p. 19.

49 Seamus Heaney, *Preoccupations: Selected Prose 1968–1978* (London: Faber, 1980), p. 57.

50 John Haffenden, 'An Interview with Seamus Heaney' *Viewpoints* (London: Faber, 1981), pp. 60–1.

51 Heaney (1980), pp. 57–8.

52 See Frieda Fordham, *An Introduction to Jung's Psychology* (London: Penguin, 1962), p. 28.

53 C. G. Jung and Richard Wilhelm, *The Secret of the Golden Flower* (London, 1931), p. 132.

54 'Editorial 1/Endodermis', *Crane Bag* 1.1 (1977), p. 4.

55 Brian Friel quoted in John Gray, 'Field Day, Five Years On', *Linen Hall Review* 2.2 (Summer 1985), p. 7.

56 See Fordham (1962), p. 65.

57 Quoted in J. Randall, 'An Interview with Seamus Heaney', *Ploughshares* 5.3 (1979) p. 17.

58 Quoted in Seamus Deane, 'Unhappy and at Home', *The Crane Bag* 1.1 (1977), p. 62.

59 Haffenden (1981), p. 63.

60 Edna Longley, 'The Aesthetic and the Territorial' in Elmer Kennedy-Andrews, ed. *Contemporary Irish Poetry* (London: Macmillan, 1992), p. 77. See also her *Poetry in the Wars* for a critique of Heaney. From a very difference stance, David Lloyd's *Anomalous States* attacks the identity politics of Heaney in keeping with Lloyd's critique of cultural nationalism that we have already analyzed in the Revival.

61 Neil Corcoran, *Poets of Modern Ireland* (Cardiff: University of Wales Press, 1999), p. 101.

62 Corcoran (1999), p. 103.

63 Quoted in Neil Corcoran, *Seamus Heaney* (London: Faber, 1986), p. 127.

64 Corcoran (1999), p. 104.

65 J. Randall (1979), p. 134.

66 See, by way of contrast, 'From Monaghan to the Grand Canal' in Heaney (1980) and 'The Placeless Heaven: Another Look at Kavanagh' in *The Government of the Tongue* (London: Faber, 1988), p. 5.

67 Patricia Coughlan, '"Bog Queens": The Representation of Women in the Poetry of John Montague and Seamus Heaney' in Toni O'Brien Johnson and David Cairns, eds, *Gender In Irish Writing* (Milton Keynes: Open University Press, 1991), p. 90.

68 Coughlan (1991), p. 99.

69 Rand Brandes, 'The Dismembering Muse: Seamus Heaney, Ciaran Carson, and Kenneth Burke's "Four Master Tropes"' in John S. Rickard, ed. *Irishness and (Post)Modernism* (London: Bucknell University Press, 1994), p. 185.

70 Brandes (1994), p. 185.

71 Thomas Docherty, 'Ana-; or Postmodernism, Landscape, Seamus Heaney' in Anthony Easthope and John Thompson, eds, *Contemporary Poetry Meets Modern Theory* (London: Harvester Wheatsheaf, 1991), p. 70.

72 Docherty (1991), p. 76.

73 Docherty (1991), pp. 77–8.

74 Richard Kirkland (2002), p. 7.

75 Seamus Deane, 'Brian Friel: The Name of the Game' in Alan J. Peacock, ed. *The Achievement of Brian Friel* (Gerrards Cross: Colin Smythe, 1993), p. 106.

76 Seamus Deane, *Celtic Revivals: Essays in Modern Irish Literature 1880–1980* (London: Faber, 1985), p. 170.

77 W. B. Worthen, 'Homeless Words: Field Day and the Politics of Translation' *Modern Drama* 38.1 (1995), p. 31.

78 Brian Friel quoted in Marilynn J. Richtarik, *Acting Between the Lines: The Field Day Theatre Company and Irish Cultural Politics 1980–1984* (Oxford: Clarendon Press, 1994), p. 35.

79 Friel, *Translations*, in *Brian Friel: Plays One* (London: Faber, 1984), p. 416.

80 Friel quoted in Paddy Agnew, '"Talking to Ourselves": An Interview with Brian Friel', *Magill* (December 1980), pp. 60–1.

81 Deane (1993), p. 106.

82 Seamus Heaney, '*Translations*', *Times Literary Supplement* (24 October 1980), p. 1199.

83 Quoted in Michael Molino, *Questioning Tradition, Language, Myth: The Poetry of Seamus Heaney* (Washington, D.C.: Catholic University of American Press, 1994), p. 23. For another excellent account of Heaney's work see Bernard O'Donoghue, *Seamus Heaney and the Language of Poetry* (London: Harvester Wheatsheaf, 1994).

84 Longley (1994), pp. 182–3.

85 Shaun Richards, 'To Bind the Northern to the Southern Stars: Field Day in Derry and Dublin' in Claire Connolly, ed. *Theorizing Ireland* (Houndmills: Palgrave Macmillan, 2003), p. 68. For a much more positive reading of Parker's play, see Terence Brown, 'Let's go to Graceland: The Drama of Stewart Parker' in Nicholas Allen and Aaron Kelly, eds, *The Cities of Belfast* (Dublin: Four Courts, 2003), pp. 117–26.

86 See Neil Corcoran's *Poets of Modern Ireland* for a challenge to criticism placing Muldoon in opposition to Heaney.

87 Longley (1986), p. 217.

88 Tim Kendall, *Paul Muldoon* (Bridgend: Seren Books, 1996), p. 55. Another comprehensive, illustrative assessment is provided by Clair Wills, *Reading Paul Muldoon* (Newcastle: Bloodaxe, 1998).

89 Kendall (1996), pp. 97–8.

90 Longley (1986), pp. 204–5.

91 Longley (1986), pp. 205–6. The reference to Edward Thomas is from Edna Longley, ed. *A Language Not to be Betrayed: Selected Prose of Edward Thomas* (London: Carcanet, 1981), p. 55.

92 Peter McDonald, *Mistaken Identities: Poetry and Northern Ireland* (Oxford: Clarendon Press, 1997), p. 99.

93 Kearney (1996), pp. 137–8.

94 Clair Wills, *Improprieties: Politics and Sexuality in Northern Irish Poetry* (Oxford: Clarendon Press, 1993), p. 61.

95 Wills (1993), pp. 61–2.

96 Ciaran Carson, 'Escaped from the Massacre?', *Honest Ulsterman* 50 (Winter 1975), p. 86.

97 Alan Gillis, 'Ciaran Carson: Beyond Belfast' in Allen and Kelly, eds, *The Cities of Belfast* (2003), p. 184.

98 Eamonn Hughes, '"What Itch of Contradiction?": Belfast in Poetry', Allen and Kelly, eds, (2003), p. 107.

99 Hughes (2003), p. 115.

100 Eamonn Hughes, '"Town of Shadows": Representations of Belfast in Recent Fiction', *Religion and Literature* 28.2–3 (Summer–Autumn 1996), pp. 141–60.

101 Sam Hanna Bell, *December Bride* (Belfast: Blackstaff Press, 1974), p. 262.

102 Hughes (1996), p. 152.

103 Walter Benjamin, *Charles Baudelaire: A Lyric Poet in the Era of High Capitalism*, trans. Harry Zorn (London: NLB, 1973).

104 Laura Pelaschiar, *Writing the North: The Contemporary Novel in Northern Ireland* (Trieste: Edizioni Parnaso, 1998).

105 Pelaschiar (1998), p. 134.

106 Laura Pelaschiar, 'Transforming Belfast: The Evolving Role of the City in Northern Irish Fiction', *Irish University Review* 30.1 (Spring/Summer 2000), p. 117.

107 Elmer Kennedy-Andrews, *(De-)Constructing the North: Fiction and the Northern Ireland Troubles since 1969* (Dublin: Four Courts, 2003), p. 275.

108 Kirkland (2002), p. 123.

109 Kennedy-Andrews (2003), p. 172. For a good account of *No Mate*'s satire on society in the North, the Republic and Britain, see Eve Patten, 'Fiction and Conflict: Northern Ireland's Prodigal Novelists' in Ian Bell, ed. *Peripheral Visions: Images of Nationhood in Contemporary British Fiction* (Cardiff: University of Wales Press, 1995), pp. 128–48.

CONCLUSION

1 Edna Longley, 'Multi-Culturalism and Northern Ireland: Making Differences Fruitful' in Edna Longley and Declan Kiberd, *Multi-Culturalism: The View from the Two Irelands* (Cork: Cork University Press, 2001), pp. 9–10. See also Edna Longley's *Poetry and Posterity* (Tarset: Bloodaxe, 2000) for more on culture and the present.

2 In her inaugural presidential address in 1990 Mary Robinson stated: 'The Ireland I will be representing is a new Ireland, open, tolerant, inclusive. Many of you who voted for me did so without sharing all my views. This, I believe, is a significant signal of change, a sign, however modest, that we have passed the threshold to a new, pluralist Ireland'.

3 Declan Kiberd, 'Strangers in Their Own Country: Multi-Culturalism in Ireland' in Longley and Kiberd (2001), p. 63. See too Declan Kiberd's *The Irish Writer and the World* (Cambridge: Cambridge University Press, 2005) for more on Kiberd's more recent engagement.

4 Roddy Doyle, *The Commitments* in *The Barrytown Trilogy* (London: Minerva, 1992), p. 13.

5 Suzanna Chan, '"Kiss My Royal Irish Ass". Contesting Identity: Visual Culture, Gender Whiteness and Diaspora', *Journal of Gender Studies* 15.1 (March 2006), pp. 1–2.

6 See the already discussed 'Floozie in the Jacuzzi' as well as 'Feminism: Personal, Political, Unqualified (or Ex-Colonized Girls Know More)', *Irish Journal of Feminist Studies* 2 (Summer 1997), pp. 37–54.

7 Chan (2006), p. 4.

8 Francis Mulhern, *The Present Lasts a Long Time: Essays in Cultural Politics* (Cork: Cork University Press, 1998), p. 158.

9 Mulhern (1998), p. 175.

10 Terry Eagleton, *Crazy John and the Bishop and Other Essays on Irish Culture* (Cork: Cork University Press, 1998), p. 327.

11 See Francis Fukuyama, *The End of History and the Last Man* (London: Penguin, 1992).

12 David Lloyd, *Ireland after History* (Cork: Cork University Press, 1999), p. 2.

13 Colin Graham, *Deconstructing Ireland: Identity, Theory, Culture* (Edinburgh: Edinburgh UP, 2001), p. xii.

14 Graham (2001), p. 172.

Select Bibliography

CHAPTER ONE: IRISH LITERATURE AND CRITICISM
IN THE REVIVAL

Arnold, Matthew. *On the Study of Celtic Literature* (1867) in *Lectures and Essays in Criticism*, R. H. Super, ed. (Ann Arbor: University of Michigan Press, 1962).

Davis, Thomas. *Essays Literary and Historical By Thomas Davis* (Dundalk: Dungalan Press, 1914).

Ellmann, Richard, ed. *Selected Letters of James Joyce* (New York: Viking Press, 1975).

Gilbert, Stuart and Richard Ellmann, eds, *The Letters of James Joyce* (New York: Viking Press, 1957–66).

Gregory, Lady Augusta. *Irish Theatre: A Chapter in Autobiography* (New York: Putnam, 1913).

Gregory, Lady Augusta. *Poets and Dreamers: Studies and Translations from the Irish* (Dublin: 1903).

Harrington, John P., ed. *Modern Irish Drama* (London: W.W. Norton, 1991).

Hyde, Douglas. *Languages, Lore and Lyrics* (Blackrock: Irish Academic Press, 1986).

Joyce, James. *Critical Writings*, Ellsworth Mason and Richard Ellmann, eds, (Ithaca: Cornell University Press, 1989).

Mac Aonghusa, Pronsias and Liam Ó Réagáin, eds, *The Best of Pearse* (Cork: Mercier Press, 1967).

MacDonagh, Thomas. *Literature in Ireland: Studies Irish and Anglo-Irish* (Dublin: Talbot, 1916).

Moran, D. P. *The Philosophy of Irish Ireland* (Dublin: Duffy & Gill, 1905).

O'Grady, Standish. *History of Ireland: The Heroic Period* Vo.1 (London: Sampson, Low, Searle, Marston and Rivington, 1878).

Potts, Willard, ed. *Portraits of the Artist in Exile: Recollections of James Joyce by Europeans* (London: University of Washington Press, 1979).

Pritchard, W. H., ed. *W. B. Yeats: A Critical Anthology* (Harmondsworth: Penguin, 1972).

Renan, Ernest. *The Poetry of the Celtic Races* (London: Walter Scott, 1897).

Saddlemyer, Anne, ed. *J. M. Synge: Plays* (Oxford: Oxford University Press, 1977).

Shaw, George Bernard. *Preface for Politicians* in *John Bull's Other Island* (London: Penguin, 1984).

Watson, George. *Irish Identity and the Literary Revival: Synge, Yeats, Joyce and O'Casey* (Washington, D.C.: Catholic University of America Press, 1994).

Yeats, W. B. *Autobiographies* (London: Macmillan, 1955).

Yeats, W. B. *Collected Letters* (Oxford: Clarendon Press, 1986).

Yeats, W. B. *Essays and Introductions* (London: Macmillan, 1961).

Yeats, W. B. *Uncollected Prose* (Houndmills, Macmillan, 1975).

CHAPTER TWO: IRISH LITERATURE AND CRITICISM
AFTER PARTITION

Anderson, Benedict. *Imagined Communities: Reflections on the Origin and Spread of Nationalism* (London: Verso, 1991).

Beckett, Samuel et al., *Our Exagmination Round His Factification For Incamination Of Work In Progress* [1929] (London: Faber, 1961).

Bell, Sam Hanna. *Erin's Orange Lilly: Ulster Custom and Folklore* (London: Dennis Dobson, 1956).

Bell, Sam Hanna, John Hewitt and Nesca Robb, eds, *The Arts in Ulster: A Symposium* (London: Harrap, 1951).

Corkery, Daniel. *The Hidden Ireland: A Study of Gaelic Munster in the Eighteenth Century* [1924] (Dublin: Gill and Macmillan, 1989).

Corkery, Daniel. *Synge and Anglo-Irish Literature* (Cork: Cork University Press, 1931).

Davie, Donald. 'Reflections of an English Writer in Ireland', *Studies* 44 (1955), pp. 439–45.

Donoghue, Denis. 'Notes Towards a Critical Method: Language as Order', *Studies*, 42 (1955), pp. 181–92.

Donoghue, Denis. *We Irish* (Berkeley: University of California Press, 1986).

Eagleton, Terry. *Heathcliff and the Great Hunger: Studies in Irish Culture* (London: Verso, 1995).

Ellmann, Richard. *The Consciousness of Joyce* (London: Faber, 1977).

Ellmann, Richard. *James Joyce* (New York: Oxford University Press, 1959).

Ellmann, Richard, ed. *Selected Letters of James Joyce* (New York: Viking Press, 1975).

Kavanagh, Patrick. *Collected Pruse* (London: MacGibbon and Kee, 1967).

Kenner, Hugh. *Dublin's Joyce* (London: Chatto & Windus, 1955).

Kenner, Hugh. *Joyce's Voices* (London: Faber, 1978).

Kenner, Hugh. *A Reader's Guide to Samuel Beckett* (London, Thames and Hudson, 1973).

Kenner, Hugh. *A Colder Eye: The Modern Irish Writers* (New York: Alfred A. Kopf, 1983).

Krause, David. *Sean O'Casey: The Man and His Work* (London: Macmillan, 1960).

McMahon, Sean. *The Best from the Bell* (Dublin: O'Brien Press, 1978).

Mercier, Vivian. 'An Irish School of Criticism?', *Studies* 45 (1956), pp. 84–7.

Mercier, Vivian. *Beckett/Beckett* (Oxford: Oxford University Press, 1977).

Mercier, Vivian. *The Irish Comic Tradition* (Oxford: Oxford University Press, 1962).

Mercier, Vivian and David H. Greene, eds, *1000 Years of Irish Prose: Part I – The Literary Revival* [1952] (New York: Devin-Adair, 1953).

O'Connor, Frank. *The Lonely Voice: A Study of the Short Story* (London: Macmillan, 1963).

O'Connor, Frank. *The Mirror on the Roadway: A Study of the Modern Novel* (London: Harvard Summer School Lectures, 1957).

Storey, Michael L. *Representing the Troubles in Irish Short Fiction* (Washington, D.C.: The Catholic University of America Press, 2004).

CHAPTER THREE: THE DEVELOPMENT OF IRISH STUDIES: CONTESTING THE REVIVAL

Allen, Nicholas. *George Russell (AE) and the New Ireland, 1905–1930* (Dublin: Four Courts, 2002).

Attridge, Derek and Marjorie Howes, eds, *Semicolonial Joyce* (Cambridge: Cambridge University Press, 2000).

Brown, Richard. *James Joyce and Sexuality* (Cambridge: Cambridge University Press, 1988).

Brown, Terence. *Ireland: A Social and Cultural History 1922–79* (Glasgow: Fontana, 1981).

Brown, Terence. *Ireland's Literature: Selected Essays* (Gigginstown: Lilliput Press, 1988).

Brown, Terence. *The Life of W. B. Yeats: A Critical Biography* (Oxford: Blackwell, 1999).

Cheng, Vincent J. *Joyce, Race and Empire* (Cambridge: Cambridge University Press, 1995).

Cleary, Joe. *Literature, Partition and the Nation State: Culture and Conflict in Ireland, Israel and Palestine* (Cambridge: Cambridge University Press, 2002).

Cullingford, Elizabeth Butler. *Gender and History in Yeats's Love Poetry* (Cambridge: Cambridge University Press, 1988).

Cullingford, Elizabeth Butler. *Yeats, Ireland and Fascism* (London: Macmillan, 1981).

Deane, Seamus. *Celtic Revivals: Essays in Modern Irish Literature 1880–1980* (London: Faber, 1985).

Deane, Seamus. *Civilians and Barbarians* (Derry: Field Day, 1983).

Deane, Seamus. *Heroic Styles: The Tradition of an Idea* (Derry: Field Day, 1984).

Deane, Seamus. General ed. *The Field Day Anthology of Irish Writing Vol. 1–3* (Derry: Field Day, 1991).

Deane, Seamus. 'Introduction' to Edward W. Said, Terry Eagleton and Fredric Jameson, *Nationalism, Colonialism and Literature* (Minneapolis: University of Minnesota Press, 1990), pp. 3–19.

Deane, Seamus. *Strange Country: Modernity and Nationhood in Irish Writing since 1790* (Oxford: Clarendon Press, 1997).

Eagleton, Terry. *Crazy John and the Bishop and Other Essays on Irish Culture* (Cork: Cork University Press, 1998).

Eagleton, Terry. *Heathcliff and the Great Hunger: Studies in Irish Culture* (London: Verso, 1995).

Foster, John Wilson. *Colonial Consequences: Essays in Irish Literature and Culture* (Dublin: Lilliput Press, 1991).

Foster, R. F. *Paddy and Mr Punch* (London: Penguin, 1993).

Foster, R. F. *W. B. Yeats: A Life Vol. 1: The Apprentice Mage 1865–1914* (Oxford; Oxford University Press, 1997).

Foster, R. F. *W. B. Yeats: A Life Vol. 2: The Arch Poet 1915–1939* (Oxford: Oxford University Press, 2003).

Gibbons, Luke. *Transformations in Irish Culture* (Cork: Cork University Press, 1996).

Gillis, Alan. *Irish Poetry of the 1930s* (Oxford: Oxford University Press, 2005).

Graham, Colin. *Deconstructing Ireland* (Edinburgh: Edinburgh University Press, 2001).

Grene, Nicholas. *The Politics of Irish Drama: Plays in Context from Boucicault to Friel* (Cambridge: Cambridge University Press, 2002).

Howe, Stephen. *Ireland and Empire: Colonial Legacies in Irish History and Culture* (Oxford: Oxford University Press, 2000).

Howes, Marjorie. *Yeats's Nations: Gender, Class, Irishness* (Cambridge: Cambridge University Press, 1996).

Jameson, Fredric. 'Modernism and Imperialism' in Edward W. Said, Terry Eagleton and Fredric Jameson, *Nationalism, Colonialism and Literature* (Minneapolis: University of Minnesota Press, 1990).

Kennedy, Liam. 'Modern Ireland: Postcolonial Society or Postcolonial Pretensions?', *Irish Review* 13 (Winter 1992/1993), pp. 107–21.

Kiberd, Declan. *Inventing Ireland* (London: Cape, 1995).

Kiberd, Declan. *Irish Classics* (London: Granta, 2000).

Kinsella, Thomas. *The Dual Tradition: An Essay on Poetry and Politics in Ireland* (Manchester: Carcanet, 1995).

Leerssen, Joep. *Remembrance and Imagination: Patterns in the Historical and Literary Representation of Ireland in the Nineteenth Century* (Cork:'Cork University Press, 1996).

Lloyd, David. *Anomalous States: Irish Writing and the Post-Colonial Moment* (Dublin: Lilliput Press, 1993).

Lloyd, David. *Ireland after History* (Cork: Cork University Press, 1999).

Lloyd, David. *Nationalism and Minor Literature: James Clarence Mangan* (London: University of California Press, 1987).

Longley, Edna. *The Living Stream: Literature and Revisionism in Ireland* (Newcastle: Bloodaxe, 1994).

Longley, Edna. *Poetry in the Wars* (Newcastle: Bloodaxe, 1986).

McAteer, Michael. *Standish O'Grady, AE and Yeats: History, Politics, Culture* (Dublin: Irish Academic Press, 2002).

MacCabe, Colin. *James Joyce and the Revolution of the Word* (Houndmills: Palgrave Macmillan, 2003).

McCormack, W. J., *Ascendancy and Tradition in Anglo-Irish Literary History* (Oxford: Clarendon, 1985).

Nolan, Emer. *James Joyce and Nationalism* (London: Routledge, 1995).

O'Brien, Conor Cruise. *Passion and Cunning and Other Essays* (London: Wiedenfeld & Nicolson, 1988).

Paulin, Tom. *The Faber Book of Political Verse* (London: Faber, 1986).

Richtarik, Marilynn. *Acting Between the Lines: The Field Day Theatre Company and Irish Cultural Politics 1980–1984* (Oxford: Clarendon Press, 1994).

Said, Edward. 'Yeats and Decolonization' in Edward W. Said, Terry Eagleton and Fredric Jameson, *Nationalism, Colonialism and Literature* (Minneapolis: University of Minnesota Press, 1990).

Shaw, Francis. 'The Canon of Irish History – A Challenge', *Studies* 61 (Summer 1972), pp. 113–53.

Smyth, Gerry. *Decolonization and Criticism: The Construction of Irish Literature* (London: Pluto, 1998).

Stanfield, Paul Scott. *Yeats and Politics in the 1930s* (Basingstoke: Macmillan, 1988).

Watson, George. *Irish Identity and the Literary Revival: Synge, Yeats, Joyce and O'Casey* (Washington, D.C.: Catholic University of America Press, 1994).

Welch, Robert. *The Abbey Theatre, 1899–1999: Form and Pressure* (Oxford: Oxford University Press, 1999).

CHAPTER FOUR: IRISH STUDIES PARADIGMS AND LITERATURE AFTER PARTITION

Brown, Terence. *Ireland: A Social and Cultural History 1922–79* (Glasgow: Fontana, 1981).

Brown, Terence. *Ireland's Literature: Selected Essays* (Gigginstown: Lilliput Press, 1988).

Brown, Terence. *The Whole Protestant Community: The Making of a Historical Myth* (Derry: Field Day, 1985).

Cleary, Joe. *Literature, Partition and the Nation State: Culture and Conflict in Ireland, Israel and Palestine* (Cambridge: Cambridge University Press, 2002).

Clyde, Tom, ed. *Ancestral Voices: The Selected Prose of John Hewitt* (Belfast: Blackstaff Press, 1987).

Corcoran, Neil. 'Discovery of a Lack: History and Ellipsis in Elizabeth Bowen's *The Last September*', *Irish University Review* 31.2 (Autumn/Winter 2001), pp. 315–33.

Corcoran, Neil. *After Yeats and Joyce: Reading Modern Irish Literature* (Oxford: Oxford University Press, 1997).

Deane, Seamus. *Celtic Revivals: Essays in Modern Irish Literature 1880–1980* (London: Faber, 1985).

Deane, Seamus. *Civilians and Barbarians* (Derry: Field Day, 1983).

Deane, Seamus. *Heroic Styles: The Tradition of an Idea* (Derry: Field Day, 1984).

Deane, Seamus. General ed. *The Field Day Anthology of Irish Writing Vol. 1–3* (Derry: Field Day, 1991).

Deane, Seamus, ed. and 'Introduction' to Edward W. Said, Terry Eagleton and Fredric Jameson, *Nationalism, Colonialism and Literature* (Minneapolis: University of Minnesota Press, 1990), pp. 3–19.

Deane, Seamus. *Strange Country: Modernity and Nationhood in Irish Writing since 1790* (Oxford: Clarendon Press, 1997).

Delaney, Paul. 'Becoming National: Daniel Corkery and the Reterritorialized Subject' in Alan Gillis and Aaron Kelly, eds, *Critical Ireland: New Essays in Literature and Culture* (Dublin: Four Courts, 2001), pp. 41–8.

Eagleton, Terry. *Crazy John and the Bishop and Other Essays on Irish Culture* (Cork: Cork University Press, 1998).

Eagleton, Terry. *Heathcliff and the Great Hunger: Studies in Irish Culture* (London: Verso, 1995).

Foster, John Wilson. *Colonial Consequences: Essays in Irish Literature and Culture* (Dublin: Lilliput Press, 1991).

Gibbons, Luke. *Transformations in Irish Culture* (Cork: Cork University Press, 1996).

Gillis, Alan. *Irish Poetry of the 1930s* (Oxford: Oxford University Press, 2005).

Graham, Colin. *Deconstructing Ireland* (Edinburgh: Edinburgh University Press, 2001).

Grene, Nicholas. *The Politics of Irish Drama: Plays in Context from Boucicault to Friel* (Cambridge: Cambridge University Press, 2002).

Kiberd, Declan. *Inventing Ireland* (London: Cape, 1995).

Kirkland, Richard. *Literature and Culture in Northern Ireland since 1965: Moments of Danger* (London: Longman, 1996).

Krause, David. *Sean O'Casey: The Man and His Work* (London: Macmillan, 1960).

Lassner, Phyllis. *Elizabeth Bowen* (Maryland: Barnes and Nobles, 1990).

Lloyd, David. *Anomalous States: Irish Writing and the Post-Colonial Moment* (Dublin: Lilliput Press, 1993).

Lloyd, David. *Ireland after History* (Cork: Cork University Press, 1999).

Lloyd, David. *Nationalism and Minor Literature: James Clarence Mangan* (London: University of California Press, 1987).

Lloyd, David. 'Republics of Difference: Yeats, MacGreevy, Beckett', *Third Text* 19.5 (2005), pp. 461–74.

Longley, Edna. *The Living Stream: Literature and Revisionism in Ireland* (Newcastle: Bloodaxe, 1994).

Longley, Edna. *Poetry in the Wars* (Newcastle: Bloodaxe, 1986).

McDonald, Peter. *Mistaken Identities: Poetry and Northern Ireland* (Oxford: Clarendon, 1997).

McKibben, Sarah. '*The Poor Mouth*: A Parody of (Post)Colonial Irish Manhood', *Research in African Literatures* 34.4 (2003) pp. 96–114.

Mulhern, Francis. *The Present Lasts a Long Time* (Cork: Cork University Press, 1998).

Pilkington, Lionel. *Theatre and the State in Twentieth-Century Ireland: Cultivating the People* (London: Routledge, 2001).

Quinn, Antoinette. *Patrick Kavanagh: Born Again Romantic* (Dublin: Gill and Macmillan, 1991).

Smyth, Gerry. *Decolonization and Criticism: The Construction of Irish Literature* (London: Pluto, 1998).

Storey, Michael L. *Representing the Troubles in Irish Short Fiction* (Washington, D.C.: The Catholic University of America Press, 2004).

Welch, Robert. *The Abbey Theatre, 1899–1999: Form and Pressure* (Oxford: Oxford University Press, 1999).

CHAPTER FIVE: GENDER, SEXUALITY AND FEMINISM IN IRISH LITERATURE

Boland, Eavan. *Object Lessons: The Life of the Woman and the Poet in Our Time* (London: Vintage, 1995).

Bourke, Angela. General ed. *The Field Day Anthology of Irish Writing: Irish Women's Writing and Traditions* Vol. 4 & 5 (Cork: Cork University Press, 2002).

Brown, Richard. *James Joyce and Sexuality* (Cambridge: Cambridge University Press, 1988).

Clear, Catriona. *Nuns in Nineteenth Century Ireland* (Dublin: Gill and Macmillan, 1987).

Coulter, Carol. *The Hidden Tradition: Feminism, Women and Nationalism in Ireland* (Cork: Cork University Press, 1993).

Cullingford, Elizabeth Butler. *Gender and History in Yeats's Love Poetry* (Cambridge: Cambridge University Press, 1988).

Cullingford, Elizabeth Butler. '"Our Nuns Are Not A Nation": Politicizing the Convent in Literature and Film', *Éire-Ireland* 41.1 (2006), pp. 9–39.

Eagleton, Terry. *Nationalism, Irony and Commitment* (Derry: Field Day, 1988).

Frazier, Adrian. 'Queering the Irish Renaissance: The Masculinities of Moore, Martyn and Yeats' in Anthony Bradley and Maryann Gialanella Valiulis, eds, *Gender and Sexuality in Modern Ireland* (Amherst: University of Massachusetts Press, 1997), pp. 8–38.

Graham, Colin. '"Liminal Spaces": Post-Colonial Theories and Irish Culture', *The Irish Review* (Autumn/Winter 1994), pp. 29–43.

Graham, Colin. 'Subalternity and Gender: Problems of Postcolonial Irishness' in Claire Connolly, ed. *Theorizing Ireland* (Houndmills: Palgrave Macmillan, 2003), pp. 150–9.

Grene, Nicholas. *The Politics of Irish Drama: Plays in Context from Boucicault to Friel* (Cambridge: Cambridge University Press, 2002).

Howe, Stephen. *Ireland and Empire: Colonial Legacies in Irish History and Culture* (Oxford: Oxford University Press, 2000).

Howes, Marjorie. *Yeats's Nations: Gender, Class, Irishness* (Cambridge: Cambridge University Press, 1996).

Hughes, Eamonn. '"How I Achieved This Trick": Representations of Masculinity in Contemporary Irish Fiction' in Elmer Kennedy-Andrews, ed. *Irish Fiction since the 1960s* (Gerrards Cross: Colin Smythe, 2006), pp. 119–36.

Kennedy, Liam. 'Modern Ireland: Postcolonial Society or Postcolonial Pretensions?', *Irish Review* 13 (Winter 1992/1993), pp. 107–21.

Kirkpatrick, Kathryn, ed. *Border Crossings: Irish Women Writers and National Identities* (Tuscaloosa: University of Alabama Press, 2000).

Lassner, Phyllis. *Elizabeth Bowen* (Maryland: Barnes and Nobles, 1990).

Lee, Hermione, ed. *The Mulberry Tree: Writings of Elizabeth Bowen* (London: Virago, 1986).

Lloyd, David. *Anomalous States: Irish Writing and the Post-Colonial Moment* (Dublin: Lilliput Press, 1993).

Lloyd, David. *Ireland after History* (Cork: Cork University Press, 1999).

Longley, Edna. *The Living Stream: Literature and Revisionism in Ireland* (Newcastle: Bloodaxe, 1994).

MacCarthy, B. G. *The Female Pen: Women Writers and Novelists 1621–1818* (Cork: Cork University Press, 1994).

McCormack, W. J. *Ascendancy and Tradition in Anglo-Irish Literary History* (Oxford: Clarendon, 1985).

Meaney, Geraldine. *Sex and Nation: Women in Irish Culture and Politics* (Dublin: Attic Press, 1991).

O'Faolain, Nuala. 'Irish Women and Writing in Modern Ireland' in Eilean Ní Chuilleanáin, ed. *Irish Women: Image and Achievement. Women in Irish Culture from Earliest Times* (Dublin: Attic Press, 1985), pp. 127–35.

Patten, Eve. 'Women and Fiction 1985–1990', *Krino* 8.9 (1990), pp. 1–7.

Quinn, Antoinette. 'A Prayer for My Daughter: Patriarchy in *Amongst Women*', *Canadian Journal of Irish Studies* 17.1 (July 1991), pp. 79–90.

Reizbaum, Marilyn. 'Canonical Double Cross: Scottish and Irish Women's Writing', in Karen E. Lawrence, ed. *Decolonizing Tradition: New Views of Twentieth-Century 'British' Literary Canons* (Chicago: University of Illinois Press, 1992), pp. 165–90.

Reizbaum, Marilyn. 'Not a Crying Game: The Feminist Appeal; Nationalism, Feminism and the Contemporary Literatures of Scotland and Ireland', *Scotlands* 2 (1994), pp. 24–31.

Sampson, Denis, *Outstaring Nature's Eye: The Fiction of John McGahern* (Dublin: Lilliput Press, 1993).

Smyth, Ailbhe. 'The Floozie in the Jacuzzi', *Irish Review* 6 (1989), pp. 7–24.

Soper, Kate. 'Stephen Heroine' in *Troubled Pleasures: Writings on Politics, Gender and Hedonism* (London: Verso, 1990), pp. 246–68.

Stevens, Robert L. and Sylvia Stevens. 'An Interview with Mary Lavin', *Studies* 86.341 (1997), pp. 43–50.

Thompson, William Irwin. *The Imagination of an Insurrection: A Story of an Ideological Movement* (New York: Oxford University Press, 1967).

Walshe, Éibhear. 'The First Gay Irishman? Ireland and the Wilde Trials', *Éire-Ireland* 40.3–4 (2005), pp. 38–57.

Walshe, Éibhear, ed. *Ordinary People Dancing: Essays on Kate O'Brien* (Cork: Cork University Press, 1993).

Ward, Margaret. *In Their Own Voice: Women and Irish Nationalism* (Dublin: Attic Press, 1995).

Ward, Margaret. *Unmanageable Revolutionaries: Women and Irish Nationalism* (London: Pluto, 1983).

Weekes, Anne Owens. *Irish Women Writers: An Uncharted Tradition* (Lexington: University of Kentucky Press, 1990).

Wills, Clair. *Improprieties: Politics and Sexuality in Northern Irish Poetry* (Oxford: Oxford University Press, 1993).

CHAPTER SIX: CONTEMPORARY LITERATURE IN THE IRISH REPUBLIC AND NORTHERN IRELAND

Auge, Andrew J. 'Fracture and Wound: Eavan Boland's Poetry of Nationality', *New Hibernia Review* 8.2 (Summer 2004), pp. 121–41.

Boland, Eavan. *Object Lessons: The Life of the Woman and the Poet in Our Time* (London: Vintage, 1995).

Bourke, Angela. General ed. *The Field Day Anthology of Irish Writing: Irish Women's Writing and Traditions* Vol. 4 & 5 (Cork: Cork University Press, 2002).

Brandes, Rand. 'The Dismembering Muse: Seamus Heaney, Ciaran Carson, and Kenneth Burke's "Four Master Tropes"' in John S. Rickard, ed. *Irishness and (Post)Modernism* (London: Bucknell University Press, 1994), pp. 177–94.

Brown, Terence. *Ireland: A Social and Cultural History 1922–79* (Glasgow: Fontana, 1981).

Brown, Terence. *Ireland's Literature: Selected Essays* (Gigginstown: Lilliput Press, 1988).

Brown, Terence. 'Let's go to Graceland: The Drama of Stewart Parker' in Nicholas Allen and Aaron Kelly, eds, *The Cities of Belfast* (Dublin: Four Courts, 2003), pp. 117–26.

Brown, Terence. *The Whole Protestant Community: The Making of a Historical Myth* (Derry: Field Day, 1985).

Cleary, Joe. *Literature, Partition and the Nation State: Culture and Conflict in Ireland, Israel and Palestine* (Cambridge: Cambridge University Press, 2002).

Clyde, Tom, ed. *Ancestral Voices: The Selected Prose of John Hewitt* (Belfast: Blackstaff Press, 1987).

Corcoran, Neil. *After Yeats and Joyce: Reading Modern Irish Literature* (Oxford: Oxford University Press, 1997).

Corcoran, Neil. *Poets of Modern Ireland* (Cardiff: University of Wales Press, 1999).

Corcoran, Neil. *Seamus Heaney* (London: Faber, 1986).

Coughlan, Patricia. '"Bog Queens": The Representation of Women in the Poetry of John Montague and Seamus Heaney' in Toni O'Brien Johnson and David Cairns, ed. *Gender In Irish Writing* (Milton Keynes: Open University Press, 1991), pp. 88–111.

Deane, Seamus. *Celtic Revivals: Essays in Modern Irish Literature 1880–1980* (London: Faber, 1985).

Deane, Seamus. General ed. *The Field Day Anthology of Irish Writing Vol. 1–3* (Derry: Field Day, 1991).

Docherty, Thomas. 'Ana-; or Postmodernism, Landscape, Seamus Heaney' in Anthony Easthope and John Thompson, eds, *Contemporary Poetry Meets Modern Theory* (London: Harvester Wheatsheaf, 1991), pp. 68–80.

Eagleton, Terry. *Crazy John and the Bishop and Other Essays on Irish Culture* (Cork: Cork University Press, 1998).

Eagleton, Terry. *Heathcliff and the Great Hunger: Studies in Irish Culture* (London: Verso, 1995).

Foster, John Wilson. *Colonial Consequences: Essays in Irish Literature and Culture* (Dublin: Lilliput Press, 1991).

Frawley, Oona. *Irish Pastoral: Nostalgia in Irish Literature* (Dublin: Irish Academic Press).

Gibbons, Luke. *Transformations in Irish Culture* (Cork: Cork University Press, 1996).

Gibbons, Luke, et al., eds, *Reinventing Ireland: Culture, Society and the Global Economy* (London: Pluto Press, 2002).

Gillis, Alan. 'Ciaran Carson: Beyond Belfast' in Nicholas Allen and Aaron Kelly, eds, *The Cities of Belfast* (Dublin: Four Courts, 2003), pp. 183–98.

Graham, Colin. *Deconstructing Ireland* (Edinburgh: Edinburgh University Press, 2001).

Grene, Nicholas. *The Politics of Irish Drama: Plays in Context from Boucicault to Friel* (Cambridge: Cambridge University Press, 2002).

Heaney, Seamus. *The Government of the Tongue* (London: Faber, 1988).

Heaney, Seamus. *Preoccupations: Selected Prose 1968–1978* (London: Faber, 1980).

Herron, Tom. 'ContamiNation: Patrick McCabe and Colm Tóibín's Pathologies of the Republic', Liam Harte and Michael Parker, eds, *Contemporary Irish Fiction: Themes, Tropes, Theories* (Houndmills: Macmillan, 2000), pp. 168–91.

Hughes, Eamonn, ed. *Culture and Politics in Northern Ireland* (Milton Keynes: Open University Press, 1991).

Hughes, Eamonn. '"How I Achieved This Trick": Representations of Masculinity in Contemporary Irish Fiction' in Elmer Kennedy-Andrews, ed. *Irish Fiction since the 1960s* (Gerrards Cross: Colin Smythe, 2006), pp. 119–36.

Hughes, Eamonn. '"Town of Shadows": Representations of Belfast in Recent Fiction', *Religion and Literature* 28.2–3 (Summer–Autumn 1996), pp. 141–60.

Hughes, Eamonn. '"What Itch of Contradiction?": Belfast in Poetry' in Nicholas Allen and Aaron Kelly, eds. *The Cities of Belfast* (Dublin: Four Courts, 2003), pp. 101–16.

Kearney, Richard. *Postnationalist Ireland* (London: Routledge, 1996).

Kearney, Richard. *Transitions: Narratives in Modern Irish Culture* (Manchester: Manchester University Press, 1988).

Kendall, Tim. *Paul Muldoon* (Bridgend: Seren Books, 1996).

Kennedy, Liam. 'Modern Ireland: Postcolonial Society or Postcolonial Pretensions?', *Irish Review* 13 (Winter 1992/1993), pp. 107–21.

Kennedy-Andrews, Elmer. *(De-)Constructing the North: Fiction and the Northern Ireland Troubles since 1969* (Dublin: Four Courts, 2003).

Kiberd, Declan. *Inventing Ireland* (London: Cape, 1995).

Kirkland, Richard. *Identity Parades: Northern Irish Culture and Dissident Subjects* (Liverpool: Liverpool University Press, 2002).

Kirkland, Richard. *Literature and Culture in Northern Ireland since 1965: Moments of Danger* (London: Longman, 1996).

Lloyd, David. *Anomalous States: Irish Writing and the Post-Colonial Moment* (Dublin: Lilliput Press, 1993).

Lloyd, David. *Ireland after History* (Cork: Cork University Press, 1999).

Longley, Edna. *The Living Stream: Literature and Revisionism in Ireland* (Newcastle: Bloodaxe, 1994).

Longley, Edna. *Poetry in the Wars* (Newcastle: Bloodaxe, 1986).

Lysaght, Seán. 'Banville's Tetralogy: The Limits of Mimesis', *Irish University Review* 21.1 (1991), pp. 82–100.

McDonald, Peter. *Mistaken Identities: Poetry and Northern Ireland* (Oxford: Clarendon, 1997).

McMinn, Joseph. 'Naming the World: Language and Experience in John Banville's Fiction', *Irish University Review* 23.2 (1993), pp. 183–96.

O'Donoghue, Bernard. *Seamus Heaney and the Language of Poetry* (London: Harvester Wheatsheaf, 1994).

O'Toole, Fintan. *Black Hole, Green Card: The Disappearance of Ireland* (Dublin: New Island Books, 1994).

O'Toole, Fintan. *A Mass for Jesse James: A Journey Through 1980s Ireland* (Dublin: Raven Arts Press, 1990).

Patten, Eve. 'Fiction and Conflict: Northern Ireland's Prodigal Novelists' in Ian Bell, ed. *Peripheral Visions: Images of Nationhood in Contemporary British Fiction* (Cardiff: University of Wales Press, 1995), pp. 128–48.

Peacock, Alan J., ed. *The Achievement of Brian Friel* (Gerrards Cross: Colin Smythe, 1993).

Pelaschiar, Laura. 'Transforming Belfast: The Evolving Role of the City in Northern Irish Fiction', *Irish University Review* 30.1 (Spring/Summer 2000), pp. 117–31.

Pelaschiar, Laura. *Writing the North: The Contemporary Novel in Northern Ireland* (Trieste: Edizioni Parnaso, 1998).

Pilkington, Lionel. *Theatre and the State in Twentieth-Century Ireland: Cultivating the People* (London: Routledge, 2001).

Quinn, Antoinette. 'New Noises from the Woodshed: The Novels of Emma Donoghue' in Michael Parker and Liam Harte, eds, *Contemporary Irish Fiction: Themes, Tropes, Theories* (Houndmills: Macmillan, 2000), pp. 145–67.

Richards, Shaun. 'To Bind the Northern to the Southern Stars: Field Day in Derry and Dublin' in Claire Connolly, ed. *Theorizing Ireland* (Houndmills: Palgrave Macmillan, 2003), pp. 61–8.

Richtarik, Marilynn. *Acting Between the Lines: The Field Day Theatre Company and Irish Cultural Politics 1980–1984* (Oxford: Clarendon Press, 1994).

Ryan, Ray, ed. *Writing the Irish Republic; Literature, Culture, Politics 1949–1999* (Houndmills: Macmillan, 2000).

Sampson, Denis. *Outstaring Nature's Eye: The Fiction of John McGahern* (Dublin: Lilliput Press, 1993).

Smyth, Gerry. *The Novel and the Nation: Studies in the New Irish Fiction* (London: Pluto, 1997).

Smyth, Gerry. 'The Right to the City: Re-Presentations of Dublin in Contemporary Irish Fiction', Liam Harte and Michael Parker, eds, *Contemporary Irish Fiction: Themes, Tropes, Theories* (Houndmills: Macmillan, 2000), pp. 13–34.

Smyth, Gerry. *Space and the Irish Cultural Imagination* (Basingstoke: Palgrave Macmillan, 2001).

St Peter, Christine. 'Petrifying Time: Incest Narratives from Contemporary Ireland' in Michael Parker and Liam Harte, eds, *Contemporary Irish Fiction: Themes, Tropes, Theories* (Houndmills: Macmillan, 2000), pp. 125–44.

Storey, Michael L. *Representing the Troubles in Irish Short Fiction* (Washington, D.C.: The Catholic University of America Press, 2004).

Welch, Robert. *The Abbey Theatre, 1899–1999: Form and Pressure* (Oxford: Oxford University Press, 1999).

Wills, Clair. *Improprieties: Politics and Sexuality in Northern Irish Poetry* (Oxford: Oxford University Press, 1993).

Wills, Clair. *Reading Paul Muldoon* (Newcastle: Bloodaxe, 1998).

Worthen, W. B. 'Homeless Words: Field Day and the Politics of Translation', *Modern Drama* 38.1 (1995), pp. 22–41.

CONCLUSION: IRISH STUDIES TODAY

Chan, Suzanna. '"Kiss My Royal Irish Ass". Contesting Identity: Visual Culture, Gender Whiteness and Diaspora', *Journal of Gender Studies* 15.1 (March 2006), pp. 1–17.

Eagleton, Terry. *Crazy John and the Bishop and Other Essays on Irish Culture* (Cork: Cork University Press, 1998).

Graham, Colin. *Deconstructing Ireland* (Edinburgh: Edinburgh University Press, 2001).

Kiberd, Declan. *The Irish Writer and the World* (Cambridge: Cambridge University Press, 2005).

Lloyd, David. *Ireland after History* (Cork: Cork University Press, 1999).

Longley, Edna. *Poetry and Posterity* (Tarset: Bloodaxe, 2000).

Longley, Edna and Declan Kiberd. *Multi-Culturalism: The View from the Two Irelands* (Cork: Cork University Press, 2001).

Mulhern, Francis. *The Present Lasts a Long Time* (Cork: Cork University Press, 1998).

Smyth, Ailbhe. 'Feminism: Personal, Political, Unqualified (or Ex-Colonized Girls Know More)', *Irish Journal of Feminist Studies* 2 (Summer 1997), pp. 37–54.

Suggested Primary Reading

THE REVIVAL PERIOD

Corkery, Daniel. *A Munster Twilight* (Dublin: Talbot, 1916).

Corkery, Daniel. *The Hounds of Banba* [1920] (New York: Books for Libraries, 1970).

Gregory, Lady Augusta. *Lady Gregory: Selected Plays*, edited and chosen by Elizabeth Coxhead (London: Putnam, 1962).

Hyde, Douglas. *Casadh an tSúgáin* (*The Twisting of the Rope*) [1901], collected in *Selected Plays of Douglas Hyde*, edited and chosen by Gareth W. Dunleavey and Janet E. Dunleavey (Gerrards Cross: Colin Smythe, 1991).

Joyce, James. *A Portrait of the Artist As A Young Man* [1916] (London: Penguin, 1977).

Joyce, James. *Dubliners* [1914] (London: Penguin, 2000).

Joyce, James. *Ulysses* [1922] (London: Penguin, 1992).

MacGill, Patrick. *Children of the Dead End* [1914] (Dingle: Brandon, 1982).

Martyn, Edward. *The Heather Field* [1899] (Chicago: De Paul University, 1966).

Moore, George. *Hail and Farewell* [1911–14] (Gerrards Cross: Colin Smythe, 1985).

Moore, George. *The Untilled Field* [1903] (Dublin: Gill and Macmillan, 1990).

Pearse, Pádraic. *The Collected Works of Pádraic H. Pearse: Plays, Stories, Poems* (Dublin: Maunsel, 1917).

Russell, George (A.E.). *By Still Waters: Lyrical Poems Old and New* (Dundrum: Dun Emer, 1906).

Russell, George (A.E.). *Deidre: A Drama in Three Acts* (Dublin: Maunsel, 1907).

Shaw, George Bernard. *John Bull's Other Island* [1904] (London: Penguin, 1984).

Stephens, James. *The Charwoman's Daughter* [1912] (Dublin: Gill and Macmillan, 1972).

Stephens, James. *The Crock of Gold* [1912] (London: Pan, 1952).

Synge, John Millington. *The Playboy of the Western World* [1907] collected in *J.M. Synge: Plays*, edited by Ann Saddlemyer (Oxford: Oxford University Press, 1977).

Yeats, W. B. *Collected Poems* [1933] (Dublin: Gill and Macmillan, 1988).

Yeats, W. B. *Collected Plays* [1934] (London: Papermac, 1982).

POST-PARTITION LITERATURE TO 1965

Beckett, Samuel. *The Beckett Trilogy* (comprising *Molloy* [1955], *Malone Dies* [1956] and *The Unnameable* [1959]) (London: Picador, 1976).

Beckett, Samuel. *Collected Poems 1930–1978* (London: John Calder, 1984).

Beckett, Samuel. *The Complete Dramatic Works* (London: Faber, 1986).

Beckett, Samuel. *First Love* [written 1946] (London: John Calder, 1999).

Beckett, Samuel. *Murphy* [1938] (London: John Calder, 1993).

Beckett, Samuel. *More Pricks than Kicks* [1934] (London: Picador, 1974).

Behan, Brendan. *Borstal Boy* (London: Hutchinson, 1958).

Behan, Brendan. *The Hostage* (London: Methuen, 1958).

Behan, Brendan. *The Quare Fellow* [1954] (London: Methuen, 1960).

Bell, Sam Hanna. *December Bride* [1951] (Belfast: Blackstaff, 1974).

Bowen, Elizabeth. *Bowen's Court* [1942] (London: Virago, 1984).

Bowen, Elizabeth. *The Last September* [1929] (Harmondsworth: Penguin, 1942).

Clarke, Austin. *The Collected Poems of Austin Clarke* [1936] (Dublin: Dolmen, 1974).

Corkery, Daniel. *Earth Out of Earth* (Dublin: Talbot, 1929).

Corkery, Daniel. *Resurrection* (Dublin: Talbot, 1942).

Hewitt, John. *Collected Poems, 1932–1967* (London: Macgibbon and Kee, 1968); a full collation of Hewitt's poetry is provided by Frank Ormsby, ed. *The Collected Poems of John Hewitt* (Belfast: Blackstaff, 1991).

Joyce, James. *Finnegans Wake* [1939] (London: Penguin, 1992).

Kavanagh, Patrick. *The Great Hunger* [1942] in Antoinette Quinn, ed. *Patrick Kavanagh: Collected Poems* (London: Allen Lane, 2004).

Kavanagh, Patrick. *Tarry Flynn* [1948] (London: Penguin Modern Classics, 2000).

Lavin, Mary. *The Patriot Son and Other Stories* (London: Michael Joseph, 1956).

Lavin, Mary. *A Single Lady and Other Stories* (London: Michael Joseph, 1951).

Lavin, Mary. *Tales from Bective Bridge* [1942] (Dublin: Town House, 1996).

MacNeice, Louis. *Collected Poems* (London: Faber, 1966).

McGahern, John. *The Dark* (London: Faber, 1965).

Moore, Brian. *The Lonely Passion of Judith Hearne* [1955] (London: Paladin, 1988).

O'Brien, Flann. *At Swim-Two-Birds* [1939] (Harmonsworth: Penguin, 1967).

O'Brien, Flann. *The Poor Mouth* [1964] (London: Hart-Davis, 1973).

O'Brien, Kate. *The Land of Spices* [1941] (London: Virago, 1988).

O'Brien, Kate. *Mary Lavelle* [1936] (London: Virago, 1984).

O'Casey, Sean. *The Shadow of a Gun Man* [1923], *Juno and the Paycock* [1924] and *The Plough and the Stars* [1926], collected as *Three Dublin Plays* (London: Faber, 2000).

O'Connor, Frank. *Collected Stories* (New York: Knopf, 1981).

O'Faoláin, Sean. *The Collected Short Stories of Sean O'Faoláin* (Boston: Little Brown, 1983).

Rodgers, W. R. *Poems*, edited by Michael Longley (Oldcastle: Gallery Press, 1993).

Russell, George (*A.E.*). *Vale and Other Poems* (London: Macmillan, 1931).

Thompson, Sam. *Over the Bridge* [1960] collected in *Over the Bridge and Other Plays* (Belfast: Lagan Press, 1997).

Yeats, W. B. *Collected Poems* [1933] (Dublin: Gill and Macmillan, 1988).

Yeats, W. B. *Collected Plays* [1934] (London: Papermac, 1982).

CONTEMPORARY LITERATURE FROM 1966 TO THE PRESENT

Banville, John. *Birchwood* [1973] (London: Panther, 1984).

Banville, John. *Doctor Copernicus* (London: Secker and Warburg, 1976).

Banville, John. *Kepler* (London: Secker and Warburg, 1981).

Banville, John. *Mefisto* [1986] (London: Paladin, 1987).

Banville, John. *The Newton Letter* [1982] (London: Picador, 1999).

Banville, John. *The Untouchable* (London: Picador, 1997).

Bateman, Colin. *Cycle of Violence* [1994] (London: HarperCollins, 1995).

Bateman, Colin. *Divorcing Jack* [1995] (London: HarperCollins, 1998).

Bell, Sam Hanna. *A Man Flourishing* [1973] (Belfast: Blackstaff, 1986).

Boland, Eavan. *Collected Poems* (Manchester: Carcanet, 1995).

Bolger, Dermot. *The Journey Home* [1990] (London: Penguin, 1991).

Bolger, Dermot. *The Woman's Daughter* [1987] (London: Viking Press, 1991).

Carson, Ciaran. *The Ballad of HMS Belfast: A Compendium of Belfast Poems* (Oldcastle: Gallery Press, 1999).

Carson, Ciaran. *Shamrock Tea* (London: Granta, 2001).

Donnoghue, Emma. *Hood* [1995] (London: Hamish Hamilton, 1996).

Donoghue, Emma. *Stir-Fry* (London: Hamish Hamilton, 1994).

Doyle, Roddy. *The Barrytown Trilogy*, comprising *The Commitments* [1988], *The Snapper* [1990] and *The Van* [1991], (London: Secker and Warburg, 1992).

Doyle, Roddy. *Paddy Clarke, Ha, Ha Ha* (London: Secker and Warburg, 1993).

Doyle, Roddy. *The Woman Who Walked into Doors* (London: Cape, 1996).

Duffaud, Briege. *A Wreath Upon the Dead* (Dublin: Poolbeg, 1993).

Durcan, Paul. *A Snail in my Prime: New and Selected Poems* (London: Harvill, 1993).

Dunlop, Annie. *Kissing the Frog* (Dublin: Poolbeg, 1996).

Friel, Brian. *Translations* [1980] collected in *Brian Friel: Plays 1*, also comprising *Philadelphia, Here I Come* [1964], *Faith Healer* [1980], *The Freedom of the City* [1973], *Living Quarters* [1977] and *Aristocrats* [1979] (London: Faber, 1996).

Heaney, Seamus. *Poems Vol. 1* comprising *Death of A Naturalist* [1966], *Door Into the Dark* [1969], *Wintering Out* [1972] and *North* [1975] (London: Faber, 1996).

Heaney, Seamus. *Poems Vol. 2* comprising *Field Work* [1979], *Station Island* [1984], *The Haw Lantern* [1987] and *Seeing Things* [1991] (London: Faber, 1996).

Kennelly, Brendan. *Cromwell: A Poem* [1983] (Newcastle: Bloodaxe, 1992).

Kennelly, Brendan. *Selected Poems* (Dublin: Kerrymount, 1985).

Kiely, Benedict. *Proxopera: A Tale of Modern Ireland* [1977] (London: Methuen, 1988).

Kinsella, Thomas. *Collected Poems, 1956–2001* (Manchester: Carcanet, 2001).

Longley, Michael. *Collected Poems* (London: Cape, 2006).

MacLaverty, Bernard. *Cal* [1983] (London: Penguin, 1984).

Mahon, Derek. *Collected Poems* (Oldcastle: Gallery Press, 1999).

Maddden, Deidre. *Hidden Symptoms* [1987] (London: Faber, 1988).

McCabe, Patrick. *The Butcher Boy* [1992] (London: Picador, 1993).

McGahern, John. *Amongst Women* (London: Faber, 1990).

McGahern, John. *The Pornographer* (London: Faber, 1980).

McGuckian, Medbh. *Selected Poems 1978–1994* (Oldcastle: Gallery Press, 1997).

McGuinness, Frank. *Plays 1*, comprising *The Factory Girls* [1988], *Carthaginians* [1988] *Observe the Sons of Ulster Marching Towards the Somme* [1985], *Innocence* [1987], *Baglady* (London: Faber, 1996).

Montague, John. *Collected Poems* (Oldcastle: Gallery Press, 1995).

Moore, Brian. *Cold Heaven* (London: Cape, 1983).

Moore, Brian. *The Colour of Blood* (London: Cape, 1987).

Moore, Brian. *The Emperor of Ice Cream* [1966] (London: Paladin, 1987).

Moore, Brian. *Lies of Silence* (London: Bloomsbury, 1990).

Molloy, Frances. *No Mate for the Magpie* (London: Virago, 1985).

Molloy, Frances. *Women Are the Scourge of the Earth* (Belfast: White Row Press, 1998).

Muldoon, Paul. *Poems, 1968–1998* (London: Faber, 2001).

Murphy, Tom. *Bailegangaire* [1984], collected in *Plays 2* (London: Methuen, 1993).

Nelson, Dorothy. *In Night's City* (Dublin: Wolfhound, 1982).

O'Brien, Edna. *Down By the River* [1987] (London: Wiedenfield and Nicolson, 1996).

O'Brien, Flann. *The Third Policeman* [1967] (London: Picador, 1990).

Parker, Stewart. *Three Plays for Ireland: Northern Star, Heavenly Bodies, Pentecost* (Birmingham: Oberon, 1989).

Patterson, Glenn. *Burning Your Own* (London: Sphere, 1988).

Patterson, Glenn. *Fat Lad* (London: Chatto and Windus, 1992).

Tóibín, Colm. *The Heather Blazing* (London: Pan, 1992).

Trevor, William. *Miss Gomez and the Brethren* [1971] (London: Penguin, 1997).

Wilson, Robert McLiam. *Ripley Bogle* (London: André Deutsch, 1989).

Wilson, Robert McLiam. *Eureka Street* (London: Secker and Warburg, 1996).

USEFUL WEB RESOURCES

The International Association for the Study of Irish Literatures (IASIL):
www.iasil.org/
The British Association for Irish Studies (BAIS):
www.bais.ac.uk/
The American Conference for Irish Studies (ACIS):
www.acisweb.com/index.php
Canadian Association for Irish Studies (CAIS):
http://irishstudies.ca/
European Federation of Associations and Centres of Irish Studies (EFACIS):
http://www.geocities.com/efacis/

Index